"Winning Mindset *is a power*
performers who give practical
These authors provide tools tha
benefit your life. If you're looking for a book to ignite or in-
spire action, you've found it! Erik Seversen has done it again
as he found some of the best leading experts to depict exactly
what a winning mindset looks like."

—JESSIE ADAMS, Founder of BelieveinU Fitness,
American Ninja Warrior

"Wow and wow! Dozens of powerful and unique perspectives
on success from people who have actually walked the walk.
Winning Mindset *is a refreshing read from cover to cover.*
I'm sure the seeds planted in one's mind from reading this
book will bear fruit for years to come."

—RICHARD BOWLING, High-Performance
Entrepreneur's Coach, Former Professional Athlete

"Winning Mindset *is a must-read for anyone looking to*
accomplish their biggest dreams in life and business but are
feeling nervous or hesitant that they can do it. Start here!
Author Erik Seversen has a gift for gathering some of the
world's greatest experts in Peak Performance and getting
them to share their top techniques in books filled with in-
spirational stories, practical tools, and the latest scientific
research that help the top athletes, business owners, and CEOs
in the world win. The whole book is powerful but reading
even one chapter can change your entire life."

—KAMILLE ROSE TAYLOR, Board Certified Peak
Performance Coach, Founder of The Ultimate LYFE

"*A winning mindset is a battle between the internal desire to perform at your best and the constant external drive to succeed at all costs. The strategies shared in the book,* Winning Mindset, *are a boon to high-achievers who want to develop sustainable, long-term performance and realize their full potential in business and life.*"

—APRIL QURESHI, Performance Coach; Author of *Simple Success Strategies for Women Entrepreneurs*

"Winning Mindset *(published 2021) is the perfect companion to James Allen's* As a Man Thinketh *(published 1903). No matter the era, culture, country, or circumstance, we share this trait with all humankind: our thoughts give rise to actions and our actions give rise to results. Erik Seversen has brought together a global band of experts to tell us their stories of perseverance as well as their recipes for success. Get out your highlighters. This book will help you think your way to a deeply significant life!*"

—JORY H. FISHER, Community Builder, Author, Business Coach

"*In elite sport, mindset is so important and can be the difference between success and failure.* Winning Mindset *emphasises the importance of the mind and how powerful the results are when you get it right. This book is a unique and eye-opening insight into the workings of the mind, with lots of amazing stories and practical examples of how to create a winning mindset. There's something in this book for everyone.*"

—STEPHEN MILLER, MBE, 6-time Paralympian, Motivational Speaker, Mindset Coach

WINNING MINDSET

WINNING MINDSET

Elite Strategies for Peak Performance

Authored by:
Erik Seversen, Alhaji Abubakar, Tania Adams, Julia Arndt, Jason Brader,
Jan Carpenter, Rose Cartolari, Molly Connolly, Liam Donnelly, Dirk
Downing, PhD, Dr. Sam Fielding, Kerry Fisher, Sven Gade, Robin Goldsbro,
Susan Hobson, Nick Holton, PhD, Richard Husseiny, Gavin Ingham, Luke
Jensen, Kirsten Jones, Kristie Kennedy, Jody Kennett, Karen Machuca,
Dr. Tim Mann, David Motto, Steven Nathenson, Anastasia Pavlatou,
Bryan Sauder, Alaina Schwartz, JD, Dr. Natalia S. Seybold, Vallerie
Skelly, Jennifer Stirrup, Serra Tumay, Corina Zanner-Entwistle

THIN LEAF PRESS | LOS ANGELES

Disclaimer—The advice, guidelines, and all suggested material in this book is given in the spirit of information with no claims to any particular guaranteed outcomes. This book does not replace professional physical or mental support or counselling. Anyone deciding to add physical or mental exercises to their life should reach out to a licensed medical doctor or therapist before following any of the advice in this book. The authors, publisher, editor, and organizer do not assume and hereby disclaim any liability to any party for any loss, damage, or disruption caused by anything written in this book.

Library of Congress Cataloging-in-Publication Data
Names: Seversen, Erik, Author, et al.
Title: *Winning Mindset: Elite Strategies for Peak Performance*
LCCN 2021916346

ISBN 978-1-953183-04-0 | ISBN 978-1-953183-05-7 (eBook)
Nonfiction, Mind, Body & Spirit, Self-Help, Performance
Cover Design: 100 Covers
Interior Design: Formatted Books
Editor: Nancy Pile
Copy Editor: Rebecca Lau
Thin Leaf Press
Los Angeles

THIN
LEAF

Thank you for reading this book. There are tools found within the following pages that can greatly benefit your life, but don't stop there. Make sure you get the most you can from this book and reach out directly to the 33 expert authors who want to help you reach your goals by performing at peak levels to manifest success in your life. Contact information for each author is found at the end of their respective chapter.

To those passionately pursuing goals and to those fighting to make positive changes within themselves and the world.

CONTENTS

INTRODUCTION

By Erik Seversen
Author of *Ordinary to Extraordinary* and *Explore*
Los Angeles, California

What does "winning" mean? Is it getting first prize at the fair for the fattest pig? Is it winning a gold medal in an Olympic sporting event? Is it creating a company and selling it for millions of dollars? Is it summiting Mount Everest? The answer is, yes. Winning is all of these things, but it is so much more. When it really comes down to it, winning is nothing more than a state of mind. Let me start with an example from my youth.

It was a cloudy April day in Tacoma, Washington. It was near the end of a heated track competition between Washington High School and another northwest school. As I rounded the fourth corner of the track, it was only me and him. None of the other runners were even close. All eyes were on us as we entered the last straightaway of the 400-meter run. Side-by-side we sprinted. My challenger inched forward, then I caught up. I inched forward, then he caught up. Sweat shaking from our hair, arms and legs pumping, lungs burning, hearts exploding, we dashed toward the finish line, and I came in just inches before the other runner.

I won—well, at least I came in before my opponent. Really, all the other runners in the race had finished long ago. We weren't fighting for first place; we were fighting not to get last place, and I succeeded at least in that. My joy was still great, though. You see, I wasn't really a runner at all. My one and only job in track, as a stocky ninth grader, was to throw the shot put. On that day, however, we were short on runners, and my coach convinced me that we just needed a body in the 400-meter race to get points, and I was going to be it.

Reflecting on the race, you could say that I lost horribly. I got seventh place out of eight runners. Another way to look at it is that I won my personal goal not to get last place. Which is correct? Well, both are correct. The difference is only in perspective. I could choose to look at myself as a winner, or I could choose to look at myself as a loser. I chose a winning mindset.

Having just shown how losing can be winning, I want to emphatically point out that I'm not a fan of participation trophies for last place, of not keeping score during kids' soccer games, nor the idea that "everyone wins and nobody loses." I do think putting our efforts against others in competition is important. I strongly believe that competition and keeping score can make us push ourselves harder, which leads us to perform better in sport, school, business, and life. This is the point of the book you are holding—to highlight characteristics of a winning mindset, so we can perform at our best and, consequently, win sporting competitions, win in business, summit mountains, and live to our fullest potential.

This book, *Winning Mindset*, is about elite strategies for peak performance. It is about creating a winning mindset within ourselves first and attracting actual wins in our lives as a result. This book explores the habits of people who win, the actions winners take, and the strategies winners employ. Basically, this book is a kit providing various tools you can use to create a winning mindset and to perform at your best.

The number one goal in this book is to provide examples from elite athletes, coaches, entrepreneurs, and more, on how to perform at peak levels. This performance can be applied to sports, school, business, and life. There are no limits to what constitutes a winning mindset, and this book will provide an array of coaches to train your mind and body as you strive toward peak performance.

Who are these coaches at your disposal? They are performance coaches, mindset coaches, neurolinguistic programming masters, hypnotists, transformational coaches, executive coaches, keynote and TEDx speakers, meditation experts, leadership coaches, sports champions, health and wellness advocates, Tony Robbins coaches, strength and conditioning coaches, authors, doctors, PhDs, scientists, Olympic and professional athletes, and more.

From the mind to the body to the spirit, the authors who contributed to this book are world-class experts in various fields who want to share their unique strategies for peak performance. These experts are from the USA, Canada, the United Kingdom, Norway, Italy, and Greece, and each wants to help you perform at your best. Also, note that each of the chapters in this book are totally independent, so I encourage you not to read from start to finish, but to select chapters from the table of contents that interest you most. As a whole, the chapters in this book offer a wide array of perspectives that create a well-rounded view of peak performance, so I encourage you to read all of the chapters.

Lastly, while reading a book is a great way to ignite action to make yourself better, nothing can replace face-to-face or online engagement, so if you connect with something one of the authors has written, reach out to them directly. Their contact information is at the end of each respective chapter, and each of these authors would love to hear from you and help you perform at your best.

Whether you are trying to figure things out and add direction to your life or you are already excelling but want to go to another level, there is a peak performer in you. I pray that something in this book helps you find and develop this, so you can live your best life.

Open up the table of contents, find the chapter that jumps out at you most, and start.

Ready … set … go!

Email: Erik@ErikSeversen.com
Website: www.ErikSeversen.com

CHAPTER ONE
WINNING ON YOUR TERMS

By Alhaji "HAAJi" Abubakar
CEO, HAAJi's WORLD
Chicago, Illinois

What exactly is a *winning mindset*? I can tell you what I think, but I believe it's more valuable if you create your own definition. Too often we are told what to think. Many of the ideas we develop early in life are greatly influenced by our community and environment. It is difficult to pinpoint where their beliefs end and yours begins. Usually, the beliefs of a group remain static, unchanged. The reality is that our beliefs can and do change, often as a result of our experiences and new awareness.

In the past, I would have told you that a winning mindset is something you are either born with or not. As for me, I definitely was not born with one. This is probably why I started, but never completed, a number of personal projects. For instance, in my college years, I wanted to begin my own clothing line. I filled a sketch book with mockups and designs. I even took a class to learn how to sew. Unfortunately, I stopped just short of taking my designs to production. Then, there was my short-lived modeling career. I found a few agencies who were actually interested in representing me. I went to a handful of jobs. But I did not keep up a self-promotion practice, as other aspiring models did, and my dreams fizzled out. There was my dream of wanting to be a physical therapist, so I could heal others. At one point, I desired to be a DJ. All of these dreams were fleeting. I believed my current abilities were a reflection of my future success, the definition of a fixed mindset.

Today, I believe a winning mindset is not predetermined at birth, but instead determined by personal growth. My definition of a winning mindset is simply understanding that continuous improvement is a must; challenging ourselves to pursue ambitious goals that stretch us; and deciding to be capable of and willing to transform different aspects of ourselves in order to achieve goals.

With a winning mindset, we understand that accomplishing a goal may take a lifetime, but this doesn't faze us. In fact, it motivates us to develop strategies to maximize efficiency as we navigate our journey.

The above is my definition of a winning mindset, and I encourage you to develop your own definition. This way you can clearly gauge success on your own terms.

As we go deeper, I'd like to explore three ideas which I believe to be the pillars of a winning mindset: autonomy, energy, and accountability.

Embracing Autonomy

Autonomy is the freedom to choose your own adventure in life. It's the power to make your own decisions without anyone else interfering. Using my definition of a winning mindset, autonomy gives me the freedom to choose my goals and the path that I want to take towards achieving them. It expands my creativity and gives me the ability to think beyond my previously held limiting beliefs. For me, autonomy is very personal. It's a reflection of the freedom we are all born with but don't always get the opportunity to express.

My Search for Freedom

My parents immigrated from Ghana to the US in the late 1980s. My siblings and I were born in Chicago, Illinois. We were the first in our family to be born in the US. This was significant because it meant that my parents placed a huge emphasis on instilling their own cultural customs onto us. These were the ideals they knew, the traditions that raised them. But being brought up in the US while following a different set of cultural beliefs left me feeling lost. At school, I never felt like I fit in. At home, I often resented my parents. I did not like that I was different. Throughout high school and even college, I felt as if I had to live a double life in order to fully express myself. Needless to say, things did not go smoothly. It was only after ending a serious relationship, because I knew that my parents would not approve of my partner, that I realized just how many of my own needs I was sacrificing for the wants of others. The feeling of living a secret life for so long had proved to be draining.

My desire for more freedom led me to finally express myself. I opened up to my family about my struggles. I shared that I did not want to live the life they wanted for me. As I had expected, they were not too thrilled about my newfound individuality. But since the idea of freedom was driving my actions, their reactions were the last thing on my mind. Eventually, I chose to pursue entrepreneurship. I started my own coaching practice as a way to support others on their journey towards personal freedom.

Once I made the giant leap toward personal freedom, I became driven to try to help others find their freedom too. My advice to others and to you is—seek out opportunities for more autonomy in your life. Challenge any restrictions, especially if they get between you and your goals. I consider the ability to live the life you want to be an expression of true freedom. And even though the decisions you make may not always feel comfortable or please everyone, they move you closer to the life of *your* dreams.

Manage Your Energy

It is often said that time is our most valuable asset. Personally, I replace "time" with "energy" in that statement. Let's say you have all the time in the world; without energy, how will you make the most of that time?

Conscious energy management is a must as you pursue goals. Since energy can only be transformed, the question becomes—how will you transform your energy, so it supports you in bringing your vision to life?

Managing energy can be considered part of the how when it comes to accomplishing your goals. In my above definition of a winning mindset, I mentioned that a winning mindset challenges me to pursue ambitious goals that I know will stretch me. This idea expresses the qualities of perseverance and discipline, both of which typically require great levels of energy expenditure. Prioritizing energy management prepares you for your worst days. Taking the time to consider both your mental and spiritual energy is a good place to begin.

Mental Energy

When your mental energy is performing optimally, you are clear and present. When your mental energy is compromised, you may be absentminded and more easily distracted. It's easy to see how beneficial increasing your mental energy can be to personal success.

Training up your focus is extremely valuable for optimal mental energy. It can be frustrating to want to focus on a particular item, while also finding it very difficult to do so. Depending on how you were raised, focus may not have been a skill that you were explicitly taught. If you had any formal education, was it mandatory for you to take a class on the topic of focus? That was not the case for me. In fact, my high school and college years were some of the most difficult times in my life due to my inability to focus. This was yet another time when my fixed mindset took charge. I assumed I simply was not born equipped with the ability to learn quickly, and I assumed all my efforts were in vain. I often thought it was unfair for my instructors to expect so much out of me. I later discovered that none of that was true, and I simply did not understand how the hardware of my brain worked.

Where Your Attention Goes, Energy Flows

Did you know that once you tell your brain what to focus on, it will direct all of its available energy towards that one thing? There's a phenomenon called *instinctive elaboration*. It's a mental reflex that is triggered, for instance, when you are asked a question. The question takes over your brain's thought process, and while your brain is contemplating the question, it cannot think about anything else.

This explains why I struggled in school for all those years. There was a discrepancy in my thoughts. At the time, even though part of me believed I could complete difficult assignments, another part of me did not believe I was capable. I didn't know it at the time, but holding these two opposing thoughts was draining my mental energy. Knowing this now, it makes perfect sense why I frequently gave up; I simply lacked the energy to move on.

In order to maximize your mental energy, you must choose to focus on the one thought you most want to believe. For me, this would have been "I can complete any assignment." By focusing on this one thought, you recruit all of your mental energy towards discovering ways to make it true.

If you want to believe that you can accomplish a goal, make sure all of your thoughts and questions are focused on the accomplishment of that goal. This will help ensure that your brain only supports thoughts that align with what you want. Be aware of any conflicting thoughts and remove them from your mind as quickly as possible. The conflict will only slow you down.

Spiritual Energy

Spiritual energy refers to anything that gives you a sense of meaning in your life. Consider your life purpose and mission. Better yet, begin by focusing on your values. Your values consist of what's most important to you in your life. Going back to my story, it was clear that living a life without freedom was draining me of my energy and my potential. Only through taking action, with freedom as the driver, was I able to discover the energy to take on challenges that I never would have previously considered. Moving towards what matters to you is energizing. But when you are in conflict with what matters to you, your energy is suppressed.

The key to managing spiritual energy is to understand what matters to you, then to honor it. Each one of us has a few top values which play a central role in our lives. My highest recommendation for managing your spiritual energy is to define your top values and find opportunities to incorporate them into your life. So, if you value travel, take trips. Maybe you value creativity? Find ways to regularly engage in creative activities, like personal art projects.

Use these questions to define your own personalized values: where do you spend a majority of your time or energy? What do you obsess about? What is most important to you in your life?

Accountability

Most people hire coaches as a way to hold themselves accountable. Many people view having a coach as a must-have when it comes to personal growth. Here's an amazing thing about the times we live in today: if you search, you will find numerous resources that offer indirect coaching. Potentially priceless information can be found when you look for it. My first suggestion would be to find a podcast or YouTube channel specifically geared towards your desired goals. It was through listening to podcasts that I decided to begin conducting my own personal feedback system that allowed me to grow exponentially.

Cultivating a growth mindset is crucial for a winning mindset. A growth mindset is rooted in the understanding that you are adaptable, and with effort, you can change and improve any area of your life. A few years back, I joined

Toastmasters as a way to improve my public speaking skills. I wanted to work my way towards speaking to a live audience, but I knew I had some work to do before I was ready. What I grew to love most about Toastmasters was the on-the-spot feedback given after each speech. I will admit that, initially, I incorrectly interpreted feedback as what I did wrong. In reality, all the feedback I ever received was supportive, with the intention of transforming me into a more well-rounded speaker. By focusing on how it benefited my growth, I was able to find joy in the feedback process. This has led me to become the undisputed area Toastmasters champion for two years straight.

When I put the feedback I received into practice, I was able to notice a rapid transformation in my speaking abilities. So, I figured, why not try this technique in other areas of my life? I began to seek opportunities to solicit feedback both in my personal and professional life. This ultimately led me to create my own personal feedback process to support me in managing my goals. I found that when you get in the habit of giving yourself critical feedback, it decreases the defensive reaction you might have while receiving feedback from others.

Reviewing Weekly

I conduct the following feedback process on a weekly basis. These statements are based on the Daily Habits Scorecard by Brendon Burchard. I've modified them to better match my personal goals:

I rate myself on a scale from 1 to 5 (1 = not satisfied, 5 = very satisfied) in the following areas:

1. Intention: I made progress towards my mission/goals.
2. Energy: I managed my energy efficiently to meet my daily goals.
3. Challenge: I challenged myself in new ways and overcame discomfort.
4. Community: I engaged with my community with the intention to make an impact.
5. Purpose: I tapped into my purpose to drive action.
6. Efficiency: I scheduled effectively to focus on high priority projects.
7. Future Self: I visualized and tapped into the energy of my future self.

I follow up the ratings by making notes of tips that I can use to make the following week even better. It's an exciting process that gives me a good look at my personal transformation. I highly recommend adopting this review process for yourself. You can use this exactly or modify it to fit your needs even more precisely. I'm sure that you will begin to see areas where your energy is placed that will allow you to continually become more efficient and focused on reaching your goals.

My core message is to focus on developing your own beliefs, tools, and techniques to succeed in your life. This is how you truly win! The pillars that I described above—autonomy, energy, and accountability—will support and enhance your winning mindset, no matter how you define it. I shared with you what has worked for me based on my experiences. How will you capitalize on enriching your own experiences?

About the Author

Alhaji "HAAJi" Abubakar is the founder of HAAJi's WORLD. He is a peak performance coach and motivational speaker. Growing up on the southside of Chicago to immigrant parents, HAAJi rose above his environment and empowered himself to create his own path in life. Now, he supports his clients on their journey to live a more empowered life. He uses research from the fields of neuroscience, mindset, human physiology, and spirituality to connect with and educate his clients. HAAJi is a lifelong student and teacher. He facilitates workshops on topics including energy management, values, and emotional empowerment.

Email: haaji@haajisworld.com
Facebook: Facebook.com/haajisworld
Instagram: @haajisworld

CHAPTER TWO
IS YOUR THINKING STINKING?

By Tania Adams
Author, Mindset and Performance Coach
Stavanger, Norway

Can you imagine how the world would be if humanity knew the secret to unlocking their potential and living in their full self-expression? What if we were given a manuscript with a step-by-step process that teaches us how to operate ourselves for best results? What would happen if we all knew how to harness the mental mechanics of the mind and have our mind working for us in a positive and progressive way? What would our thought process be like? How would we relate to one another and how would we perform in our everyday life? This is a subject I began studying 26 years ago. It is a topic I am truly passionate about, and I am excited, today, to tell you the good news—that this is possible. Anyone can do it.

A winning mindset is our ticket to freedom and happiness. It's the gateway to our true potential and ultimate success. A winning mindset takes a holistic approach where all aspects of our life are in balance. It's when we truly know ourselves and how to harness our creativity. It's wanting the best for others because we support their success, and it's living consciously, being awake in the here and now, and operating from the flow state.

Throughout my journey and life experience amidst the path of self-development from discovering and uncovering my human potential and embodying the steps and process of change that resulted in my own personal transformation, I was astounded to learn about the radical change and vast possibilities that are available for everyone. I wanted this for everyone, as I could see and sense how humanity would enormously benefit from learning how to operate for successful results and how this knowledge would revolutionise the world. I knew in my heart that this was an integral piece of information that people needed to become aware of, and this was the reason I became a coach and specialised in mindset, performance, and wellbeing.

Surprisingly, this vital mindset and performance information has been around for thousands of years, but sadly, not at the forefront of education. The mystics, world inventors, and historical changemakers all spoke of this untapped potential within us, where we could mine from the unlimited well of creativity and avail of our God-given mind power. Socrates said, "Know thyself." William James, the grandfather of humanistic psychology, maintained that deep attentional focus was associated with genius, observing, "The education that could teach attention would be the system, par excellence." Buddha said, "You and your world are composed of your thoughts, the wise person controls their thoughts."

So, how do we harness this great potential? It all boils down to the structure of a winning mindset, understanding the key parts and components of a successful strategy that we can learn and implement to enhance and empower our general way of thinking. Just like making a cake—when we know the ingredients and process, we can bake a perfect soufflé! Equally, when we want to look and feel better, we physically train our body and change our diet by following a health and fitness regime over a period, and then we begin to see results. This is the same way as training our mental health—we must go to the mental gym and train our brain! It's such an important and life-changing part of our wellbeing that brings so much value, not just for ourselves, but for everyone and the planet. You see, when you begin to focus your attention towards attuning your mind, and you start strengthening and building new mental muscles, very quickly you will experience the change because the brain flourishes with a growth and empowered mindset.

Neuroscience research has shown that we can rewire our brain because the brain is changeable and adaptable. Scientists have named this "neuroplasticity." This means that when we transmute thought and energy combined, either on a repetitive basis or when a vast amount of attention and emotion (energy in motion) has been directed towards a specific thought process, whether it be of a positive or negative context, then we can create new neurological pathways and build new beliefs, and, depending on the nature of our thought, we can either empower or disempower our mental programming. You may have heard the phrase by Donald Hebb, a Canadian neuropsychologist, "Neurons that fire together wire together!"

Therefore, we must live more consciously and police our thoughts because our words are powerful. They have an emotional weight. The meaning that we give towards the communication we express and receive, as well as the amount of attention and emotion that we expend, will determine the level of impact and how the information becomes stored in our mind, which we can liken to a filing system. When I finally gained the realisation of how we really are 100 percent responsible for our experience of reality, our interpretation, and how every word functions to create this experience of reality, I began attuning my awareness to the vibratory coherence of the words that I use as this was a huge insight and gamechanger. To put it simply, every single thought we have, as we become conscious of it, will cause a ripple effect. If we think sad thoughts, we will become sad, and if we continue thinking them, we could burst into tears or become depressed. On the other hand, if we have happy thoughts and we feel happy, laugh, and get into good humour, then we will feel better.

Instead of focusing on things that hold you back in life, focus on things that help you to flourish and make you a better human being. Instead of imagining negative scenarios that will most likely never happen, use your imagination wisely by bringing your mind to the present. Use your mental energy towards focussing on things that will benefit and empower you and others.

Be aware that what you focus on prevails. You literally craft your own mind by choosing what you pay attention to. Of course, you can hardly control what happens around you throughout your day, but you can control your interpretation of a situation and how much it affects you. To be more specific, you have the power to choose *what* affects you and to construct your own neural connections.

The mind is vastly intelligent; it has enormous potential, and it's our greatest asset. Sigmund Freud said, "The mind is like an iceberg, it floats with one-seventh of its bulk above water." Therefore, six-sevenths of the mind is subconscious. In today's scientific research, studies have estimated that human beings think between 60 to 70 thousand thoughts a day, and 90 percent of those thoughts are the same thoughts as the day before and have been for some time. Most of our thinking activity is subconscious, and this amounts to 95 percent of brain activity, including our habits and patterns, automatic body function, creativity, emotions, personality, beliefs and values, cognitive biases, and long-term memory. The latter five percent is our conscious cognitive activity, which includes sensations, perceptions, memories, feelings, fantasies, and everything inside of our current awareness, the here and now, the powerful present.

Freud also said that we were merely puppets of the subconscious, as 95 percent of our mind is on autopilot and, therefore, running the show. For example, have you ever realised that you have driven yourself home or taken public transport and arrived at your destination, but haven't really been paying attention? Or when performing tasks or playing a well-known tune on a musical instrument, it can suddenly seem much more difficult when you go from being absent-minded to consciously thinking about it. Brain scans have revealed that when your mind wanders, it switches into "autopilot" mode, enabling you to carry on doing tasks quickly, accurately, and efficiently and without conscious thought.

We can liken the mind to a computer, the hard drive is the mind and the software is the programming. Since the beginning of time on planet Earth, human beings have absorbed and recorded information (software), which has imprinted on the mind and become our programming. In our early stage of life, we begin learning from our parents, peers, guardians, tribe, and teachers. By the time we reach seven years of age, the brain has been osculating in a theta brainwave state, soaking up, absorbing, and imprinting the fundamental learnings that shape our life. Then as we grow and evolve in our journey from childhood to adulthood, we alternate through the various brainwave states and build upon our memorised behaviours and automatic habits, imprinting and conditioning our mental programming, which becomes and reinforces our unique identity and personality.

Each of us is an artist who paints our own canvas. We are the director of our movie, the producer of the song we sing, and the author of the story we tell. It's time to get in the driving seat of your thoughts and realise that you are the thinker of your own thoughts and consciously take hold of the reins. Even when the thoughts appear to just pop up, it's vital to realise that we have the choice to continue them. A great way for you to begin exercising your power is to become aware of the vital difference between (1) your thoughts as just thoughts and (2) your thoughts as reality. Be especially aware of creating any negative thought attacks, which can start with one thought that you could have dismissed. Otherwise, if you continue to feed the negative thoughts, they will grow and expand, and you become weaker until they overwhelm you.

All of us experience an internal dialogue, a "little voice," and an internal monologue inside our head that can either be positive or negative. Depending on its context, it can have a profound effect on our performance and reality. Consider this, many people go on diets to lose weight, some people diet continuously and often they yoyo with their weight. Whilst being mindful of what we eat is imperative because we are what we eat, equally we must be conscious of our *mental* diet and the types of thoughts we think and digest. The best mental diet is a good balance of alkalised thoughts, a selection of savoury thoughts that we feed ourselves through our internal and external communication on a regular basis. This includes the gift of praise and recognition, which is a powerful combination that adds great value and works wonders with both our internal dialogue and external communication to others. Be aware that the most important words we say are the ones we say to ourselves. The opposing diet would be of an acidic nature with toxic thoughts that wouldn't feel good or digest well and would pollute our mindset.

An example to illustrate this point is when a person consistently talks about their problems or illness, repetitively telling themselves and others about it, and sometimes giving a detailed description. Similarly, this happens if we give too much attention to bad news carried by the TV, media, and people. We must be careful with our mental environment because the danger of this approach from expending too much focus and energy towards a situation is that the person who's telling the story and the people listening can imprint it on their mind and add their energy to the topic of conversation, so it becomes magnified.

However, the good news is that this is equally as powerful when we digest and record information of a good and positive context, as this will empower our mind and wellbeing, lift our state, and energise us. Therefore, we must be mindful of our mental diet, our internal dialogue. We must act as the gatekeeper of our mind and choose wisely from an unlimited choice of mental health foods by selecting only those with the highest life force. Ultimately, we must be an alchemist and turn our base words and thoughts into gold.

Now that you have realised the true nature of how you create your reality and that to improve the quality of your life, you must improve the quality of your thinking, be aware that you will always experience your thoughts as real. It's important to understand that your thinking is your sole input into the creation of your personality, your personal reality.

To help you maintain a healthy mind, it's important to relax your mental house, especially as the mind is constantly processing a vast amount of information, and, depending on the nature of your thought process, there can be too much noise contamination, which clouds the mind and your reality. Just like a lake, if the water is continually stirred, then it becomes murky and muddy, and you cannot see clearly. Once you stop stirring, the mud settles, and the lake becomes clear. This has the same effect on your mind. There are various forms of meditation widely available that can help you with the process of relaxation. However, the main aim is to relax your conscious mind and then move into the relaxation of your deeper mind, the subconscious. Through this approach, something special happens. As the mind chatter calms down, the energy relaxes, and you reach a clear state of mind. The natural flow of life force within you can express itself more freely, so you connect with the underlying driving force of energy, and, as a result, you are able to operate from your true nature.

Operating from your true nature is the purpose of mental and physical relaxation. Everyone has the capacity to function in an effortless state of well-being, but it takes practice to slow down the fast pace of thinking, quieten the noise, and relax your energy. However, like everything, practice makes perfect. The more you consciously hone a different approach, then you will experience the change and begin to live more powerfully in the present.

A great practice that you can start doing now is to take a walk in nature and go on a "sense safari." Allow yourself a timeout with some head breathing space. Immerse yourself in your surroundings, connect with everything around you, and engage in a myriad of senses. Let any thoughts that arise pass by like clouds passing in the sky, and let them go with no attachments. This approach will help to clear your mind, stimulate the senses, relax your energy, and bring you into the powerful present.

Another important and valuable exercise to stimulate and enhance your creative potential is the art of visualisation. This approach is extremely beneficial when you tap into the power of your visual sense and dream about your ideal life. Albert Einstein said, "Imagination is everything, it is the preview of life's coming attractions." Use your imagination wisely and think about aspects of your life where you want to excel—your health, relationships, finance, and career, whatever areas you seek growth and life improvement in. Be aware that it's also important to include other people in the success of your goals, as this has proved to have a powerful effect with the life-forming process.

Whether you can visualise or not, a great resource that will help you to excite and empower your mind cells is a vision board. This will enhance your creativity and it's a powerful contribution to manifesting your lifestyle, as your reticular activating system (RAS) will become stimulated, and you will begin to attract things into your life just like a magnet—hence, the law of attraction.

A vital ingredient that must be included when you are visualising is to be single-minded, which means having your thoughts and feelings about your goals all moving in one direction. You must believe without doubt that whatever you are visualising will come about. This is the secret that Jesus revealed thousands of years ago. He taught people how to harness their greater mind power and to believe with no opposing thought. It's also the formula that the super achievers and successful athletes have used throughout time.

Your whole mind must be congruent and moving in one direction. There must be no division in your mind. Therefore, all your attention and energy must be focussed on your goal, your end outcome, without even a tinge of doubt. Through this approach something amazing happens—the vast subconscious of your greater mind becomes available, and as a result, you turbo-boost yourself to your goal. It's a kind of magic that happens when you use the whole of your mind and operate as a holistic person, as you will move from being double-minded to single-minded and release a vast amount of power through the process of whole-brain thinking. You will tap into the unlimited treasure within and harness the innate intelligence that permeates life. This is the great potential and power that we all hold individually and collectively. Each of us is born with this gift, and it's our God-given birthright to thrive and shine.

So now you know that a winning mindset is a game of strategy, and you can consciously choose the aroma of your thinking by manipulating the variables of thought and smartly using your mind. Harness your potential by cultivating your mental strength and fitness to be sound of mind and sound of body. Be aware that you have the formula to empower and enhance another frame of mind. This is the art of a thriving mind culture and the answer to attaining mind mastery.

About the Author

Tania Adams has a strong background with 30 years of frontline communications, sales, and leadership skills within the corporate, retail, and media sectors. She began working as a coach in 2002, and she specialises in mindset, performance, and wellbeing. A running theme of expression from Tania's client testimonials is about their profound transformation, and she frequently receives feedback from clients on how their lives have radically changed for the better from their work with her. Tania is passionate about the power of human potential and has an in-depth understanding of human behaviour and how the mind is conditioned for either success or failure. Her professional experience of almost 20 years has spanned three continents, where she's worked with some of the biggest companies in the world, including Walmart, Tesco, Credit Suisse, BBC, Vodafone, and Calvin Klein.

Tania has gained invaluable experience in her field throughout her journey as a coach. The person who has inspired Tania the most and caused the greatest impact on her life is Dr Tony Quinn, originator of the The Educo® Model. https://www.educoworld.com/

Websites:
https://www.linkedin.com/in/taniaadams/
https://www.taniaadams.co.uk/
@tania_adams_coach

CHAPTER THREE

THE BURNED-OUT PEAK PERFORMER

By Julia Arndt
Peak Performance Coach
Lake Tahoe, California

The greatest gap in the world is the gap between knowing and doing.
—John Maxwell

Do you consider yourself a peak performer? Smart, driven, highly successful? Over the years, from high school to college, to landing your dream job in one of the world's leading organizations, you have proven over and over again that you can work extremely hard to get what you want.

But how do you keep your high achiever status alive without the sacrifice of burning yourself out, struggling with work-life balance, and eventually questioning if your role or company is the right fit for you?

As an introduction during an offsite team-building event for my job at Google in December 2016, my colleague David shared brief profiles to recognize all the people on our team for their outstanding work during the year. My profile was a little comic figure, sitting at a table with a coffee cup in hand, surrounded by a raging fire. The little figurine had a speech bubble that said, "It's fine."

I was handed the "award" for frequently showcasing unwavering resilience. I was known as the person who "walked through the fire" and found something positive in every situation. I stuck through difficult experiences and was able to connect with my stakeholders in a way that few could. I felt extremely proud of the title; it was exactly what I wanted to stand for and be identified with.

Little did I know that only 18 months later, I would be diagnosed with burnout and anxiety. It turns out that as resilient as I thought I was, I wasn't. I had, for years, created unhealthy patterns of which I wasn't aware.

I identified as a peak performer my whole life. I developed what people call "grit" early on. I had a passion to work hard, ambition, and discipline. These traits got me really far in my life. Elementary school was easy for me, I was a straight A student. That changed quickly when I got to high school. All of a sudden, I came home with a few Cs and Ds on my evaluations, and I wasn't happy. My sister, who was two years older, remained a straight A student throughout high school, and I wanted to be the same, to make my family proud. After the first two years of struggling and feeling defeated by my average grades, I found a system. If I would come home from school, rework all of my classes, copy what I had written down neatly during class, and then study for a few hours, I could keep up. It quickly became my obsession. I loved having organization and structure in my notes, and my grades started to reflect what I worked so hard for.

Even though my dad was a high school teacher, my parents never put pressure on me to deliver great results; it was the opposite. When I was only 15, my dad used to tell me I was too hard on myself. But for me, it was my way to get recognition from him for my hard work and discipline.

I completed high school with straight As and got accepted into three universities. I understood, hard work pays off. After improving my English skills during a six-month stay in Bournemouth, England, I returned to Germany to start college. I studied international management with a focus in finance in Germany. After that I completed a six-month internship at the Volkswagen Group in Braunschweig before going abroad. In my first year studying for my end-of-year exams, I lost 15 pounds from the stress. I didn't know any other way; I was fine, and I knew that's what I had to do in order to perform and get a good job afterwards.

I continued my double bachelor's degree for one and a half years in Marseille, France. Again, good grades were the status quo. I went to Sydney, Australia, for my second six-month internship at the German-Australian

Chamber of Industry and Commerce before returning to France to do my master's degree in brand management and marketing.

I graduated with honors both in my bachelor's and master's degrees, and I took in my second foreign language, French. And even before finishing my master's degree, the offer letter from Google was on the table. Jackpot. Working so hard for most of my life continued to pay off.

When I got to Dublin the first day, I was proud of myself and felt accomplished. I spoke three languages fluently, had amazing degrees from renowned schools in Germany and France, and had a few powerful internships under my belt. But while meeting my new work colleagues, I quickly realized I was just one of many successful multilingual graduates. People who got hired by Google commonly spoke four or five languages, interned at consulting companies, graduated from the top colleges in the world, and often even had multiple passports. We all moved to Dublin for our first job after college, working at the European Headquarters in an account management role, and we all knew that Dublin was just a stop-over. One to two years until we got the first promotion to move into the next role. The rat race was on, and the competition continued: who hit their sales targets first, who could shine with extraordinary customer stories and special projects, in addition to their core job. We all knew how it was done. We had learned over many years—even though we were on average only 25 years old—that hard work paid off. But "competing" with the best and brightest didn't get us that quick reward that we had become so used to. And that started to create a stressful pattern of long office hours, additional (voluntary) weekend shifts, and extra projects. We hoped that if we just put more in, it would eventually pay off.

Although I was excited to be surrounded by so many amazing, bright colleagues who later became my friends, it also nagged on my confidence. All of a sudden, I was "just" one of thousands of very bright people. I regularly met people who, being two or three years younger than me, had already achieved more, spoke more languages, and had more work experience.

You get the story. In my life, I always reached high and achieved high. What I set my mind to, I got.

Defining the Burned-Out Peak Performer (BOPP)

The burned-out peak performer (BOPP) is extremely self-motivated and self-disciplined, hard-working, and reliable. Their core belief is that working hard is the key to success and finding fulfillment in life. *I have worked hard my whole life, I'm so busy and I have zero time, I want to please everyone, so they like me and see the value in me, and I'm very good at what I do, and it will pay off.*

BOPPs are results-driven, externally motivated, and thrive with recognition and approval from others. They believe that life is competitive. They are confident on the outside, insecure on the inside (impostor syndrome alert!), and are never really satisfied with their results. With hard work and dedication, they have always been the best at everything they set out to do (even though they might not fully believe that they are, in fact, one of the best).

No matter if male or female, the BOPP is identified by a high level of attributes often associated with the masculine—drive, organization, structure, power, success, strictness; being very ambitious and competitive; and often aggressive where and when necessary.

A BOPP's qualities are developed very early in life. Often starting in high school, the BOPP was a straight A student, always committed to do the best work. The BOPP enrolled successfully in a top-notch college, based on all the great work, extra-curricular activities, and outstanding referral letters that they collected. They were the top students at the top college, outperformed everyone on exams, and graduated with honors.

Shortly after, or even before the completion of their college degree, they landed a job in one of the world's leading companies, such as a tech, consulting, or any other company that most people would "die" to work for. In a matter of a few years, BOPPs rise to earn high incomes in comparison to their peers. They continue to strive for recognition from others at work in the form of positive feedback from their managers, always seeking the next promotion, higher salary, and stock option packages.

The BOPP always excels at what they do, and if they don't, they know exactly what they need to do to get what they want. And so, they have developed the unhealthy habits that come with "success." Working hard and late, not taking breaks, pushing through extreme fatigue and sickness, being completely out of tune to signals that their body gives them.

One of the things that BOPPs weren't taught in school, college, or entering the highly appealing tech and consulting world was how to continuously perform at their best to climb the corporate ladder, while consistently dealing with high levels of stress, high-pressure deadlines, being connected to devices 24/7, and still having a somewhat decent work-life balance.

There are no mandatory programs in the "best companies to work for" today that prevent people from burning out, that teach them methods and tools to optimize their workflow, navigate high-pressure environments swiftly, and keep them accountable to take care of themselves.

People aspire to work in the tech and consulting world, but nothing prepares them for this type of environment. The results are that one in five employees suffer from mental health issues. Two hundred million workdays are lost to depression each year. Work-related stress costs the US economy nearly $300 billion per year, and the estimated cost to the global economy is one trillion dollars per year in lost productivity (WHO, May 2019). The United Kingdom Department of Health and the Confederation of British Industry have estimated that 15 to 30 percent of workers will experience some form of mental health problem during their working lives (WHO Report on Mental Health, May 2019).

Sustaining Performance Over Time

In an environment where everyone is the best, how do you sustain your performance over time and avoid burning out? Start by taking action now. Right now. Don't wait. That is the best advice I can give you. Start to look at your habits and routines, and ask yourself how they help you to consistently perform at your best. Do you finish your workday feeling accomplished? Do you go to bed feeling satisfied and happy?

The first step to that is to create awareness about where you are at. For example: how do you spend the first 60 minutes of your day? On your phone scrolling through social media? Or treating yourself with self-care practices to be at your best for the rest of your day? Track your time. Write down your thoughts. How do you feel? What are you grateful for? How are your stress levels? That's your status quo. From there, you can start to make adjustments. Create new routines. Test out new systems.

One of the biggest realizations I had when I went through my burnout was that my company had amazing benefits in place to help me through this period of time: medical leave, EAP programs, mental health resources.

But why, up until this point, had I never heard about how to prevent getting to burnout in the first place? It's because we are all still learning. Mental health is just starting to become part of the conversation. We like to make corporations responsible for how we feel and slip into the victim role. *I have all these meetings, all these projects.* But you have a choice. You choose how you live your life. You choose how many meetings you accept, how many projects you take on, how you respond to your competitive colleagues, and how many breaks you take. You choose with awareness. You choose when you are conscious. There is no other way.

I didn't know what a mental health condition was until I was diagnosed with one. I always considered myself a really aware person. I was physically active, ate well, and slept at least eight hours per night. You grow with your experiences, and when I burned out, I understood that I had effectively ignored the signals of my body for far too long.

There were signs—difficulty sleeping, digestive problems, negative thoughts, constantly feeling on edge. These were just a few symptoms that slowly started to become part of my day-to-day life. In the end, I didn't feel like myself anymore. Even though on paper I led a dream life, I felt empty.

After a three-month medical leave, I decided to leave my corporate job to dive deeper into the question, "How can peak performers sustain their performance over time without the sacrifice of burning out?" From my own personal experience and from training over 6,500 people from companies like Google, Facebook, Microsoft, Uber, and Swisscom, I identified the most important components to develop the next workplace superpower. I developed the Peak Performance Method.

The Peak Performance Method is a three-dimensional model that combines mindfulness, productivity, and leadership tools to help peak performers create a set of unique skills to continue to deliver high performance without sacrificing mental and physical health.

Based on initial research, applying Peak Performance Method tools in your day-to-day life for only ten consecutive weeks results in significant improvements in the following areas: stress levels decrease by up to 45 percent; depression is reduced by up to 71 percent; sleep quality improves by up to 48 percent; and there's a 26 percent increase in performance and a 41 percent increase positive mindset.

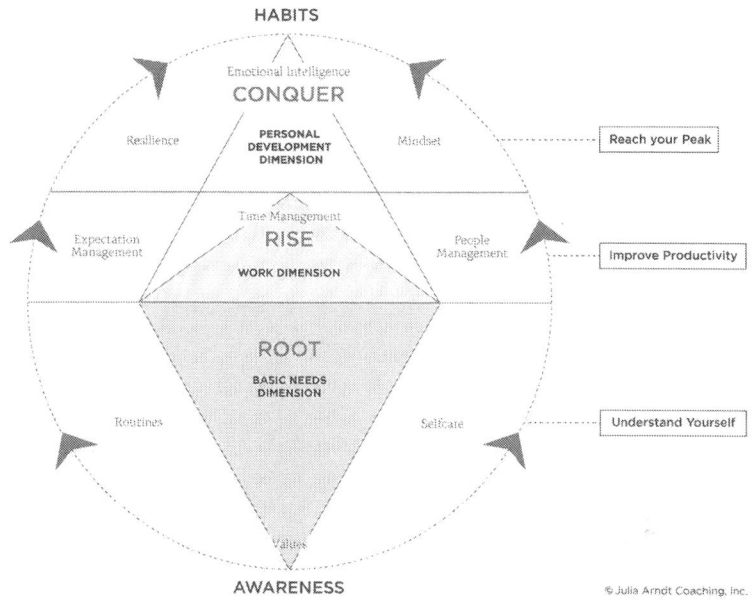

In order to break the burn-out cycle, you need to start adapting your routines, your habits, and your behaviors to build sustainable performance tools over time.
—Julia Arndt

Yoga and meditation, for example, are great tools to manage your stress levels, but if you don't know how to manage your time effectively, set boundaries, and create the right mindset that gets you there, the best 30-minute yoga session won't help you sustain your performance over time. You need to dig deeper than that.

Many people think that by leaving their role or their company, they can fix the problem. They forget that the set of routines and habits that got them there won't miraculously be fixed when they start anew. On the contrary, after their initial six-month honeymoon phase at their new job, they find themselves exactly where they were before: working too many hours and having difficulty prioritizing their tasks and sustaining their concentration and focus throughout the day.

Based on the Anatomy of Work Index 2021 (Haas School of Business, University of California, Berkeley) nine in ten US workers are experiencing burnout today, which can be responsible for up to half of annual employee turnover (Kronos, 2017).

Don't let this be you.

Don't wait until you experience your first panic attack or you feel so burned out that you can't get out of bed anymore. Start now. No more excuses. Not even the excuse that you don't currently feel burned out, overworked, or unproductive. There is always room to grow. Having a winning mindset isn't a short-term phenomenon. To excel and continue to excel, it is important to recognize that we need to take care of ourselves as we compete with other superstars in our respective fields. Through self- care and positive routines, resilience and mindset to keep our winning mindset strong, we can not only become amazing, but we can continue to do amazing things over time.

About the Author

Julia Arndt is the founder of the Peak Performance Method (PPM), a unique model combining critical productivity, mindfulness, and leadership tools to help forward-thinking individuals and organizations develop the next work-place superpower through scalable programs. Julia is a stress management trainer, international speaker, and the host of the "STRESSD" podcast.

Julia originally hails from Germany, has lived in five countries over the last 14 years, and speaks three languages fluently. After working at Google in Silicon Valley for 7.5 years while the company grew from 30,000 to 100,000 employees, Julia has been running her own consulting and coaching business, helping over 6,500 employees at innovative companies like Google, Facebook, Microsoft, Uber, Swisscom, and many more understand the effects of stress on body and mind, move beyond burnout, and build a mindful lifestyle that delivers focus, high energy, and productivity.

Email: julia@peakperformancemethod.com
Website: www.peakperformancemethod.com

CHAPTER FOUR
PERSISTENCE

By Jason Brader
Collegiate Director of Sports Performance
Center Valley, Pennsylvania

Life is ten percent what happens to you and ninety percent how you respond to it.
—Lou Holtz

Life is difficult. Plain and simple. Regardless of social status, age, or gender, life isn't easy. Growing up, I often wondered what it would be like to have money. I'm not talking about Bill Gates' or Elon Musk's money, but enough money to live comfortably. Life was tough growing up in Bethlehem, Pennsylvania. Bethlehem is known for the toughness and grit that Bethlehem Steel characterized. I remember looking out my window as a kid and seeing the gigantic rusted steel stacks across the river. Those steel stacks represented a blue-collar work ethic and the never-quit attitude my parents instilled in my brother and me from an early age.

My parents had my twin brother and me late in life. Both were previously married and had adult children. My father was 58, and my mother was 44 years old when we were born. My father was retired and worked part-time as a crossing guard. My mother was a waitress and earned $3.15 per hour at Bethlehem Steel's headquarters. I remember her walking 2.5 miles to and from work every day. She never complained or made excuses. She did what was necessary for us to survive regardless of how she felt. She was hard-working, and I respected her for it. Her message was simple. Whatever you choose to do, give everything you have and strive for greatness. These words echoed in my ears throughout my life. Mediocrity wasn't in my vocabulary, and I wanted to create a path to success. She taught me to be relentless in everything I did. It didn't matter how difficult the situation was, it was my choice how I attacked any obstacle in my way. At the time, I could have never imagined how tough life would become or how her lessons would guide me through some of the darkest days in my life.

When I was 12 years old, I got my first job as a paperboy. Every day, my mom and I woke up at four in the morning and delivered 100 papers around the neighborhood. My mother and I created some great memories on these early morning walks. While we walked, I told her of my hopes, goals, and dreams. She was a great listener and always gave me great advice. Regardless of what challenges I was facing, she always had a solution. I didn't have a ton of confidence at the time, and she was able to offer me encouragement. I had a stammer, and it made me very self-conscious. Kids from around the neighborhood and school would mock me relentlessly. Life was difficult, but she made sure that I knew she had my back.

Like most 12-year-old boys, I didn't like waking up at four in the morning. However, I knew I wanted to improve my life. It wasn't comfortable, but it was necessary. I enjoyed being independent and purchasing my own things. My mother and the paper route taught me discipline, work ethic, and an entrepreneurial spirit. These early mornings taught me that if I wanted something bad enough, I had to go out and get it. It didn't matter that I was poor or didn't have a big house. It didn't matter that my parents had limited education and connections. What mattered was my attitude and effort. A winning attitude directly impacts effort. When your attitude is great, you have no other choice but to win. Winning is exactly what I did.

I began playing football in seventh grade, and it changed my life. Up until this point, I begged my parents to allow me to play, but we could not afford the fees for the youth league. Finally, when I reached seventh grade, I could play for the school's team. For years, I listened to my classmates talk about their youth football games and how well they did. It was brutal listening to these kids brag about their accomplishments. Now I was able to suit up and get the opportunity to showcase my ability on the football field. What I lacked in size, I made up for in toughness. I was relentless and loved the sheer physicalness of the game. It didn't matter how big, strong, or tough the guy in front of me was. If I was able to stand, I was going to compete. That year I was the only seventh grader to start, and I made an immediate impact. I had instant respect from my coaches, teammates, and opponents. My dad never had the opportunity to play sports when he was growing up, so this allowed us to create a bond. He loved sports, and my parents enjoyed watching me excel on the football field.

I couldn't wait for high school. I had big time aspirations and knew that football was my ticket out. The football field was the great equalizer. Nobody cared where I was from, how I talked, or what I owned. All that mattered was how I performed. Immediately I became a starter on the freshman team, and the coaches knew that I had a ton of potential. Eventually my body caught up to my skills, and I matured into a great football player. I focused on building my body and worked hard in the classroom. Life was good, and I was carving out my niche.

After the season ended, I started to train. I rode my bike to the racquetball club almost every day and envisioned myself playing college football. I pictured myself rushing for thousands of yards and winning awards. In my mind, if I could see it, I would achieve it. This was my primary focus until I noticed my dad's health declining. He smoked since he was a teenager and was a drinker. He spent a lot of time drinking at the social club, smoking, and gambling. These behaviors took a toll on his health and our family. Eventually, years of hard living caught up with him, and he was diagnosed with lung cancer. We were devastated with the diagnosis, and my life was changed in an instant. To make matters worse, my mother began having chest pains. At the time, I told her that it was probably from stress. Little did I know that her chest pains were from inflammatory breast cancer. Eventually her chest pain became so severe we rushed her to the emergency room and received the official diagnosis. My world was crashing around me, and life would never be the same.

While my friends were concerned about dating, sports, and being teenagers, my brother and I were consumed with taking care of our parents. This was my life until my father and mother passed away ten months apart during my junior and senior years. My brother and I found ourselves homeless with little hope and resources. We were on our own, and it was time to make a decision. Do we become products of the system or find a way to win?

Adversity can either make or break an individual. It can become a catalyst to achieve greatness or an excuse to explain failure. Regardless of who you are or where you're from, it is something we all will face at some point in our lives. When I lost my parents, I was at a crossroad in my life. I was in survival mode and had a decision to make. Was I going to allow my circumstances determine my fate, or was I going to make the best of my circumstances?

Persistence

The starting line is always crowded. Everyone is eager and ready to start the race. Weeks, months, and sometimes years of preparation finally come together for one race. This is the moment that everyone has been waiting for and an opportunity to showcase all the hard work. Initially adrenaline is the driving force. The body is strong and ready to perform. The gun goes off, and everyone accelerates from the starting line. As the runners get settled into their race, several begin to separate themselves from the pack. The distance between the runners begins to grow and everyone is finding their pace. This is the point where legs become heavy and lungs begin to burn. Thoughts begin to wander and apprehension begins to creep into the conscious mind. As the race continues, people begin to drift further and further back. At this point, people slow their pace and some will quit. It is decision-making time. This is your defining moment. Do you break through or break down? Most people won't blame you for quitting. Some people will applaud you for even trying. How do you respond? Do you listen to the voice that tells you to continue moving forward or listen to the one that tells you to quit?

Everyone is faced with these decisions on a daily basis. Do we listen to the voice that seeks pleasure and avoids pain, or do we listen to the one that moves us closer to success? The average person decides to quit or slow down. However, the champion pushes forward into the unknown and embraces the pain. Instead of turning down, they decide to turn up. The pain becomes their ally and fuels a newfound strength. This is the opportunity they have been waiting for. This is their chance to find out what is inside them. It is an opportunity to break barriers and realize new possibilities. When the lungs begin to burn, this is where the paycheck is earned. This is where average meets good and good advances towards greatness. Peak performance is realized and your unique potential is discovered.

A method I have used throughout my life to keep focused is visualization. I picture myself tapping a wall with a sledgehammer. When I begin, the sledgehammer leaves little dents. As I hammer the wall, my arms begin to tire and burn. However, I know that eventually I will become adapted to the burning sensation and those small dents will weaken the wall. Eventually the small dents become large breaks until eventually the wall tumbles down. I know that the only way I could lose is if I quit hammering.

Remember that anything worth your time should, and will, be challenging. Don't expect the wall to come tumbling down after one strike. Be ready to hammer until that wall buckles. If you aren't willing to do the hammering, someone else will. The feeling of regret will always outweigh the burning sensation associated with hard work. It will be hard, but ultimately it will be worth it.

Set a Standard and Stick with It

"Tough times don't last, but tough people do." I remember my best friend whispering this to me at my mom's funeral. I was at an all-time low and was scared. I was poor, alone, and emotionally drained. I wasn't feeling very tough at the time. Actually, I was feeling pretty vulnerable, weak. As the priest made his final remarks before he lowered my mother into the ground, I made a promise to myself and my parents. I was going to commit to doing whatever was necessary to carry on their legacy and create my own. I was going to become the first person in my family to graduate from college, become a collegiate All-American running back and hall of fame athlete. I was going to start a family of my own and become a successful and productive member of society. I was going to use all my hardships as motivation. Motivation not only for myself but for others who faced similar adversity. I knew I was tougher than the situation and that God had made me strong for those who were weak. I wasn't going to stop when I was tired but was going to stop when I was finished. After I finished, I was going to reset and repeat. This was my process in everything I did.

No One Owes You Anything

Just because you have endured hardship, doesn't mean anyone owes you anything. Never expect more from anyone than you expect from yourself. After I graduated from college, I created a highly successful sports performance business. During this time, I worked day and night developing my business, and I helped some of the premier athletes in the world. Everything my athletes and I achieved was earned. I wouldn't have wanted it any other way. This was always my mindset when I was an athlete and businessman. However, this wasn't the way I felt when it came to my personal life.

When I was in college, I began drinking on the weekends to celebrate victories. This eventually became part of my process when I reached my goals. It was also an escape mechanism I used to cope with my demons. I didn't realize at the time, all the emotional baggage I stored when I lost my parents. My me-against-the-world attitude helped me overcome adversity, but it eventually was leading to my demise. I had a family, successful business, and a great life to the casual observer. This wasn't the case, and I was struggling. I drank, gambled, and almost lost everything I achieved over two decades. I wanted it to be easy and felt sorry for myself. I thought the world owed me something because I came from nothing and became something. I wasn't who I wanted to be, and I needed to change. I decided to take the same get-it-done approach and start from ground zero. Just before my oldest daughter's twelfth birthday, I told my wife I was finished drinking and gambling. This was the turning point in my life.

The world didn't owe me anything, but I did owe myself, my family, friends, and athletes my best. Every day I focused on my sobriety, and eventually those days turned into weeks, months, and years. Long nights of drinking and gambling became nights I bonded with my wife and children. Initially I felt regret for the time I'd lost hurting myself. This pain was soon replaced by a newfound confidence that enabled me to pursue my lifelong dream of becoming a collegiate strength and conditioning coach. I embraced the mindset that the world didn't owe me anything. I owed the world the best version of myself.

After almost a year of being sober, I told my wife I wanted to sell my business and pursue college coaching. I contacted over 100 BCS football strength and conditioning coaches and had only three replies. One of those coaches was Scott Cochran at the University of Alabama. I was so fired up because he was one of the top coaches in the country. Alabama had just won the National Championship, so I had to jump at the opportunity. Initially I planned on staying the summer and returning to my family and business. It was extremely tough leaving everything and everyone behind, but I needed to do what was necessary to achieve my goals. The summer turned into 14 challenging months of extreme highs and lows. I had an amazing experience that allowed me to create life-changing relationships and work with some of the top football players and coaches in the world. Eventually I was hired by Kurt Hester at Louisiana Tech University and received my first full-time opportunity as a collegiate strength coach. I successfully sold my business on June 1, 2019, and was able to rejoin my family in Pennsylvania when I was hired by Albright College as the director of sports performance.

Expect Things to Get Tougher Before They Get Easier

My life's journey was anything but easy. In retrospect, I wouldn't have wanted it any other way. All the ups and downs and peaks and valleys have shaped me into the person I am today. I have enjoyed financial and professional success. I've also been humbled by self-imposed hardships. I've gained a unique perspective because of these experiences. I have learned that when I accepted that life was hard, I was able to relax and begin living. When I left my family, I returned to living like a spartan. I reverted back to survival mode. By doing this, I was able to enjoy the simple things in life and reflect on my journey, a journey that started as a poor kid from Bethlehem and had moved to becoming a highly respected person who had beaten the odds. A person who is marvelously flawed as well as unique. A person who has an unrivaled spirit that is willing to push the limits to reach his goals.

Remember that regardless of how far you may have fallen or how desperate you may feel, everything that you need to succeed is already in you. All you need to do is take that first step towards your goals. Expect it to be challenging and don't wish it to be any other way. Your legs will become heavy and your lungs will burn. Remember to continue to push forward and don't stop when you are tired. Only stop when you win!

About the Author

Jason Brader is a husband, father of three, entrepreneur, collegiate strength and conditioning coach, inventor, and mentor. He founded, developed, and sold FASST Performance, which was one of the top sports performance facilities in the country for almost two decades. During his career, he has worked with some of the top teams and athletes in the country. Jason is a highly sought-after motivational speaker who has spoken to business leaders, schools, teams, and athletes across the country on topics such as leadership, growth, human potential, goal setting, and overcoming adversity. He recently authored the book, *Why Not Me*. The book is a self-help memoir highlighting Jason's life—overcoming addiction, beating adversity, and reaching your unique potential. You can read more about Jason on his website and learn how he can help you or your organization improve performance.

Email: jason@jasonbraderfasst.com
Website: www.jasonbrader.com

CHAPTER FIVE
EMPOWERED ACTION CHANGES THINGS!

By Jan Carpenter
Founder, Turn Over a New LEAF, Resilience Coach
London, England, United Kingdom

Be the change you want to see in the world [starting from within].
—Gandhi

The most successful people say that persistence is their secret ingredient. The first step is going from idea to action. And, I'm talking about action that changes things, the right kind of action. I'm talking about the type of action that people with a winning mindset take daily, the type of action that leads to success (whatever that is for you).

Yet living with poor health and wellbeing can scupper our plans. Challenging stuff can happen in life, and it can, knowingly or not, be the reason why we "don't" or the reason why we "do". Unknowingly, it can chain us to our past, depleting our best efforts to be successful, to break the mould and stand out, to be our desired future self.

My deepest *why* derives from enduring a big trauma in my early teens—a family breakdown—before which there was a lot of change and bullying. This unknowingly resulted in deep-seated negative emotions of anger and guilt, which, with no one to talk to, incubated through my teens, culminating in rebellion at school. These unconscious emotions would pop up at times when

I was advancing my career in a stressful professional role, as unhelpful waves of emotion and relationship issues, which, over time, caused an autoimmune condition. I had a hunch to listen to the bodily messages and to take action to protect my health from worsening. My health, wellbeing, and peak performance has significantly improved, as have many other people's, since founding Turn Over a New LEAF and integrating Havening Techniques into our inventive transformational LEAF model, which is to Let-go, Empower, Act, Flourish.

I write this chapter with you in mind. I invite you to grab a notebook and engage a different perspective. Answer the questions along the way to ignite awareness and action.

Peak performance simply means giving a specific task, or situation, 100 percent of your effort, energy, and strengths. In a peak performing state, you create the internal conditions to ignite your potential and flow, to grow beyond your comfort zone, to embed and sustain that until it becomes second nature. To that end, I will demonstrate how we use Timothy Gallway's formula for peak performance: Potential minus Interference = Performance (p-i=P) (Gallway, 1997, Inner Game of Work).

Along the course of the 2020 COVID-19 pandemic, research as shown by mentalhealth.org, Sleep Council, imperial.ac.uk, and the United Nations has uncovered a corresponding rise in ambient stress and a decline in the quality of sleep, diet, and exercise. These four factors ignite the "great negative stress cycle." This generates a vulnerable electrochemical landscape within the mind and body, escalating unhealthy electrical brain frequencies and generating toxic stress chemicals, both day and night. This is what we call interference when the body is in survival mode. According to CIPD, mayoclinic.org, Huan Song et. Al., and bbc.com, when endured for too long, it can become chronic and traumatic, contributing to mental and physical "dis-ease", and/or relationship challenges and various levels of stuck-ness, including inertia, problem-focus, or foggy thinking. Negative stress affects work performance. The CIPD notes the correlation between a rise in negative stress during the pandemic and a concerning rise in presenteeism.

You, like all of us, are a mixture of strengths and weaknesses. You may have potential, which is hidden from you and the world at large. Our potential can be unknowingly scuppered by poor wellbeing habits and internal emotional interference. At any one moment, we have a mixture of conscious/unconscious and helpful/unhelpful emotions, thoughts, and beliefs that drive our behaviours. Our own "inner stuff" can sometimes be our biggest obstacle to letting the best version of ourselves shine through. Our capacity to get out of our own way may be one of our biggest strengths. When you reduce the interference of stressful emotions from within yourself and tune in to peak performance states, you empower your potential to ignite and deliver your best performance, tapping into your creativity, flow, and strengths.

The LEAF Model

Here I'll explain our LEAF model: Let-go, Empower, Act, Flourish:

"Let-go" can be achieved using Havening Techniques® (explained later), enabling you to weed out unwanted emotions and related symptoms and behaviours, stemming from past trauma, which might have accumulated over a lifetime, sapping you of the essential energy required for peak performance. Note any unhelpful emotions or behaviours you'd like to stop in your personal or work life.

"Empower" involves using Havening Techniques, coaching, and neuro-linguistic programming (NLP) to tap into what we truly want in life and using the power of imagination and intention to associate it with peak performance, goals, and outcomes. What is the goal that you need peak performance for? What desired outcome do you want to achieve from that? What is your "why" that's so important to you about this? What energising, positive emotions do you hope to gain more of? What would you do differently if you took the braver path?

"Action" involves experimenting with and forming "little and often" wellbeing habits to reduce the level of stress toxicity in your body and forge a path towards a positive stress cycle. Deliberate actions to improve your mood, breathing, nutrition, rest/sleep, and fitness with the intention to optimise your brain, gut, heart, nervous system, and your whole self to thrive, whatever the external adverse conditions. What "little and often" actions do you/can you take to engage your positive stress cycle every day? Action changes things! What action will you take every morning that will start you off in your optimal self?

All of this is aimed at helping you to "Flourish". That is, to deliberately integrate a balance of the following wellbeing domains into your life every day:

- Healthy body
- Emotional wellbeing
- Productive thinking and creativity

- Positive relationships
- Optimal communication
- Engagement/flow

And with those wellbeing domains at play in your daily life, it helps to generate greater levels of the following peak performing outcomes:

- Psychological safety (inner calm)
- Energy (get-up-and-go)
- Positive Mental Filters (emotions, thoughts, beliefs, attitude)
- Neuroplasticity (brain resilience)
- Growth mindset (stretch)
- Mental and physical health (comfort)
- Synergy (spark/creativity)
- Community (belonging)
- Meaning and purpose (spiritual)
- Accomplishments (achievement/contribution)
- Authentic happiness (joy)

In truth, peak performance is unique to everyone. Take a moment to note which domains and outcomes are your strengths and where you may have gaps.

Havening Techniques®

The remainder of this chapter illustrates how we use Havening Techniques to help clients achieve various LEAF domains and outcomes. Havening Techniques is a subtle yet powerful psychosensory technique rooted in the latest neuroscience, founded by Dr Ron Ruden 20 years ago. More recently, it has attracted research from UK universities including King's College London confirming its efficacy in helping to address internal interferences that result in stress-related mental and physical ill health and work performance.

Havening Techniques® engages our inherent biological systems to permanently heal, strengthen, and empower our minds and bodies
—Dr Ruden

Havening reduces the internal interference caused by negative stress, traumatic stress, and vicarious stress, all of which can too easily become "encoded" into the amygdala (the trauma centre of the brain) when four conditions known as "EMLI" are met: a threatening EVENT takes place (i.e., job loss/change/incident, death, relationship crisis, mental or physical ill health event, performance failure, etc.), with the MEANING "I could lose something I'm attached to" (i.e., not winning/attaining a much desired peak performance outcome), at a time when there is a "vulnerable electrochemical LANDSCAPE" within the brain, and there is a perception of INESCAPABILITY, that is, feeling trapped or unable to control or influence the situation. Encoded traumas can be big, small, and/or incremental, momentary, endured in childhood and/or adulthood, and/or experienced in the first, second, or third person.

Briefly note any big or small encoded traumas you have endured in your life that could possibly be interfering with you reaching your desired peak performance and outcomes.

Once trauma is encoded, the biological alarm system is set up that can cause an array of "fight-flight", subtle to overt, and distressing involuntary symptoms (i.e., fast heart rate, sweaty palms, butterflies, foggy thinking, anxiety, pain, etc.). Unresolved traumatic stress endured over a long period of time generates an internal toxic environment that can quietly gnaw away at our capacity for peak performance, depleting capacity in our resilience bucket and, over time, creating a fixed mindset, suppressing our immune system, and gradually causing a range of stress related "dis-ease".

Note down any "fight-flight" symptoms you observe in yourself and in what situations.

Now, I invite you to do a basic Self-Havening session. Read through this paragraph first before following the procedure. Note down your desired peak performance goal. Momentarily recall any stress/tension linked to that which brings up any stressful emotions (e.g., fear, worry, anger, frustration, etc.) into working memory to activate the amygdala. Note down your discomfort rating of the stress/tension out of 10 (10 = high discomfort/0 = low). For learning purposes, aim for no more than 5/10. Use Havening Touch by rhythmically stroking your face and arms in a downward motion and hands in a circular motion. Harper et al.'s research in "Taming the Amygdala" found this action generates calming delta brain waves, "feel good" neurochemicals, and a neurobiological sense of safety in the mind.

After which, we use various subtle yet powerful techniques, involving a mix of distraction, imagination, sensory input, and intention, to help measurably reduce the perceived level of stress, creating a window of time to let go, build resilience, and tune in to the empowered peak performance (growth) outcome.

Now identify two off-topic activities you enjoy doing, for example, cooking, admiring trees, hiking, etc., and one fantastically positive experience in your life and how that felt. Then, while doing Havening Touch, imagine yourself actually doing them, describing each one in turn for two minutes out loud. After that, note down your out of ten rating again. Then repeat, each time enriching the experience with what you're seeing, hearing, smelling, and positively feeling until you notice your score has reduced. Now describe your desired best peak performing outcome, you at your utmost best, in flow, with empowered positive emotions. Then repeat the following statements several times in turn:

- What if I was [state the positive emotion you feel right now] more of the time? (i.e., happy, calm, excited, brave.)
- I deserve to feel [this positive emotion] more of the time.
- I can see myself being grateful for [this positive emotion] more of the time.

Observe the results, note how you feel!

LEAF blends in a selection of Havening Techniques for four significant outcomes:

L   To LET-GO of unwanted emotions caused by "encoded' traumatic stress, thereby freeing up energy and capacity to focus more on the performance task.

E   To EMPOWER desired outcomes, goals, and performance mindset.

A   To enact a momentum of resilience ACTIONS and routines to enhance neuroplasticity over time, for a growth mindset and to learn and adapt more easily and effectively.

F   To ignite a shift from limiting to empowering beliefs to broaden potential to FLOURISH in your desired peak performance outcome and life.

With generous permission from three of our clients, I illustrate here how we're using Havening and our LEAF model to achieve wellbeing and peak performance in various ways.

Our first case study is about Frank whose peak performance goal was to optimise his personal relationships and to feel a sense of authentic happiness. Relationships are a core part of our existence. When managed well, they provide a well-spring of happiness and vice versa. Emotions are at the core of all our relationships, whether personal or business.

Frank has a strong belief in harmony and service through relationships, and an interest in helping to solve other people's problems. He believes that doing good brings good. At times, he would find himself being accommodating to the detriment of his own desires or needs being met. He would also have sudden panic-like feelings, shortness of breath accompanied by feelings of inadequacy, overwhelm, and dread. This might occur when helping others or when doing day-to-day or performance activities. Not that people would easily have spotted this as he was skilled at hiding it, but the level of energy it took being on-guard and ready for the next attack and then recovering each time, was immense.

It transpired that the root of Frank's trauma stemmed back to his childhood when he felt a sense of responsibility to make his then distressed single mother feel better, but was unable to do so. This was at a time when there was a long period of arduous "ambient" stress. Both mother and child were vulnerable electrochemically and, therefore, increasing the likelihood of stress or trauma being encoded.

Multiple therapies later, nothing truly worked until Havening Techniques. Now Frank reports, "I feel myself again", "I had no idea I could feel this safe and resilient", and "I'm free to communicate openly with people", and "I have the choice to accommodate others if I choose to." After just three sessions of Havening/LEAF, his peak performance goal was made far easier to achieve. Potential minus Interference equals Peak Performance. By showing Frank his potential and eliminating the interference from his childhood experience, Frank was able to perform better.

Our second case study is about Sandra. Her peak performance goal, as a paid-by-the-hour contractor, was to not let severe hay fever stop her from working and to work optimally. For three months of the year, from March to May, when the cherry blossom tree is in bloom in the UK, Sandra would have flu-like symptoms, swollen eyes and joints, and she would be scared to go outside in case it worsened. This caused a corresponding negative impact on her mood, which negatively affected her performance at work. She had to take time off work when it got really bad, and this was exacerbated by the looming idea that her contract could be ended at any time with two weeks' notice.

With some investigating, it became evident that Sandra's allergy started after a traumatic pregnancy, 18 years before. We used Havening Techniques to let go of the unhelpful traumatic emotions that were still attached to the memory of the event. After two brief sessions, the hay fever was gone and continues to be gone three years later. Sandra no longer feels unsafe going out for those three months of the year and can actually stand underneath a cherry blossom tree with no ill effects.

The wellbeing outcome was that she got her healthy body back. The peak performance outcome was her high level of motivation, commitment, and performance.

Whilst this relates to a transitory auto-immune condition, we know that the symptoms of autoimmune diseases can worsen with stress and, on un.org, Harvard recently cited a study by Huan Song et al. finding a causal link between traumatic stress and autoimmune disease for a higher proportion of people. Hence, the use of Havening can have a radical positive effect on the pain and discomfort of such physical health conditions for the advantage of peak performance.

Our third case study is Emma, whose peak performance goal was to perform at her best in a divorce court hearing. The desired accomplishment in this case was to be one of the 20 percent of self-litigating women who win such cases, a learning opportunity for career advancement, and a symbol against misogyny.

The odds were stacked against her. Even though she felt prepared from an evidential basis, she was concerned that all the emotional strife under the surface, endured from a challenging and abusive childhood that echoed through her life and relationships, would come out in the hearing, and she'd be considered unhinged, her evidence belittled, and walking straight into the 80 percent of self-litigants who fail.

After just three Havening LEAF sessions, she was primed and ready to restart the legal proceedings. The outcome was that she presented herself in line with that 20 percent performance zone: emotionally stable, compassionate, and determined. She came out feeling more positive about the outcome than she had previously expected.

So, to summarise: Potential minus Interference equals Peak Performance means first having an empowered peak performing outcome, being clear on your deepest "why", associating with what you want to see, hear and feel, and setting some short- and long-term goals with that end in mind.

Secondly, Havening is an effective tool to help you reduce inner interference and smooth the way to that end in mind. When you push beyond your comfort zones, there is a tendency for the body, life, and the universe to push back. It might feel stressful, painful, and a struggle. If you push through those barriers and persist on, leveraging them as opportunities to heal, using Havening, you have the potential to break through your own wellbeing and peak performance ceilings. No one ever said this was going to be easy, yet creating a winning mindset and reaching peak performance can be made easier using Havening and the LEAF model.

About the Author

Jan Carpenter is the founder of Turn Over a New LEAF, certified Havening Techniques® practitioner and trainer, personal performance coach, and NLP practitioner. Turn Over a New LEAF brings a selection of highly effective tools, technology, and scalable coaching to enhance wellbeing, positively impacting on personal performance and workplace performance.

Jan enables peak performance outcomes by helping customers to improve on six wellbeing domains through the lense of his innovative LEAF model—Let-Go, Empower, Action, Flourish—delivered through online one-to-one sessions and workshops.

Throughout Jan integrates the practical neuroscience of Havening Techniques to empower transformation. The overall outcome being enhanced wellbeing and performance, towards flourishing in the humdrum of life or in any particular endeavour we set our mind to.

With gratitude for your active participation in this chapter. Join us on a LEAF workshop or for a one-to-one session. Remember: Action Changes Things!

Email: info@turnoveranewleaf.co.uk
Website: turnoveranewleaf.co.uk
LinkedIn: linkedin.com/in/turnoveranewleaf

CHAPTER SIX
LEADER, KNOW THYSELF

By Rose Cartolari
International Leadership Advisor and Executive Coach
Milan, Italy / New York, USA

He who cannot change the very fabric of his thought will never be able to change reality, and will never, therefore, make any progress.
—A. Sadat

For over 30 years, I have worked in large organizations, from American Express to UNICEF and as an entrepreneur/co-founder and COO of a successful multinational pharmaceutical company. Currently, I act as an advisor and coach to senior-level leaders and entrepreneurs. The patterns are always the same: the most successful leaders are those who are deeply grounded, so self- and situationally-aware that they are able to effectively interact with others, as well as emerging market conditions. They have deep understanding, poise, and vision. They are calm in the face of instability and rapid changes, and they are adept at handling complexity and constant evolution. They are comfortable holding and seeking opposing ideas at the same time, are at ease concentrating on targets and developing deep competencies while still being able to change quickly. They have a mindset that allows them to win while others fail.

A deep grounding is their "core," the key to their dexterity and agility as well as long-term achievements. With ambiguity becoming one of the defining features of the workplace today, being able to stand strong in the midst of uncertainty is crucial to success.

In fact, one of the concepts gaining a stronghold in the field of leadership and leadership development is the notion that leaders must be able to renew their own capabilities and styles, and to create cultures in their organization that are ready to handle any type of issue that may come up. Key to this is a leader's ability to reinvent themselves and to know how, what, and when to do it. It involves taking the time to reflect, develop self-awareness, and be ready and nimble in adapting and updating based on changing needs, while holding firm to well-defined core values and principles.

In order to explore a winning mentality and to help you perform at the cutting edge of your chosen work, this chapter will explore what real (and useful) self-awareness is and why it is critical for leaders to start getting deeply acquainted with themselves. With the pressures I see so many leaders facing today, it is easy to focus on fixing external problems and processes and to jump into action. However, real transformation of opportunities, of workplaces, of communities, and of performance—both individual as well as collective—is about transforming people, not just transforming processes, and then asking or expecting people to follow suit. So, if we want to have the right mindset to transform our reality, we need to start with transforming ourselves. And the first step to changing ourselves is self-awareness.

The Changing Landscape of Leadership

The world today, entering the spring of 2021, is unpredictable, disruptive, rapidly changing. The only way to stay "stable" is for people and organizations to show that they are resilient, can quickly grasp changing and foggy situations, and can think and act ahead of the curve. In the face of unprecedented changes, the very meaning of what leadership is today is changing, and leaders now have to find new and different ways of creating both a long-term and sustainable future for their organizations as well as delivering strong results today.

Leaders can rarely enjoy the "smartest person in the room" status as technology, globalization and diversity of teams are shifting our notions of needed skills. They are, therefore, required to move from a "command and control" role to one of inspiring, motivating, and empowering increasingly diverse teams. They need to be able to identify, nourish, and sponsor experts in a range of fields who are "smarter" than they, themselves, are, and certainly more knowledgeable in certain areas, as well as finding ways to mobilize everyone towards a common objective.

Not all leaders have this capability. Often those who lead us today were promoted because of their technical and business capabilities, but now they are required to quickly adapt and update to newer skills that are required to lead. This means expanding on growth-focused behaviors: flexibility, curiosity, openness, perspective taking, iterative thinking, the ability to receive and understand data (feedback) of all kinds, and having enough humility to respond.

These are all characteristics of a growth mindset and emotional intelligence, two of the key skills for leaders today.

Founded on research by Carol Dweck, a growth mindset is the belief that abilities (such as intelligence and talent) can be developed and cultivated through hard work and effort. On the other hand, the belief that a person is born with fixed abilities, that can rarely be altered, is called a fixed mindset.

Emotional Intelligence, a concept made popular by Daniel Goleman, refers to a person's facility in recognizing, managing, and using their own and others' emotions in ways that help a person understand emotional needs, tensions, and dynamics in a group and, ultimately, empathize, diffuse conflicts, and overcome challenges.

Seems Obvious, So What Is the Problem?

Developing a growth mentality and emotional intelligence skills means working on yourself. It requires having a strong emotional grounding and awareness, being clear minded in the midst of turbulence, and being able to develop a listening skill that can pick up even weak signals in churning markets.

And while this notion resonates with many, on a conceptual and intellectual level, most leaders (most people, I would venture to say) don't really want or like to work on themselves. Why is that? There are several reasons:

- Many just don't see the need. These people are multi-talented, focused, and highly accomplished. They have worked very hard to get to where they are, having made it past much of the competition to have finally "arrived" at an important place. It's very hard to see further space for improvement. And from their point of view, they're not wrong. Those skills and attitudes got them promoted many times. It is hard for them to always see themselves as a work in progress because it means they have to question themselves, often undermining that very thing that they believe is the key to their success. However, this often leads to an incorrect sense of their own performance and can lead to a sort of complacent self-confidence. It also means they are less likely to seek out feedback for improvement. Not surprisingly, research has shown that the more experienced a manager is, the less able they are to truly judge how effective they are.

- Self-improvement takes courage. For leaders, it's not easy to accept that all they learned and all they know, all they have achieved and accomplished is no longer valid or best-in-class. It's hard to bow to the notion that they have to update, change, adapt. These leaders are being asked to give up something that has functioned for them and brought them success, for something else that is uncertain. Risk taking is difficult for all of us, and the more experienced or "in charge" we are, the harder it is to put ourselves up for discussion, to be put "in play."

- Finally, many of the leaders today, at least in the corporate world, are no longer "spring chickens," and so their learning and habits have been embedded for years. Certainly, learning things after 50 is not like learning things at 20 or 30—you just don't have the same mental or physical energy and flexibility. It's much harder to push yourself, to work on yourself.

For these reasons, many of us stop entering into growth conversations with ourselves. This is the big challenge of the corporate world, because if we really want to transform our organizations, we need to start transforming ourselves first. Otherwise, all we will see is the multiplication of "growth" jargon and hype throughout organizations, but with little or no change. So, a potentially game-changing mindset transformation is often reduced to a compliance-based, politically correct action or annoying verbiage.

Self-Awareness: The Game Changer

A huge body of research shows that when we know and see ourselves clearly, we have a clearer picture of gaps in our skills. It allows us to both notice and understand better our strengths as well as areas for development. This, in turn, allows us to understand where we can benefit from input in making decisions, in nurturing cultures of openness, and in motivating and inspiring employees towards shared goals.

Greater self- and situational-awareness also drive a leader's ability to recognize their biases, emotions and behavior, and situational awareness allows them to be in tune with the people around them. In other words, it makes leaders more emotionally intelligent. It becomes a powerful tool to influence and impact those around them and strengthens not only their performance, but that of their teams and organizations, which, ultimately, is the role of leaders.

From all the research conducted on this matter, two types of self-awareness emerge:

1. Internal—which focuses on our ability to understand our inner workings, what we care about, what drives us, our passions, fears, triggers, and feelings.
2. External—which represents how others look at, feel, and think about us, with respect to our behavior and how we appear to them.

Of course, being self-aware in one area does not mean that you are also self-aware in the other. In fact, there is very little correlation between the two. But the higher your internal self-awareness is, the more you will be able to ground and center yourself. The better you will be at recognizing and overcoming triggers that destabilize you. By having an intimate knowledge of your inner workings, you will be able to decrease reactivity, and better manage stress and anxiety.

On the other hand, having a clear picture and understanding of how others see you makes it more likely that you will be able to have closer connections with people and satisfaction in your relationships. A great way to do this is to use a 360-degree evaluation tool to get real-time feedback and then use the information to enter in deeper conversations as well as behavior change.

Developing Better Overall Self-Awareness

To develop better self-awareness, I would propose these four simple steps:

1. *Go out of your way to be curious about why you do what you do.* It's hard to maintain a sense of who you are when you are called to answer to so many different kinds of problems on many different fronts. So, keep asking yourself questions and get feedback. *How do I respond to certain things? Why did I respond in that way? How do I handle issues/people/*

things that are uncomfortable? How do I handle not being comfortable with or not knowing something?

2. *Be honest and open about wanting to improve and actively seek feedback and work on yourself.* This will not only give you valuable input for your own growth but will signal to others that you value growth and that you support everyone in growing and working on themselves. The more open leaders are with showing that they desire feedback and constant improvement, the more likely the organization will follow suit.

3. *Zoom out.* Take some time to get a higher-level perspective. Take a step back and look at the 360-degree context. *What should I focus on? What is distracting me? What will this problem look like in a week? In a month? Who else should I talk to in that context?* This type of deep thinking allows for better clarity and provides an opportunity to model how to process and react without fear of decision making in ambiguous or changing situations.

4. *Intentionally seek out perspectives, ideas, people, and skills that are not your own.* Take a moment to ask yourself: *whose perspective am I not taking here? Who would disagree with this and what would be at the root of that disagreement?* Actively encourage opposing viewpoints and alternative perspectives to avoid groupthink.

Ultimately, qualities like trustworthiness, reliability, vision, and understanding are what will drive individuals and teams to perform at their peak and to take on a world which is changing constantly and rapidly. The more resilient and growth-minded leaders are, the more successfully they can lead themselves and their organizations.

However, we need to go beyond that. The required change is deeper, more personal, and more sustainable. Leaders need to take the first step in knowing themselves more deeply and showing up more authentically.

In the end, it's a matter of taking one crucial step: begin with yourself. That is the only way we can all become what Satya Nadella, CEO of Microsoft, defines as a "learn-it-all" rather than "know-it-all" kind of leader. And that is how, as leaders, we can all help our communities, organizations, and ourselves to perform in ways that are worthy of our role.

About the Author

Rose Cartolari is a leadership advisor and executive coach whose 30-year career includes management roles in large organizations such as American Express and UNICEF, teaching in elite business schools in the US and Italy, as well as co-founding and serving as COO of Scharper Pharmaceuticals. Having lived internationally her whole life, Rose's consulting practice spans across continents and she is fluid in working with diverse cultures and perspectives. Her expertise in growth mindset, creating top-performing teams, and leadership upskilling has helped hundreds of executives be successful, energized, and influential. Rose is a member of the Forbes Coaches Council and writes and speaks internationally on issues related to leadership strategy, personal empowerment, and culture change.

Website: www.rosecartolari.com
LinkedIn: https://www.linkedin.com/in/rosecartolari/

CHAPTER SEVEN

FROM SCARCITY TO MASTERY: EVOLVING THROUGH TRANSITIONS WITH THE ATHLETE MINDSET

By Molly Connolly, CPC, ELI-MP
Founder of Ipseity Life Coaching, Athlete Transition Coach
St. Louis, Missouri

Lose yourself in the joy of the process, not the accolades of "success."
—Christopher Bergland

Over the past decade or more, mindset has been discussed as what sets elite athletes apart from their competition. Businesses have jumped on the mindset bandwagon trying to develop their employees with skills such as resiliency, grit, and motivation in order to meet company objectives. Yet developing a mindset isn't a one-flip switch. It evolves over time, and, honestly, it requires digging deep within ourselves.

As a former collegiate athlete and an athlete transition coach, I've experienced and seen firsthand the effects of what our past experiences, thoughts, and emotions have on our mindset, specifically with the scarcity and mastery mindsets, and our ability to perform.

In this chapter, I'll share what I call the cycle of the athlete mindset and what areas people can develop to help move from a scarcity mindset to a mastery mindset.

All client examples provided are from former collegiate athletes. Their experiences occurred as they transitioned out of sport or involved methods they learned through sport before applying strategies from the cycle of the athlete mindset.

Scarcity Mindset

The scarcity mindset, simply put, is the belief that resources are limited and even the belief that there can be a lack of necessary resources within oneself. With the scarcity mindset, there's never enough money, never enough time, never enough fill-in-the-blank. *I'm not smart enough, not thin enough, not fill-in-the-blank enough.*

Sadly, the scarcity mindset has shown up in every single one of my clients. Why? Because its toxicity is everywhere within our culture and our own negative self-talk, our inner critic.

Even the basic notion of winning and losing is a perfect example of the scarcity mindset. How it works is that an athlete constantly questions their self-worth based on whether they win or lose when, in fact, performance doesn't equate to self-worth. The scarcity mindset feeds off of comparing ourselves to others and can even be comparing ourselves to our past self when going through a significant change.

Mastery Mindset

Mastery mindset is not the opposite of the scarcity mindset, but more about being present, enjoying the process, and acknowledging the opportunity for growth from any outcome. A person with this mindset has learned how to trust themselves and is aware of what impacts their confidence in situations. By continuously practicing self-growth, this person shifts their perspective to "being" versus "doing" or "having." The mastery mindset is developed over time with constant curiosity and perseverance. But how? Here's where the cycle of the athlete mindset comes into play.

The Cycle of the Athlete Mindset

The athlete mindset is developed not only through certain qualities and actions, but also through a specific set of skills or disciplines centered around thought and emotion. Over time, these disciplines can move an athlete from a scarcity mindset to a mastery mindset, no matter their athletic ability.

During my time as a collegiate athlete, I was completely unaware how these disciplines (or lack thereof) would allow me to accelerate my growth in self-discovery, career, relationships, and even finances. Now, I use these with my clients as they pertain to their own goals and objectives when developing a mastery mindset and transitioning out of their sport.

Self-Awareness and Self-Acceptance

First and foremost, self-awareness and self-acceptance are the most critical disciplines in developing the mastery mindset. You can't have one without the other, and they allow the rest of the cycle to be as efficient as possible through self-growth.

When I mention self-awareness, I'm specifically referring to your beliefs, values, responses, and even your thoughts and emotions. By knowing what they are and where they come from, you're able to select the beliefs, values, and responses that serve you best. You're able to set a foundation to walk your talk. As you practice self-awareness, you'll begin to notice changes within your environment and within others.

One of the biggest aha moments with self-awareness is "reality vs. the story." A client of mine, Anna, discovered one of her two core values was connection, yet she was having a difficult time with certain friendships, especially now that her collegiate swimming career was over. In one of our early sessions, she elaborated about a recent get-together where both her and her friends were upset. Eventually the blame fell to her. Anna went on to explain that she only tried to help and do what was right. We examined "what was right," and she realized this was her "story." Technically, "what was right" can be viewed differently and separately for each individual. When recognizing that her value of connection was pushing her into situations, she started asking herself if she really needed to be involved or was involving herself unnecessarily in order to feel connected. Anna was able to not only develop her self-awareness, but honor her value of connection with others.

Building off of self-awareness is self-acceptance, especially when viewing life from "reality vs. the story." At this point, we need to reexamine ourselves and how we approach situations. Here, there is no judgment. You accept who you are and where you are, right here, right now. You acknowledge that the past experiences, beliefs, and values you reviewed for self-awareness made you who you are and helped set you up for where you want to go.

In the first few months of starting my coaching business, I had a friend, Megan, reach out for coaching. Let me start out saying Megan is a badass. As a previous Division I collegiate soccer player, her drive for perfection and desire to go above and beyond appears in everything she touches. For her, authentic connection is a value she holds high on a pedestal. Whether it's her career, her relationships, where she lives, or what she does for fun, she pours her heart and soul into it.

To my surprise, we discovered a high level of imposter syndrome within her. Megan was constantly running into walls of self-doubt and feeling not good enough when she didn't have all the answers. Learning and research were key to her feeling secure in her recommendations at work, yet they were overly time-consuming. The majority of her tactics came from previous experiences and knowledge, but incorporated new technology or products that would make the process more efficient.

Once we exposed these gaps, Megan was able to level-set herself. She acknowledged her expertise and passion for wanting to learn new things. Her solution was to continue to share her knowledge and strategies while asking to learn more from others in specialized areas. Riding this wave allowed her to not only gain self-acceptance, but allowed her value for authentic connection within team members over time.

The interplay between both self-awareness and self-acceptance creates your own personalized method of self-compassion. It is important for high achievers to remove perceived expectations from others (and ourselves) to become our true selves and move into the mastery mindset.

Trusting the Process

As you practice and build self-awareness and self-acceptance, you begin to trust the process. You're able to start where you are and explore the process leading to your results. You know what bothers you, what lights you up, what you value, and why. You're able to focus in the moment by trusting yourself that what you're doing is all part of the process. Here you begin to make decisions based on previous outcomes and experiences while building resiliency, determination, and passion for the task at hand.

During a session Ryder was exploring determination and resilience while trusting the process. He brought up the continuous improvement method, also known as aggregating marginal gains. By becoming 1 percent better than you were the day before, you'll be 37 percent better a year from the day you started (1.01 to the 365th power = 37.78). Ryder explained he used this formula when he was a collegiate football player and tries to apply it in his everyday life. Of course, the opposite is true. If you decline, let's say due to an injury or lack of motivation, by 1 percent every day, you'll have a substantial aggregating marginal loss in performance (0.99 to the 365th power = 0.03). Ryder's example strengthens the notion that each and every one of us is a continuous work of increasing or decreasing progress.

Rinse and Repeat

As you work through the first two areas of the cycle of the athlete mindset, self-awareness and self-acceptance to trusting the process, you'll begin to see what's working and what is not. You loop back to self-awareness when reviewing the process and accepting where you are in order to make slight adjustments to the overall approach.

Think about it this way—progress is better than perfection. Where you are is still in progress, there is no end point. It's not "When I have this, I will do that." There is no such thing. You're always in motion. You're always changing. You're always in transition. When you do this enough and see the outcomes, you're able to trust yourself.

Refining these three disciplines on a consistent basis allows you to become more efficient and increase your mastery mindset. In fact, the disciplines become habits, making the conscious unconscious, which leads to the next stage of the cycle: the flow state.

The Flow State

When were you so heavily involved in a task or conversation, that you lost track of time? Or when did life slow down, and your movements felt effortless and already predetermined? Maybe the feeling was more about perspective, and you were more aware and observant than participating or performing? Moments such as these are called being "in the zone" or the "flow state," also known as synchronicity.

But how does the flow state happen? It happens through connection to the present moment. Practicing the prior disciplines over time while doing something you're passionate about allows you to narrow the gap until the connections meet.

Here authentic connections become imperative to move closer to the powerful "flow state." As you expand your awareness and acknowledge who you are, the connection between the two leads to an authentic connection to self. The connection amplifies outward to the connection with others, to your environment, and to life as a whole.

Overlapping the discipline of trusting the process pushes you slightly out of your comfort zone and expands your risk-taking, allowing for additional self-growth. Not only do you trust the process, but you build confidence and intuition of when to trust your gut. Then that confidence builds even higher allowing you to make quicker decisions that align with your true self.

Applying the Athlete Mindset During Transitions

When using the cycle of the athlete mindset, it's imperative to give yourself grace during a new or significant transition. Why? Because you're human! Think of one of your top skills or passions. How long did it take you to develop and use it with ease? If you're an athlete, you know it's taken years, if not decades, to get to where you are. Why would it be any different for a large transition? In the next section, I share different ways clients have used the disciplines of the athlete mindset cycle during their transitions.

Developing the Disciplines

Reflection is key to mastering each of these disciplines. If it wasn't necessary, athletes wouldn't spend hours reviewing previous performances to learn and prepare for what's next.

I give each of my clients a reflection journal that consists of a handful of questions to help them process the session and what happens between sessions. Use these questions as you work your way through the disciplines to shed light on your insights and areas for growth:

- What are you experiencing?
- What new connections are you making?
- What has real meaning for you?
- What has challenged you?
- What are the greatest insights or new understandings?
- What is missing from the picture?
- What do you need more clarity on?

Starting with the self-awareness and self-acceptance client examples, the more Anna and Megan practiced these disciplines, the easier they became ingrained. Of course, the toughest part is executing the disciplines when they're needed most—in the moment.

For Anna, practicing self-awareness came from identifying the moment where her value of connection was being neglected. Discovering those moments where your values are being challenged or neglected allows you to see what's not serving you. Ask yourself the following questions:

- How are you thinking and feeling when your values are being honored versus when your values are being challenged or neglected?
- What in your current life allows you to honor your values?
- What is one achievable step you can take over the next week to incorporate your values more often in your daily life?

Megan was able to practice self-acceptance by level-setting her expectations of her work performance. Expectations from ourselves and others are difficult for most high achievers. When you're experiencing self-doubt, ask yourself the following:

- How is my lack of acceptance holding me back right now?
- What's preventing me from being more accepting of myself?
- How can I use this insight to enhance my performance or next step?

Ryder's discussion about the continuous improvement method really came down to the fact that we're a constant work in progress. Yet, how do we work on trusting the process? Usually in this discipline we have concrete goals and plans, yet, at times, they are so large it can take years to accomplish. In order to build resilience and confidence when trusting the process, you would need to evaluate the progress and determine what changes are necessary. As you're working through your goals, ask yourself the following questions:

- What are the advantages and disadvantages of staying true to your goals or plans in the current situation?
- What is working well for you and what is not?
- How can you adapt your current strategy to slightly stretch yourself out of your comfort zone?
- How will you celebrate your small wins as you work through trusting the process?

Developing the flow state encompasses the disciplines above, yet a few simple tactics can heighten the sense of connection. Continue to use reflection and draw upon the last time you experienced the flow state.

- Describe the experience in as much detail as possible.
- What parts of the experience were memorable?
- What made it so special?
- What can you replicate from the experience to bring yourself to being fully present?

Evolving to a Mastery Mindset

Since change is constant, no one stays in the mastery mindset. It's a life-long practice. Each experience of the disciplines gives you the opportunity to gain new knowledge and information. You strive for continual improvement, knowing that results, whether that's losing the championship game or accepting the new job, do not get in the way. Here, you realize you can't make a mistake as it's all part of the process. You remove expectations from self and from others. You enjoy the process while not focusing on the destination.

About the Author

Molly Connolly, CPC, ELI-MP is a former Division II athlete and has been a competitive swimmer for over 25 years. She started Ipseity Life Coaching to help former college athletes transition to a life outside of their sport with confidence and clarity. Molly overlays her experience with the athlete mindset to her client's everyday life to help them move out of their comfort zone and achieve personal goals all the while discovering who they are once their athletic career has ended.

Molly is a certified professional coach, Energy Leadership™ Index Master Practitioner, and COR.E Transitions Dynamics Specialist™ through the Institute for Professional Excellence in Coaching (iPEC). She has also served as the communications board chair for ICF Nebraska and on the marketing committee for the Midwest Regional Coaches Conference.

Download your free "Developing the Athlete Mindset Disciplines" guidebook at the website below.

Email: molly@ipseitylifecoaching.com
Website: https://www.ipseitylifecoaching.com/
LinkedIn: https://www.linkedin.com/in/mollyeconnolly/
Instagram: @ipseitylifecoaching

CHAPTER EIGHT
THE POWER OF BELIEF

By Liam Donnelly
Professional Triathlete
Guelph, Ontario, Canada

If you ask any high-performance athlete or coach about the pillars of performance, they will likely mention how sport is both physical and mental—you need to have the physical ability to meet the demands of competition, and you need to have the mental toughness and experience to match physical ability. While I agree these are essential components of performance, I think we often overlook a third, equally important aspect—the emotional.

I believe our thoughts and self-talk are a powerful tool that can either elevate or inhibit performance. Understanding ourselves and being aware of our emotions are essential to maximizing our potential on any given day. Emotions can influence performance, and we can influence our emotions.

When I look back at my career as a professional triathlete thus far, I can connect almost every race where I under-performed to feeling nervous, anxious, or "out of my league" on the start line. Likewise, almost every performance where I have punched above my weight class has been preceded by feelings of excitement, confidence, and self-belief. As an athlete, I have always preferred to be the favorite instead of the underdog, leveraging the expectations of others as confidence that fuels performance. But, very importantly, I have realized that intrinsic belief is much more valuable than validation from others. When belief comes from within, there is less doubt and more conviction. This internal fire can uplift our performance far beyond our physical and mental capabilities. This is the *power of belief.*

The Power of Belief

Mindset can be performance-enhancing. In fact, leveraging my emotions to create self-belief is the single biggest tool I have used to elevate my career as a professional triathlete.

The first time I truly understood the power of belief was before the 2018 Junior Pan-American Championships in Brasilia, Brazil. Going into that season, my only goal was to represent Canada for the Junior World Championships in Gold Coast, Australia. The selection criteria were difficult, and I knew that my best chance of qualifying was to place in the top five in Brasilia.

For context, the year prior at the 2017 Junior Pan-American Championships, I finished in 32nd place. That was my debut international championship, and it was quite apparent that I was lacking experience and confidence at that level of competition. My mom told me after the race, "I will never forget the look on your face as you were being called on to the start line. You looked scared to death."

Fast-forward to 2018 in Brasilia, I approached the race with a very different mindset. I remember combing through the start list the day before the race and having this aha moment of confidence where I thought to myself, "I really believe I could win this thing." I got on the phone with my coach that night, and all I can remember saying to him was "There is absolutely no reason why I can't win tomorrow." He said, "You're right, you could win," and just like that, I was ready.

Spoiler alert, I did not win the race.

I finished in fourth place, within seconds of the winner, in a break-through race that qualified me for my first World Championships. But, more importantly, I realized that no matter what race I step into, no matter who my competitors are, no matter what challenges lie ahead, my biggest asset is self-belief. If I was ever going to win a race, I would have to stand on the start line believing it was possible. I had to have a winning mindset even before the race began.

And that was a big win for me.

The Science of Belief

Having a winning mindset is not just about sporting success. The lesson I learned in Brazil is a lesson I have since applied to almost every aspect of my life. Understanding that our emotions can be controlled and leveraged to elevate performance has led to breakthroughs in my academic success, managing stress and workload, dealing with adversity, and so much more. Do I think you can also use the power of belief to improve performance in your daily life? Absolutely.

This claim goes beyond just anecdotes. Scientific research is beginning to uncover the scope of our control over our emotions. There are four main chemical substances produced by the neurons in our brain, known as neurotransmitters, that are responsible for various aspects of happiness: dopamine, serotonin, oxytocin, and endorphins. While these occur naturally from complex neurological processes, a McGill University study, led by Elisabeth Perreau-Link, suggests they can also be intentionally triggered through our thoughts and emotions.

Understanding that it is possible to manually increase production of these neurotransmitters is a powerful tool for performance. Increased dopamine leads to higher levels of motivation, enthusiasm, and confidence, which can lead to better productivity, higher cognitive ability, or greater perseverance through adversity. Serotonin and oxytocin make us feel happier and more supported, which can help strengthen our personal relationships with family, friends, co-workers, or significant others. Endorphins increase our ability to deal with physical pain, which certainly has strong implications for endurance athletes like myself. Controlling our emotions has the potential to play a significant role in improving all aspects of our lives.

In my own experience, self-belief is the key to triggering these neurotransmitters. Once I begin to have confidence in my abilities, I am able to produce greater levels of dopamine, serotonin, oxytocin, and endorphins. In turn, this increases my physical, mental, and emotional capabilities, which leads to an improvement in performance. This performance then creates more confidence, which in turns leads to additional neurotransmitter production, and the cycle continues. Entering this sort of positive feedback loop is exactly what has helped me elevate my performance in my triathlon career thus far.

To Be or Not to Be

For many people, it is inevitable that nerves, stress, or doubt will take control of emotions preceding any sort of high-stakes performance. It is completely natural to feel helpless in fighting off these forms of performance anxiety. Cultivating a relationship with your emotions is a long process that takes time to develop. Through this process, the goal is that the "uncontrollable" starts to become controllable. Where before you may have been at the mercy of your emotions, you will start to realize that you have a choice.

Nerves or excitement? Stress or gratitude? Self-doubt or self-belief?

Next time you are standing in front of a challenge, take a moment to actively recognize the "uncontrollable" emotions you are feeling, such as nerves, stress, or self-doubt. Then, ask yourself, "What if I can replace these feelings with something more productive? For example, what if I can replace my nerves with excitement? What if I can replace my stress with gratitude? What if I can replace my doubt with belief?" Over time, you will begin to realize that you can use your emotions to either enable performance or inhibit performance—the choice is yours.

Mindset of Gratitude

Using your emotions to your advantage is not something that needs to be reserved for your greatest challenges or when you need to pull off the performance of a lifetime. It is a practice that can be drawn upon every day to improve the quality of your life. One particular tool that I use in my own daily life is a *gratitude mindset.*

I started pursuing a university degree at the age of 18 and made my professional triathlon debut at the age of 19, meaning that for the last three years of my university studies, I was balancing the responsibilities of being both a full-time athlete and full-time student. On an average day, triathlon was taking up about five to seven hours of my time, and managing this workload as a student was more challenging than I could have ever imagined. I felt overwhelmed, stressed, and burnt out too many times to count.

Switching to a mindset of gratitude was the greatest shift I could have made for my mental health, happiness, and success. A gratitude mindset can be used to change your outlook on your responsibilities, whether this be your training sessions as an athlete, studies as a student, long work hours as an entrepreneur, or whatever else is on your plate. Instead of seeing these responsibilities as burdens, someone with a gratitude mindset sees these as a privilege and an opportunity.

As a full-time student and full-time athlete, a day with three training sessions, three classes, and a group meeting could be overwhelming, stressful, and exhausting just to think about. With a shift to a mindset of gratitude, a day like this becomes much different—it is an exciting day with three opportunities to work on my craft as an athlete, three opportunities to soak up as much knowledge as possible in school, and another opportunity to work with my peers on a project I am passionate about. You can see how with this mindset, you may be able to trigger production of the "happiness" neurotransmitters and enter into the positive feedback loop of performance.

Now, I am not perfect—nobody is—so always having a mindset of gratitude is still a work in progress for me. While I may not be able to approach every day with this mindset, being cognizant of it and trying to put my most grateful foot forward each day has certainly had an impact on my life. I believe being able to pursue our dreams and passions is the greatest privilege we will ever have. Some days are tougher than others, trust me I get it, but if you have a passion in your life that you feel is weighing you down, just remember, you are still one of the lucky ones.

Imposter Syndrome: Your Own Worst Enemy

For many, building self-belief and confidence to improve performance is no easy task. People of all ages and careers are crippled by "imposter syndrome": the internal belief that you are not as competent as your peers or that your merit, skill, or achievements do not warrant your current opportunities. Imposter syndrome manifests itself in many ways—the athlete who feels out of their league at their championship match, the student who does not feel as smart as their peers in their degree program, or the co-worker who does not feel capable at their new job.

I personally have felt imposter syndrome many times in my life. I have felt this in the classroom when my peers talk about concepts I have never heard of. I have felt this on the start line of the 2017 Junior Pan-American Championships, where I finished in 32nd place. I even felt this when I was approached to co-author this book.

It is okay to have these thoughts of doubt enter your mind. It is how you respond that really matters. Imposter syndrome is no different from any other type of doubt, nerves, or stress. You can let it inhibit performance, or you can challenge it with emotions that will enhance performance. Certainly, if you can create negative thoughts in your head, you can replace them with positive ones.

One effective method is to start actively identifying reasons why you are going to succeed in your daily environment. With practice, it will become easier for your brain to identify reasons to have confidence and belief, and over time, you will start to develop a bias for replacing self-doubt with self-belief. This small step forward can stimulate production of the neurotransmitters and allow you to enter the positive feedback loop of elevated performance. As imposter syndrome becomes more prevalent, having control of your mindset is perhaps one of the biggest competitive advantages you can have in this world. This is the winning mindset.

The Power of Belief—Believing in Your Power

Life is full of challenges. When the odds feel stacked against you, and it is unclear whether you have any chance at success, remember that you can choose how to respond: doubt or belief. Emotions can influence our performance, and we can influence our emotions. Believing in yourself may just be the tipping point that sways the odds in your favor.

The power of belief can elevate your performance in sport, your confidence in a business meeting, your comfort in your personal relationships, and your perseverance through difficult times. Once you realize that your emotions are a tool that can be leveraged, you realize that your potential is limitless.

About the Author

Liam Donnelly is a Canadian professional triathlete. He has represented Canada at all levels of international competition, including multiple North American Championships, Pan-American Championships, and World Championships. He continues to train and compete in pursuit of qualifying for the 2024 Paris Olympic Games.

Liam is a recent graduate of Ivey Business School at Western University, one of Canada's most prestigious business programs. He was a Western National Scholar, Academic All-Canadian, and competed for Western's varsity cross-country and track and field teams.

Liam is also an accomplished speaker and is passionate about seeing others achieve success through gratitude, happiness, and self-belief. He is committed to developing local youth and grassroots sport communities. Liam is interested in social impact and sustainability through data-driven entrepreneurship, and recently founded Strident, a company that hopes to make custom and affordable training programs accessible to runners of all levels.

For further inquiries, you can reach Liam at liam@liamdonnelly.ca.

CHAPTER NINE

TRAIN YOUR BRAIN: YOUR PATH TO PEAK PERFORMANCE

By Dirk Downing, PhD
Founder, Zoning In: Peak Performance Coaching
St. Louis, Missouri

"The wait on the top of the hill, Nick, looks excruciating," said golf analyst Peter Kostis to his partner in the booth, Nick Faldo.

Faldo, golf's former world number one, responded, "He looks calm though, doesn't he?"

"He" referred to a 43-year-old Tiger Woods as he waited in the fairway of the par five 15th at the 2019 Masters Tournament. Woods then sat at 12 under par and was the co-leader. He now faced one of the toughest shots in golf, a 227-yard shot into a treacherous green with water short and a big slope just behind the hole that had a reputation for punishing shots not hit with the purest of contact. Calm was the opposite of what most would be feeling in that moment.

Yet, on this April day, in spite of a 10-year drought in major championships, a cascade of injuries, and a divorce, Tiger did look calm. He was also ready. He hit a masterful shot—a towering high draw right that landed softly, right where he aimed it, about 25 feet right of the hole. He went on to win the Masters that day, earning his fifth green jacket, and his 15th major.

We can't know specifically what Tiger was thinking during that testing moment on the unforgiving 15th fairway. However, his uncanny sense of calm and his ensuing elite performance shows us what is possible even when circumstances and possibly our own past performances are stacked against us.

So ... imagine you are in your own high-pressure moment, whatever that may be. Not on a warm spring day at Augusta National, but the moment you engage in one of the important performances of your life. What can you do to achieve a calm and focused mentality when the pressure is on? It's what you do *now*—and between now and then—that matters.

What follows here are some of the same tools I have given to my clients for building a strong mental game. They can easily be your tools as well.

First: Grow Your Elite Mental Game

Elite performers have refined qualities that extend beyond the tactical, strategic, and sometimes athletic mastery of each performance. What are these qualities? Strength that comes through challenge and positivity. We can train harder, bounce back faster, and maximize our game more often when we pursue these qualities. They are like fertile land necessary to grow any elite mental game.

Choose Challenge

Every morning, world-renowned photographer, artist, and entrepreneur, Chase Jarvis, takes a brutal cold-water plunge. "I gotta get my ass in that freezing cold water because I'm going to get good at being uncomfortable," Jarvis says on his *Unlocking Your Creative Potential* podcast. Elite performers are able to perform when others might get anxious because they engage in difficult moments all the time. Some have had tough experiences happen unexpectedly while others have found their flow and routinely manufacture difficult moments. The idea is simple: put yourself through something tough, and, in doing so, you become better equipped for whatever comes next.

It's important to recognize here that there is a difference between something that is difficult and something that is simply taxing. A challenge to test your nerves can be as impactful as a challenge that tests your muscle. Great workouts can be a good start for some, but also consider fresher challenges that you are less familiar with. Try a sport or exercise you've never done (say, yoga or rock climbing), study a new foreign language or musical instrument, or maybe volunteer somewhere outside your comfort zone. It is the act of routinely stepping into new situations that keeps us on our toes as we go forward. And here, as with many training strategies, appropriate balance is key. The goal is for the challenge to push us, but not make us so uncomfortable that we get burnt out. It's a rhythm that takes time and adaptation to master.

Practice Positivity

Instead of asking, "Are you a glass half full ... or a glass half empty person?" Let me ask you this: "What fills your cup up?"

When great performers show up on game day, they have made a habit of filling their cup *every* day and, in doing so, have primed themselves to respond positively and productively to whatever situation comes their way. Positive doesn't always sound corny and fake. Positive thoughts are those that help you take control. No matter the situation—good, bad, or in between—great performers are able to see the bigger picture and focus on something productive that will propel their performance forward. If you're bringing your A-game to a performance, positive thoughts will help that performance be even better. If you're struggling, positive thoughts will help you get back on track.

So how do you train this ability to "fill your cup up"? One good place to start is a positive psychology exercise by Dr. Martin Seligman called "Three Good Things." I recommend my clients engage in this exercise for at least two weeks prior to game day so that they have significant time to build their positivity.

Here's how it works: as you engage in your daily life, try to make it a point to recognize the good things that happen. At the end of each day, pick your top three things. Relive those parts of your day and act as if you are experiencing those same moments and feelings again. Write about those moments in your journal.

On tough days, this positive reflection will take some effort and creativity. But, over time, it gets easier. After all, even on days where you don't win or you fail to achieve a goal, you *do* learn, and learning is positive. Often, I hear my clients say, "At first I couldn't think of anything to write about ... Now I can't narrow it down to just three things!"

Second: Maximize Your Training

As we go after peak performance, we need to level up consistently. After all, those who feel like they are constantly getting better are the people who have a strong, long-term motivation to keep improving. It's a fun feeling! I once had a PGA tour golfer tell me that the most motivated he ever was to go out and practice was right after he won.

If improvement—or leveling up—is a great motivator, it also brings two challenges. First, it's hard for elite athletes to improve. What does Simone Biles do after she earns a perfect ten, for example? But for others, it's easy to get stuck and not see any improvement at all. They get stuck in their development and find it difficult to recognize *any* improvements, thus losing the feeling of gaining competency. This can turn practice, training, and game days into a physical and emotional grind that often disappoints. Joshua Foer, in *Moonwalking with Einstein,* calls it the "okay plateau," or the simple but profound idea that no one can maintain the same quantitative improvements as they did when they first started out.

So how can you continue to feel you are gaining competency as you train? By setting achievable small goals and redefining success.

Set Achievable Small Goals

The better we get, the more leveling up requires creativity and an outside-the-box approach. Challenge yourself to chunk out your development each day. Set realistic, but small challenging tasks and goals that will push you and keep you feeling accomplished each step of the way. Pick a repetition or a goal that you haven't achieved much or often, and make it your challenge for the day—and then celebrate that chunked-out small achievement. The mind is habit-forming. If you're a person who can get in the rhythm of feeling successful in practice every day, then it becomes like a familiar habit—a way you feel about yourself and your ability to improve and get things done.

Redefine "Success"

In addition to being creative and setting achievable but challenging short-term goals, we need to also redefine and be realistic about what it means to level up. For example, if you are a golfer who averages 80 each round, to go from shooting 80 to 75 is much harder than going from 100 to 95. In fact, it is more statistically significant for a golfer who averages 80 to improve by two strokes than it is for a golfer who averages 100 to drop their average by five shots. I know this sounds obvious; however, when I come across clients who are stuck, it often comes down to this narrow-minded thinking about improvement. They believe they *should* be leveling up "big" because they are working hard, and they don't recognize the small daily improvements they are making.

I once had a friend and former collegiate golfer say, "Dirk, second place is just the first loser." I remember laughing when I heard that—in part because of how absurd it seemed, but also because of how popular that mentality can be among talented and driven performers. You don't have to get stuck in this way of thinking. You can and should acknowledge your smallest successes. A winning mindset isn't always about first place.

According to Carol Dweck, people who operate in a fixed mindset view success and failure as zero sum. You either get the win, or you don't. This type of thinking devalues qualitative improvements and devalues learning. How can you make it a habit to recognize the mini-wins that occur every day? Remember the payoff: the simple act of recognizing these mini-wins keeps your energy and motivation in a strong place, so you can continue your journey toward excellence.

Third: Plan Your Game-Day Game

Up to this point, everything has been about building a mental strategy before, between, and leading up to a game day or BIG performance. But what about game day? What about when you're stepping up to the plate for a crunch-time performance? These strategies, if built properly, allow you to maximize your performance on game day.

Appreciate Your Calm

First, as you step up to that moment right before your big performance, think about the new mental strength you have created. In essence, you have built a new foundation by choosing challenges, practicing positivity, setting achievable small goals, and redefining success. So now, at crunch time, what some might feel as a pressure-packed moment doesn't feel that way anymore.

Name Your "Go-To" Thought

As you approach a big performance event, pick a specific "go-to" thought or phrase that can become your private secret weapon to calm you and put you in touch with your best game. For "Steve," who was out playing golf with three buddies on a hot August day, his go-to phrase brought a peak performance. As he stood on the tee box of a daunting par five, the wind picked up considerably. His golfing friends started to heckle and tease. "Uh-oh, Steve ...," they laughed, thinking he couldn't perform in the wind gusts.

But, calmly standing over his ball, Steve simply said, "Not a big deal," and proceeded to smoke his tee shot right down the middle. Later in the round, one of his buddies tried the same phrase, "Not a big deal," and proceeded to hit a *terrible* shot.

For Steve, the calm—even cocky—"Not a big deal" put him in a confident mindset that enabled him to hit a spectacular shot. That particular phrase didn't work for his buddy, and it might not work for you, but other phrases will.

When we are performing our best, we tap into well-established thought patterns that have been cultivated through many mental reps. Because each performance is nuanced and often has several mini-performances within it, great performers often have many "go-to" thoughts that help them deliver in each specific moment. These thoughts simultaneously prevent us from engaging in distracting thoughts while also helping us to lock in on the necessary information we need to deliver.

Imagine it is game day, and you are getting heckled by a friend, your competition, a colleague, or a boss. What would be a mental place you could go to restore a sense of calm and confidence? What could be your trained "go-to" thought that will help you deliver in this moment?

Control Your Energy Level

One of the first times I remember thinking a lot about energy and how to harness it, was back in undergraduate school. My roommate, Gabe, was a master at creating and spreading enthusiastic energy. One day when I was exhausted after a brutal night studying, Gabe burst into the apartment and said in a loud whisper, "Boys ... LET'S GO!" And at that moment, I was amped up and ready to go shoot hoops.

Two years later, I was training for my first marathon on a trail in Columbia, Missouri, when I cramped up on mile eleven. I was set to run 16 miles that day, but once my muscle seized, I wanted to quit. As I gazed into the distance of the beautiful tunnel created by the lush trees surrounding the trail, I remembered my roommate and his contagious, "LET'S GO!" Suddenly my pain was diminished, and I was energized. I got back into my running trance and knocked out the last five miles.

In order to deliver our best performance, we need to have the ability to control our energy level. People tend to have a lot of energy (potentially too much nervous energy) on game day and not enough energy during the grind to get to game day. In both circumstances, it's important to have strategies in place that allow us to control our energy level, so we can appropriately calm ourselves down or pick ourselves up depending on what is needed.

If you need to bring more energy to training, use your own experience. Imagine you are a week out from the biggest performance of your life, and you are stressed, sleep-deprived, and can't seem to focus on anything. What strategy could you employ? Try thinking of a memory or a time when you felt effortlessly focused and full of energy. What did you feel like and do? When you are in the thick of stress that is sapping your strength, what memory could you visit to amp up your energy level?

And if you want to protect against having too much energy or negative energy in a big moment, try taking a deep, slow breath, and remember your go-to phrase. Remember, no one gets to control our energy better than we do.

The Evolution of Your Mental Game

What happens after you build your foundation, maximize training, and plan your game-day strategies? Have you reached the pinnacle of elite mental performance? You're off to a great start! But just remember, your mental game, by definition, evolves as you do. The specific phrases and encouragements that work well for you at one time, may not work in several years. To continue to evolve, you will need a mental game that can stretch with you. You will need to value and prioritize time spent reflecting on past performances—good, bad, and neutral.

When you go after peak performance—as in, your absolute best performance—you are giving yourself license to be idealistic, optimistic, open-minded, and creative in your journey as you look to maximize *yourself*, instead of replicating what has already been done. We need to know ourselves. More specifically, we need to know ourselves well during those moments when we face challenges, randomness, bad luck, misfortune, and pressure. If we know ourselves and our tendencies in those moments, then we have a chance to create strategies to improve in the future. No matter what our limits might be, we always have the ability to move the needle one way or the other. Which direction it moves is entirely up to you.

About the Author

Dr. Dirk Downing grew up in Saint Louis, Missouri, active in golf, swimming, diving, baseball, basketball, and football. His love of sports and interest in the mental aspects of performance led Dirk to earn his PhD in sport psychology at the University of Missouri, Columbia, where he worked extensively with a wide variety of Division 1 collegiate athletes. His research led him to work with world-ranked PGA tour professionals, studying the best mental performance practices of elite athletes.

Dirk is owner and founder of Zoning In: Peak Performance Coaching. Dirk currently works with many athletes—from high school and collegiate to those who simply want to enjoy themselves and their game more on the golf course. He also coaches beyond athletics, providing training to entrepreneurs as they work to improve their daily motivation and engagement in building their own businesses.

Email: dirkmd23@gmail.com
Website: www.ZoningInPPC.com

CHAPTER TEN
THE ACCELERATED GROWTH MODEL

By Dr. Sam Fielding
Elite Mindset Mentor, Sponsored Athlete
Caroga Lake, New York

If you change the way you look at things, the things you look at change.
—Wayne Dyer

Performance is based on having a solid foundation. It doesn't matter what your discipline or what you're striving to achieve. If you're the one doing it, the number one factor that creates success is you. As a lifelong athlete and student, I love to dive deep into material, both in my athletics and work. From seeing what happens when you go deeper and deeper into a subject or practice, I've realized that, often times, the deeper you go, the more confusing and complex things get, until you get to the point where you begin to completely lose focus, scattering your energy so far that you feel like you're going backwards.

Here's the magical thing. Keep digging deeper, and you'll start to see that what you thought was digging you deeper into one thing, is actually taking you deeper into THE ONE thing. And that is your consciousness—who you are and why you are here.

In anything, as a novice you begin at the bottom and start to build your base of knowledge. You start with the fundamentals and you learn the basics. Say it's skiing. You learn how to deal with your equipment, get your boots on, step into your skis, and feel what it feels like to stand on snow with things strapped to your feet. Then, as you progress, you start to learn how to move on skis; you learn how to stop on skis, and eventually you learn how to turn. From that foundation, you start to move up and refine those skills until you feel more proficient. Then you gradually progress off the bunny slope and learn how to ride a chair lift. Now you're back at the bottom, broadening your foundational base, and then you start to build back up. Every time you add a new element, you're back at the bottom rebuilding your foundation. But eventually you get to the point where you've pretty much covered all of the basics and have built your foundation, but you want to refine everything to get better and better. You realize there's an endless world to explore in just skiing alone.

You dive in, you begin to live skiing; it starts to become part of your identity, and you *are* a skier now. You might even move to an area where you can ski all the time, living in a mountain ski town. It's bliss for a while, until you hit the point where you start to plateau and wonder if you're going to get beyond this one point where you don't feel progress. Now you're at that nebulous point of wondering what you really need to focus on. Is it your boots? Do you need to get better custom boots? Is there a ski that is better for what you want to do? Maybe you should move to another resort because you're just not feeling things click.

Sometimes, in the process of learning and finding a passion, we develop a kind of tunnel vision, and we completely forget to step back and take a big picture look at what the whole point is. We become so absorbed in the process, we completely forget the purpose. Forget the purpose, and you forget who you are. You're so far into your created identity that you start to make choices that have nothing to do with what you want, and before you know it, you're on the rollercoaster of life wondering why you just can't find success no matter how hard you try.

So, you have to get back to that ONE thing. To excel, you need to simplify. Simplify to one main focus and devote your life to practicing that. Your entire day, your entire focus will be your ONE thing. Find the most important principle that is holding you back and focus on that with the dedication of a warrior, and you'll accelerate your success regardless of what you're aiming to accomplish.

How do you identify the ONE thing?

You probably already know what it is, but to really uncover it, there's a process. I'm going to break it down for you. Here are the ground rules to life ...

The Reality of Human Life

There will be times when things are in flow, and you're feeling like life was made for your design (because it is), and you'll feel amazing. Opportunities will come, benchmarks will be achieved; you will want this state to last forever.

Then there are other times when we're frustrated, blocked, confused, feel like a fraud, can't seem to do anything right. We get injuries, have unexpected challenges, losses. There will be times of despair so deep that you will think it will never end. When those down moments come, and you feel irritated, everything bothers you, you're anxious and feeling like things are falling apart, and you're physically sick, you'll do anything to get out of those states. But, when you're feeling good again, you completely forget all of the things that you said you would do to change the negative state that you were in when everything was craptastic.

It doesn't have to be this way. The changing states of energy are a fact of life, but you are actually in control of those states. They are not unfortunate circumstances; they are the reality you create. You actually create your physical reality from your energetic reality. But when you're in a good place, you tend to coast. You get complacent and don't take action to create the state you want. As a result, things stagnate, and then you get into a rut, again.

Getting out of this state is very simple. It doesn't take changing your life, your job, your partner, your trainer, or doing any other thing immediately, even though it feels like it. All you need to do is learn to read your energy and understand how to shift the negative state to one that you want. Practice this skill, and you will be able to shift at will to the desired state. Want to feel like your life is a vacation every day? Then do it. You're the only one stopping you.

This is an absolute necessity. If this sounds like some pie-in-the-sky woo-woo talk, let me give it to you straight. This is not some nice-to-have thing reserved only for the people who can afford the luxury to think about their feelings. This is pretty much the reason you are here on this earth, and it is available to everyone.

Why do you need to practice shifting your mental state? Think about what happens when you are chronically stressed—you get sick. You are literally making yourself physically ill by keeping yourself in a state that isn't where you should be. Imagine the times when you're sick or injured, or let's say you get a medical diagnosis that scares the crap out of you. Maybe you're watching a loved one with a terminal illness? What are you wishing for in that moment?

That you did something differently. You can learn how to avoid going down that road.

There are no such things as small issues in your life. The challenges you face in achieving your aspirations are symptoms of the larger issues in your life. Uncovering these issues is one of the most important things you will do in your life. So, the solution to your problems and identifying the blockages (your kryptonite) is not just doing one isolated thing to fix a problem, like getting new boots or better skis. It's part of a larger process that will bring you greater satisfaction and joy in all of your life.

When I work with clients, I teach them what I call the accelerated growth model to gain the awareness they need to not only identify the blockages, but how to handle them both inside and outside of their main ambitions. Here's the breakdown of the accelerated growth model.

Accelerated Growth Model

First, you need to believe that you can do whatever you're trying to do. If you don't, then you need to fix this first. Your limiting beliefs might be your own, but they might be from something that you accepted from someone else in your life. You need to question whether or not your limiting belief is true, and if it's not true, get rid of it. Don't know how? Get help. See a professional, do hypnosis, talk to a friend or mentor, but get rid of it. If you don't get rid of a limiting belief, it will limit your success.

You have to believe that you can handle change. Discomfort isn't always bad. Most people have a distorted view of what they can or cannot tolerate. You need to push your boundaries to expand them. Discomfort is the sign that you've found your boundary. Just as the "good" feelings we have provide information, the "bad" feelings that we have are information too.

Second, you need to know your "why." Your why is what drives you. This is your fuel. If you don't know why you're doing something, you'll give up as soon as it gets hard. Look for the root of your actions because your why needs to be what drives you. Not what your family expects of you, what you think others want of you, or what you believe will make you happy—these are less important than being driven by your why. No "thing" will make you happy, doing the things that you enjoy will make you happy. This is an important idea to maintain.

You have to be able to shift your perspective because you only have one perspective, and it might be wrong. Acknowledging that you might not be seeing the reality of a situation is one of the most powerful things that you can discover while making changes in your life. If you only have one perspective, you'll eventually hit a wall, because you'll never see your blind spots. They're called blind spots for a reason. Again, here, get help from someone you trust. This is not a sign of weakness; this is a sign of courage and growth. Thinking that you can and need to do everything by yourself is not only wrong, it will stop you dead in your tracks. Life is not a solitary event. You have stories in your head, and some of those stories are holding you back. Find the stories that are your excuses and upgrade them to new stories. Don't remain stagnant because of excuses.

Do not buy into the belief that you only have so much time to accomplish something. Time is irrelevant and will only stress you out if you focus too much on it. Don't buy into the idea that you are too old, too young, too late to start something. If you are breathing, and I'm assuming that you are since you're reading this, it's not too late.

If you put time into the center of the picture, you will start to lose focus on what matters. It will start to squeeze you like a vice, and you'll be completely paralyzed.

You need to focus. You need to be able to single-mindedly focus your attention on the primary blockage that is holding you back. You'll find the answer to this in what's most important to you. Don't know what's important to you? GO back to your "why."

Your attachment to the *way* to get there is probably it. Let go of how, and focus on what issues are holding you back. When you know what your kryptonite is, then you can focus on that 24-7—yes, even while you sleep—and you will accelerate your success.

Don't know what your kryptonite is? What is the most frustrating thing that happens to you repeatedly? Whatever that is, identify that and then do the opposite of what you normally would do. This helps you play your own game. You need to have your own internal focus to know what is the right choice for yourself. Not what someone else has done. Trying to copy someone else is a sure-fire way to end up in confusion and frustration. You need to understand that your internal feedback is the most important thing to guide you. Surrender to what life gives you. Ninety-nine percent of the time your plan is just a plan.

In the odd event that the one percent plays out, celebrate. Otherwise, make the right next choice. Don't know what the right choice is? Go back to your why.

About the Author

Dr. Sam Fielding is a mindset and high-performance coach, who teaches groups and individuals her unique accelerated growth model to identify individual blockages that are holding them back from success. After becoming a professional ski patroller and sponsored skier after learning how to ski in her early 20s, she began to teach others how to identify the fast track to achieving their goals. As a doctor of acupuncture, she realized that if she didn't help people identify and upgrade their beliefs and thinking, they would never be able to break the patterns of behavior that lead them to illness in the first place. Using her unique life-transforming process of the accelerated growth model and "energetic intelligence," Sam has helped numerous clients not only achieve the success that they are hoping for, but also find a greater sense of purpose and joy in all aspects of their life. To learn more about working with Dr. Sam please email her or visit her website.

Email: sam@drsamfielding.com
Website: www.drsamfielding.com

CHAPTER ELEVEN
THE HERO'S JOURNEY

by Kerry Fisher
Transformational Life Coach, Yoga Instructor
New York, New York

We are what we repeatedly do. Excellence, then, is not an act, but a habit.
—Aristotle

This message is for you: *you can live the life of your dreams. You can be the person you dream of being. You can.*

Did you hear that? Let me say that again. I want you to really take this in. Take a deep breath in through your nose and a long breath out through your mouth.

You can live the life of your dreams. You can be the person you dream of being. And you will. You will.

You are reading this for a reason. You are here to be all the things you dream of being. To do all the things you dream of doing. It's time to throw off your chains. Today is the day.

You were born for a reason. You are here for a purpose. You know it. You feel it. But you doubt it. Why is that?

You were trained to doubt—trained to doubt yourself. Trained to discard what you knew in your heart, so you could fit into the group. No more. Starting today, you can open a new chapter. You can become the person you know you are deep in your soul.

Let me tell you a little story. When you were born, you knew exactly who you were. You knew exactly why you were here. You were born perfect in every way. Babies are pure and blissful. They know wonder. They know joy. They can lie and stare at their hand and be endlessly amazed. They live fully in the moment. They don't worry about what's going to happen next week or next year. They know who they are, and they are happy to be who they are.

Babies aren't trying to change. They don't think, "Gee, if only I had different colored hair or different colored eyes; a better brand of diaper; a nicer crib." No, they are happy with who they are. Because they know who they are, and they know why they are here. They are here to live, to experience all that life has to offer. To express the fullest version of who they are.

Babies laugh when they're happy and cry when they're sad. They aren't scared to try new things. They don't lie there, thinking, "Hmmm, I would love to crawl, but what if I fail?" No. Instead, they try to crawl and fail, try to crawl and fail, and then eventually, they learn to crawl. And then walk. And then run. Babies don't give up. They don't get upset with themselves when they can't do something right away. Instead, they try and fail, try and fail, practice and fail. Until they succeed. Right?

But then what happens?

Babies grow up. People start to tell them that they can't do this and they can't do that. Their parents, teachers, family, friends, everyone telling them what they can and cannot do—who they should and should not be. Gradually, the veils fall down, the mask slips on. The true self gets hidden. They assume a false identity and live a life they didn't really want—they live by rules and restrictions made by others. They lose who they are to become who everyone else wants them to be.

You know what I'm saying? You can feel the truth when it hits you, can't you? We all can.

It's time to drop the mask, to uncover who you really are. Because you are here for a reason. You are here for a purpose. You can live the life of your dreams. You can have it all. You can be the person you have always dreamed of being. Let's start now.

The Path Is Winding

The journey to living the life you imagine, to being the person you dream of being is not for the faint of heart. The path is winding. You will reach the highest peaks and fall to the darkest valleys. When you are at one of the soaring peaks, it feels great. You stand there victorious with the world at your feet. Success is yours. You feel invincible, like you have finally arrived. All is well. The only problem is that you don't stay up there on those exalted peaks forever. Inevitably, you fall down into one of the valleys, and it's those moments when you are tested. Those moments can discourage you, make you doubt yourself, make you question your decisions. They might even bring you to your knees. We've all been there; we've all had those moments. Moments when we are unsure, moments when we wonder if we have chosen the right path.

What if we could simply change negative thoughts? What if we could change our mindset? What if we start to look at everything, absolutely everything, as a lesson, as something that is happening *for* us instead of something that is happening *to* us? What if we had the same equanimity towards our failures as we do towards our successes? That, my friends, is one of the most important shifts to make. That is part of what having a winning mindset looks like.

In life, we crave the moments of soaring success. Let's be honest. Those moments are wonderful, and they feel great. They make us feel like we are on top of the world. What about the moments of failure, though? We don't relish those, do we? But what if we did? What if we looked at those hard experiences as gifts? What if we look with new eyes and see that it's in those moments of failure where there is the greatest chance to learn the most? This is where the magic happens, where we learn that our mess can become our message.

When you learn to stand up when you want to stay down, you are getting stronger, becoming battle-hardened. Those events can make you better and more capable, not just stronger, but also more compassionate, understanding, kinder, softer. A better version of you.

The hero's journey is not about the moments of success. No. The hero's journey is about the moments when life knocks you down, and you use your tools to get back up. Let's begin.

Prepare for the Journey

Preparation is always the most important part of any journey. The hero's journey is no different. You can take steps to ensure that wherever you are on your journey, you can keep pushing forward, step by step, moment by moment, moving towards your goals and dreams.

First, you must gain *clarity* around your goal. Next, you create a *funnel of focus* so that you have a plan for getting to your goal. Then, it is time to create a *winning mindset* so that you are able to continue moving forward even when obstacles are placed in your path. Finally, it is time to take *action*.

Clarity: Clear Vision

The first step is gaining clarity on what you want to accomplish, on the goal you are moving towards. This is the most essential step of all because once you have a crystal-clear vision of your destination, you have a guiding light to aim towards.

To gain this clarity, the use of journaling is very effective. Sit down when you have some quiet time and allow yourself to write every single thing you want to accomplish, all your hopes, all your dreams. Don't hold yourself back here, you're creating an ideal vision of the person you plan to be, the life you plan to live. This will be your guiding light, your North Star.

Once you have this ideal self-blueprint, it's time to break it into manageable steps. This is where you shape your goals. Make a list of all the goals you want to achieve and pick one overarching goal you plan to achieve over the next three to five years. Now, break it into its smallest component parts. List all the skills you need to acquire, all the people you will need on your team, all the steps you need to make to move towards your goal. Continue to revise this list until all the pieces that need to be accomplished are listed.

Once you have this master list, you need to break it down even further to what you need to accomplish over the next year, quarter, and month. Take the needed time to create a plan to lead you strongly in the direction of your long-term goal. This leads you to the next step, which is focus and goal setting.

Focus: Your Blueprint for Success

Once you gain crystal-clear *clarity* on what you are aiming towards, it's time to focus. This is where you create a blueprint for your success.

You have the big goal you want to accomplish over the next three to five years. Now it's time to break it down. Look at the list you made of skills you need to acquire, the steps you need to take, and the people you need to contact, and decide what you need to accomplish this year. Find the action or the combination of actions that would have the greatest impact on moving you towards your goal. Your yearly goal will be the key to moving forcefully in the right direction. It's what guides you.

Now that you have your goals for the year, it's time to break the yearly goals down into quarterly goals, things you want to accomplish over the next three months. After that, break it down to what you need to accomplish this month, this week, and finally, what you will accomplish today. Each day, review the goals you plan to accomplish that day. Take action each and every day in the direction of your goals, even if it is a simple action. Consistency is the key. Keep the forward momentum as you maintain focus.

Take time to remind yourself of your long-term goal and your yearly goal to keep yourself motivated. However, each day your main focus is on the tasks for the day. This single-pointed *focus* creates a blueprint for progress towards your ultimate goal. The year-end goal is your guidepost, but you now know what you need to do this quarter, this month, this week, and today to get there. This is a key aspect of peak performance. What steps can you take each day to move in the direction of your ideal self, your ideal life?

Now that you have gained clarity and you have a single-pointed focus, it's time to get into a champion's *mindset.* This is a key aspect of performing at your peak. You prepare yourself for battle, knowing in advance that you will hit obstacles along the path.

How do you do that? You do that by creating a *winning mindset.*

Winning Mindset: Steeling Yourself for Action

The *winning mindset* consists of three steps: (1) believing you can do it; (2) clearing the blockages; and (3) leaning into discomfort and getting comfortable with the uncomfortable.

Step 1: Belief

The first step is your belief system. You must believe you can achieve your goals in order to actually achieve them. This might seem obvious, but it is something that many people overlook when moving towards their goals. Belief is the most powerful predictor of success in life.

Affirmations are incredibly useful in creating a belief in yourself and your ability to attain your goals. You can find affirmations online or in books, or you can create your own. Here are some affirmations that create the mindset of a champion:

- "I achieve my goals with ease and grace."
- "I step into my power, and I accomplish every goal I set out to accomplish."
- "I am guided by my North Star and use it to guide me to take action each day in the direction of my dreams."
- "Every day in every way I am getting more confident, more competent, and more courageous."

Use any of these affirmations or create your own. Once you are comfortable using affirmations, create your own affirmations that are personalized to you and your specific goals.

Step 2: Clearing the Blockages

The next step is to remove any blockages you may have. These blockages are typically thoughts and beliefs left over from your childhood or ones that you have unconsciously picked up from those around you. They might be ideas like "I am not enough," "I can't do it," or "People like me can't accomplish things like that."

We all have these unconscious and subconscious blockages, but the good news is that we can rewire our beliefs, rewire our brain. You can do this by using affirmations as discussed above, but it is also extraordinarily helpful to use meditation to clear these old, outdated beliefs.

Meditation can take many forms. It can be as simple as sitting quietly and focusing on your breath. You can sit and simply pay attention to your thoughts. You can also use guided meditations, which are amazing because you can find meditations geared towards the exact blockage you are trying to clear.

There are a lot of great apps and free meditations online, so spend some time finding one that is suitable for you or simply create your own personalized meditation practice. It doesn't have to be fancy, just take a few minutes each day to relax and tune in. If you haven't ever meditated before, you might just find that a daily meditation practice can change your life. Try it.

Step 3: Leaning into Discomfort, Getting Comfortable with the Uncomfortable

When you are on the path to becoming the person you dream of being, to living the life you imagine, you will meet obstacles. There will be moments when you try new things and need to learn new skills in situations that are not familiar to you. This can become uncomfortable or create feelings of unease. This is to be expected on the hero's journey.

The path to becoming the very best version of yourself is not a smooth one, so it is essential that you have some simple practices to fall back on when the going gets tough. You already learned about affirmations and meditation; now it's time to add one more tool to your toolbelt. Breathwork.

Doing a simple breath exercise when you notice that you are moving into a difficult or stressful situation can be invaluable. The Navy SEALs created a breathing technique called box breathing, which is a great tool for reducing stress and keeping yourself on an even keel.

The way to do box breathing is to inhale through your nose for five seconds, hold your breath for five seconds, exhale through your mouth for five seconds, and then hold your breath out for five seconds. That is one round. Repeat for three to five rounds, and then take a break. It is interesting to note how you feel before you do box breathing and how you feel after you complete the box breathing routine. Use this technique anytime you want to increase your joy and decrease your stress. It's a game changer. Try it right now and see how you feel afterwards. Three rounds will only take 60 seconds.

Taking the steps towards improving your beliefs about yourself, clearing the blockages, and learning how to lean into discomfort will create the winning mindset you need to move powerfully in the direction of your dreams.

As an additional resource, you can check out the website listed at the end of this chapter to find links to meditations, breathwork practices, affirmations, and other resources to help you clear any blockages.

Take Action: Time to Just Do It

Once you've gained the clarity and focus needed to create a winning mindset, it's time to roll up your sleeves and take action. This is the place where the pedal hits the metal. Each day, take inspired action in the direction of your goals.

Keep in mind your ultimate goal guiding you on your journey and take action each and every day in order to move confidently in the direction of your goals one step at a time. This is where all your work pays off. It's where the magic happens. This is also where patience and dedication are required.

You'll need to have the patience to take action day after day even when it doesn't seem like you're making any progress. Remember, the journey of a thousand miles begins with one step. Take that step. And then take another step. And another. Don't get discouraged. It's often at this moment that you are tested the most, where there will be problems to solve and mountains to move. Work diligently, moment by moment, day by day, week by week, and year after year.

Your dedication is the key to this action step. You will be tested, and it's all part of the journey. It is helpful to remember why you're doing all this work. Keep your ultimate goal in mind, let it be your guiding light. It is essential to remember that behind every successful enterprise is years and years of hard work and dedication. Be dedicated to your vision and don't let anything stand in the way of taking steps each and every day.

Patience and dedication to your grand vision for your business, for yourself, and for your life is the secret to actually attaining the life you dream of. It's the secret to peak performance and a winning mindset.

In closing, remember that the hero is forged in the fire. The hero has the clarity, the focus, the winning mindset, and the ability to take inspired action each and every day in the direction of their dream. The hero is a warrior, marching with purpose, dedication, and drive towards the fulfillment of their ultimate goals and dreams. Be that hero, be that warrior.

About the Author

Kerry Fisher is a wellness educator, transformational life coach, and motivational speaker. She teaches people simple tools for extraordinary living.

Kerry was raising a family and working as an attorney when she began a daily yoga practice. Yoga was the perfect antidote to her hectic lifestyle, so she decided to take instructor training. Kerry left her law career, so she could dedicate herself fulltime to teaching people how to live the best life possible.

As a former competitive gymnast and dancer, Kerry has had a lifelong fascination with wellness. She is a lifelong learner who has completed training across a variety of disciplines, including peak performance, mindset, anatomy, physiology, neuroscience, meditation, mindfulness, breathwork, Thai yoga massage, and yoga.

Kerry is a mom of five and has been married for 25 years. She strives to live a kick-ass life, and her mission is to show people that they can too. Please check out her website for meditations, breathwork exercises, affirmations, and other helpful resources.

Email: theyogateachers@gmail.com
Website: theyogateachers.com
Instagram: @theyogateachers

CHAPTER TWELVE

OUR BELIEFS: THE DEEP FORCES OF WINNING

By Sven Gade
Professional Certified Coach
Fort Lauderdale, Florida

Whether you think you can or think you can't, you're right.
—Henry Ford

The Common Challenge

Carlos is an open-minded, dynamic, and easy-going leader with an MBA from an elite European business school. Before he was hired by a start-up company in Latin America last year, he already knew the hectic busyness of this environment. Carlos loves to solve problems and get stuff done. He rushed into action but overall progress was rather slow, even though he worked really hard. Reviewing this later, he concluded that he'd totally omitted to plan and prioritize properly. It's not that he doesn't know about project management, he was just carried away by his belief: "There is no time to lose." Carlos isn't unique in this belief.

Our beliefs are in us; they influence what we do; they are present when we make decisions. Some of our beliefs touch us consciously while others stay below the surface, not even noticed by us. Our beliefs are formed by our experiences, the wins, and the defeats in our lives. Our parents and our teachers plant them under our skin—knowingly and unknowingly. Some of our beliefs change over time, and some stay with us forever. They are always by our side, powerful companions. They shape our development. In fact, they define us.

The Inner Winner

Looking at the story of my life so far—all the highs and lows, as a professional, as a family man, and as an athlete—has led me to discover my personal beliefs. Here are those that are most empowering for me.

Dreams Come True

During my time working for DHL, I had the opportunity to work in very different roles and lead teams in all parts of the world. I will never forget when I started to work with a new team in South Florida. A bunch of great individuals, but unfortunately too busy with internal battles and not able to demonstrate their collective value to the organization. After some tough team sessions, we were able to jointly agree on our standards of working together and gradually improve our performance. To my surprise, I really loved this emotional and mental turnaround, and I devoted more attention to it than to the actual service we were providing to our customers.

As part of the process, I hired a trainer named Kevin to teach us better interpersonal communication skills. After a full-day training in August 2012, Kevin and I met over dinner in a small restaurant near my office. I was about to take the last bites of the roasted duck, when he looked gently at me and started a discussion: "I have seen you with your team, have you ever thought about becoming an executive coach?" These words changed my life for good.

I was fascinated by the idea of working at nothing other than my passion and also becoming my own boss. But why would I leave an organization that was so instrumental in my professional growth? And how would I be able to establish a business in a market with which I am not familiar? And even if I did, how could this generate sufficient income for me?

Nevertheless, the thought of taking a new direction kept spinning in my head. Kevin continued to inspire me. He explained what it took to be a good coach. I found a great institute to study coaching, got some practice, and became certified. People that I admired became my advisors, and, with some private clients, I slowly started to run a little side business.

After almost two years of preparation, I spoke with my boss about the plan of launching my own boutique coaching firm. He offered me a contract to co-facilitate a newly designed leadership development program. My employer became my first business client! Today, five years later, my reality is close to the vision I had for myself. It was not always easy, but I never regretted a single moment of this journey of mine.

Dreams of our future appear randomly and touch all aspects of life, not only career, but also relationships with family and friends, sports, adventures. We just need to hold on to them and play creatively with them. Don't dump "crazy" ideas too quickly, and give yourself time to make your dream come true.

Together We Make It Happen

Before I became the director of a change program in 2003, my boss briefed me jokingly, "I have only two problems: my topline and my bottom line. Everything else is fine." He tasked my small team and me to improve basically everything that our warehousing division in Europe did. There was no big budget, no external support for us, except a small consultancy firm that was not focused on logistics but on people and change. This company gave us a whole new perspective on fostering collaboration and teamwork.

Our "learn-shops'" were real game changers. On a late autumn day, we gathered about 40 people in Frankfurt, Germany to develop new ideas and boost the productivity in our warehouses across Europe. Early on, my colleague from Belgium took the podium and gave a talk about a project in which she'd failed miserably. The atmosphere in the room changed magically, and it touched everybody. The scene was set to enter an open and honest discussion of operational shortcomings, which would lead to solutions for all parties involved.

In one of the following break-out sessions, a colleague presented an on-going project, the progress made, and the roadblocks. It was a loud and clear call for help. In another room, two colleagues debated the pros and cons of a productivity tool. They stimulated the attendees to chime in. Not to decide who was right, but to generate ideas to make the system even better.

Our program gained great momentum from those learn-shops and various other interventions. After three years, we reached our financial goals. No doubt, we modified our infrastructure, systems, and processes. However, primarily the change happened because the 16,000 people in our organization were stepping up, giving one another a hand, and jointly making it work.

Team members bring collaboration to the next level when they care about each other, help each other, have each other's back. Human connections let us thrive. The way we approach other people determines how we engage and create relationships with them. When we meet others with an intention to listen, to understand them and get a different perspective without any judgment, we will be able to solve problems, handle conflicts, unite teams, and create a winning mindset together.

Keep On Going Strong

Every year, I go with a friend on a bike trip in Europe. We cycle for a week, always starting from where we left off the year before. Over the years, we followed the Atlantic coastline from Germany to Gibraltar, and soon we will finish our ride from Glasgow, Scotland to Istanbul, Turkey.

It was a rainy morning in Wehe-den Hoorn in the north of the Netherlands on the second day of our tour in 1998. Nevertheless, we got on our bikes heading towards Den Helder, a 70-mile ride. Mid-day, the weather worsened, the strong headwinds blew the rain right into our faces. We had no thoughts about Den Helder, let alone Gibraltar. We were just pushing hard to make it to the next village. With the slowest pace ever, we finally arrived at our destination for the day, as wet as fish. Before we could even ask for a room, the receptionist brought us a nice hot cup of coffee. After all the struggling in the weather, we felt accomplished.

The goals in our life keep us moving forward. Our win-plans determine the direction and steps to take, they allow us to focus on the process, not the result. We start these big projects by dividing them in smaller chunks. They then turn into items on our daily action-list, with those related to our important goals being the first ones to tackle. And when things get tough, when every step is heavy, I see myself cycling against the rainy winds in the Netherlands. I remain optimistic, see it as a challenge and not a problem, and focus on "the next village to reach."

Does that mean to never give up? Almost. If you lose your reason for going further, you're on the wrong track and better change your course. However, if you can reconnect with your "why," you'll get the energy to cope with pain and setbacks.

Dreams come true, together we make it happen, and *keep on going strong* are the beliefs that personally work for me. They may sound like a universal formula, but they have my stories, my very own interpretation behind them. Start to discover your individual beliefs.

Here's a good place to start: draw your "lifeline" of the last ten years. Consider the impactful events and turning points in this period along the horizontal axis. Go up and down on the vertical axis by the degree of feelings of success, happiness, pride—*winning*—in your very own definition. Mark higher on the vertical axis for positive feelings and lower on the axis for the opposite. What empowering beliefs let you reach the peaks? Write them down. How will they support you to achieve your goals and continue to win?

The Untapped Potential

We've looked at empowering beliefs. Now, let's look now at the other side, our limiting beliefs, those that mask our possibilities, that prevent us from fully utilizing our potential. My boss had great plans for me in 2005. He wanted me as country manager in Spain. However, everything changed, and I was given the role as country manager in Denmark instead. Less revenue, fewer people, bigger problems. I was convinced that I deserved better but wouldn't admit it openly.

And how did I perform? Not very well at all. I was too full of myself and concerned about my career, and I'd underestimated the work to be done. When things got worse, I blamed others or looked for scapegoats. It was hard to take, but I failed in my role and gave up after two years. Many months later I began to realize how my limiting belief of "deserving better" was at the root of not delivering the expected results, even overshadowing other empowering beliefs.

Some of our limiting beliefs are very present, for example, when we lack self-confidence. Others are more hidden, as in the case of my Denmark experience. No matter the circumstances, you can spot those beliefs and transform them. It is your choice, a choice of winning.

Going through our daily life, our brain deals with a whole microcosm of immediate thoughts that relate to our beliefs. Some of them we are aware of, but many others, we are not. There are thoughts that derive from our empowering beliefs and others that rather work against us and prevent us from winning. They creep in out of nowhere and let us remain with a self-talk that might sound like, "I cannot do that," "I am not creative," "This is against me personally," or "I am too old / too young / too whatever." We all have our patterns of self-limiting beliefs. Nevertheless, they can be changed! Let's take a look at some proven methods.

The Powerful Pause

Carve out some time for yourself at the end of the day, just five to ten minutes will make a difference. Create a mentally relaxing environment for yourself. I like to run; others have a meditation practice. You might want to sit down in nature or listen to music that calms you. Find your best approach, totally up to you.

As you pause, go over your day and recall your highlights. They are your source for self-confidence and resilience. Ask yourself, "What am I proud of? What did I truly enjoy?" Then reflect on your lowlights, without blaming yourself or feeling a failure, and search for learning opportunities. When you write down your daily findings, patterns of productive and unproductive behaviors will emerge over time.

Take a moment and go deeper. Neuroscience teaches us that the events around us first trigger our thoughts, which then cause our emotions, and they finally determine our behavior and our decisions. Let me give you an example: you host a meeting and people show up late. You think there will not be enough time to cover the agenda; you feel rushed, and you start to talk over others or cut them off. Pretty bad, isn't it? Now, if you really want to improve, you need to find the root cause, your thought. It actually might come from an even deeper belief, in this example, for instance, "We are working on a mission impossible."

Your daily reflection time will raise your self-awareness. After a while, you will catch your self-talk "on the go" and realize its impact on your actions. Here are some instances of generally unproductive behaviors and the beliefs that possibly caused them: not delegating because "nobody is as good as I am." Not saying no because "I want to be liked by everybody." Being defensive because "admitting a mistake is bad for me." Being distracted because "every email has to be answered immediately," etc.

Here is the point: the story that you're telling yourself is not necessarily true. What if it is not, and it just holds you back? Take the following steps to transform your limiting thoughts and beliefs. Come up with a different behavior, one that is not following your usual thought process. See yourself acting with a new positive behavior and think about all the new opportunities it opens for you. Take a pen and a paper, and write down everything that comes to your mind. Do this for three to five minutes. Pay no attention to spelling and grammar. Just keep writing non-stop, get it all out on paper, everything matters. Read your notes a few hours or a day later, and if you want, repeat the exercise once more. Quite quickly, the compelling reason for your new behavior will emerge with mental pictures associated with it. This is your vision for improvement!

Experiments for Winners

The best way to make positive changes is to design and conduct an experiment, a very specific situation, to start your new behavior. If you are still hesitant, ask yourself, "What is the worst that can happen?" Be realistic and make it bearable. Go in your experiment and focus on the process, your feelings, and your thoughts. Keep your winning mindset in check, and don't look immediately at the outcome. Write down your takeaways.

I once worked with a client, Heather. Her leader was disappointed about her being completely silent when meeting with her teammates. Heather told me, "My colleagues are much more experienced. If I say something wrong, they will get a bad impression of me." When I asked her, "What do you believe they think about you if you don't say anything?" She quickly saw that speaking up would be low risk for her. In the very next meeting, Heather made one comment, her first contribution to the team discussions. She shared with me afterwards that she felt proud of herself, and she felt she helped the team to be more effective.

When your first experiment works, let other experiments follow. As you go along, implement some routines that make your new behavior stick. Heather, for instance, aimed at the beginning to make at least one comment in every meeting. Continue to observe yourself, take notes related to your process. It is about consistent practice, not an occasional effort. Over time, your thinking will change based on the experiences you collect. And ultimately, all these small changes will affect your limiting beliefs. They turn into something that sounds like this, "I am capable," "I am protected," or "People are trustworthy."

At the end of the day, your mindset is the reflection of the story you are telling yourself. The better and more positive your story is, the higher your chances are to win.

About the Author

Based in Fort Lauderdale, Florida, Sven Gade is an executive coach, team coach, and workshop facilitator. As the founder of LeaderTrip Coaching®, Inc. he draws from more than 25 years' experience as a senior executive in the logistics industry, mainly at DHL, where he worked with global and cross-cultural teams.

Sven is an approachable and recognized authority in the field of leadership and teamwork. He holds a master's degree in mathematics from the University of Hamburg, Germany and earned the designation of professional certified coach (PCC) from the International Coach Federation (ICF) and Certified Team Performance Coach™ (CTPC) from Team Coaching International (TCI). Sven is a certified practitioner of the Emotional Intelligence assessment by Genos, an Australia research company.

Email: sgade@leadertrip-coaching.com
Website: www.leadertrip-coaching.com

CHAPTER THIRTEEN

YOUR INNATE WINNING MINDSET

By Robin Goldsbro
Founder of Level Seven, Transformation Coach
Leeds, England, United Kingdom

*We seldom realize that our most private thoughts and emotions are
not actually our own. For we think in terms of languages and images
which we did not invent, but which were given to us by our society.*
—Alan Watts

It seems to me that before we can cultivate or realise a winning mindset, we
must understand what we mean by "winning", "mind", and "set".

Let us first explore the idea of "winning". What does it mean to win?
Winning for what purpose? And, if one is to win, does someone have to lose?

What do we mean by "mind"? What is the real purpose of the mind? Is
it our brain's capacity to understand information and retain knowledge, or
to hold a single idea long enough for it to be realised? Could it be something
beyond matter and something we don't truly understand?

What does it mean to be "set"? To be set for what purpose? Does it mean
immovable, inflexible or rigid, or does it mean something else?

Does a "winning mindset" mean to be focused on achieving a single outcome at the expense of everything else by utilising the power of mind?

The Rise of the Focused Human

For millions of years, we, humans, have been evolving. The size of our brains has increased and with it our capacity for many things. It's our human nature to learn, grow, and work to better ourselves. It's this drive that has made us the dominant species, moving us out of the trees and into the plains, and then from hunter-gatherers to farmers, from the cave to modern homes, from plants concocted remedies to synthetic, over-the-counter medicines.

It's a truly remarkable feat—through working together in small groups and tribes we've done the impossible. I'm of the mind that it couldn't have been achieved without a winning mindset.

Humans are often so caught up in our own heads, we don't realise our ancestors have been laying down the foundations for a winning mindset for millions of years. Like an oak tree, we see the leaves and the fruits, and we watch it weather a storm with its branches being thrown this way and that; but after the storm has passed, we don't stop to consider what kept it standing. It's not what we see—the leaves and branches blowing, but what we don't see—the roots and foundations of the tree.

This is what I want this chapter to be about—our roots and foundations. Just like the logic of a tall building, the higher we want to go, the deeper and stronger our foundations need to be if we're going to have the mindset to win.

We're Off Course

It's useful to know that the foundations our ancestors set down for us have been predicated on a world of natural selection and physical things. It's relatively recently that our way of life has changed so significantly that we can go to the supermarket for food. For most of our existence, it's not been like that. We've had to remain focused on living and gathering what we really need to survive. But here's the thing—we don't live in that world anymore, yet we're still operating like hunter-gatherers. The focus our ancestors have been developing for us is now *hunting* for significance—quick fixes. And we're *gathering* stuff. We still have all the incredible focus we've always had, but it's become misplaced.

In the past, if you relaxed your focus for too long, you could go hungry or get eaten by something else that was hungry. This is the world we were designed for, so our Darwinian mindset encourages us towards short-term, finite goals. Because of natural selection and our need to push our genes into the next generation, competition and exploitation exist.

We don't like to see ourselves like this because we're educated and reasonable people, and we don't see that it's also our education system that perpetuates our misguided focus.

The System

Our current ideas about education started in the Industrial Revolution. The big idea was to lure people out of the countryside, where we'd been succeeding for millennia, to work in factories. The bait was simple. Education and the promise of a regular income, fulfilment, status, and opportunities. It would be a fair system—it would be based on meritocracy. You would get rewarded (money) in line with your effort (time). All you had to do was work hard and conform. Those who worked hardest and put in more time would get the better jobs in the factory, and those that failed could go back to the farm.

Today, our educational system is based on the same idea. Here are a set of things we want you to learn and know, so you can work in the factory in the name of prosperity. We'll grade you on the basis of suitability for life in the factory, get you to compare yourself with your peers because it will ignite your Darwinian origins and make you fight to get your genes into the future.

Layer on top the core principle that if the capitalist factory is to remain open, it needs someone to consume its goods and services. Taking full advantage of our historical tendencies, it encourages us to consume, and we're indoctrinated to build on the ideas of comparing ourselves with others, who learned in the educational system, and we define ourselves through bourgeois comparisons.

The truth is that capitalism needs comparisons to fuel it. Comparisons make us look for differences rather than similarities on which we might connect. This is not a dig at growth and prosperity, only that external prosperity reaches a threshold at a much lower rate than we might expect, at which point it leaves us internally impoverished. Ultimately, we can never have enough stuff (that we don't really need), and it doesn't lead to fulfilment.

Why Is All This Relevant?

I want to awaken you to the truth. We're in a mindset trap, and the first step to escaping the trap is to realise you're inside it and to see it for what it is.

We're preconditioned to believe the answer is in gaining more of something, so that's what we focus on. Except we don't call it focus, we call it distraction. We're on the lookout for the "next best thing", the right diet, workout, technology, promotion.

The pursuit of more information is to help us achieve this. We think to ourselves, "If I can just access more information, work harder, and acquire more knowledge, my performance, mindset, and motivation will be improved." But there is never enough, and so the endless cycle of unfulfilled striving continues, and we're all doing it.

Our ancestors knew and accepted a different reality. They didn't work for a living—they lived for a living. Something else was driving them, and they thrived because of it. They had less stuff and with that, less distractions, less competition within the tribe, and they were rich and successful because of it.

Let me illustrate for a moment. Consider cave art and embellishments on early tools. These are not the acts of people who were scraping an existence. They're the work of successful people with a culture who inherently knew that winning was having more time to do what you love. They knew that less of something creates a space for something else. More energy, more time to think, time with self and to just be. And all without fear of judgement.

Our early human ancestors had a winning mindset, and you can see its legacy around you today. But they were lured by a magic trick and a promise to leave the tribe. As they left the tribe, their ego was fuelled, and this created internal friction. Our ancestors weren't battling with the factory owner for their ideas of winning. Winning for them came from within. A winning mindset first starts with a battle to win back your own mind, and our ancestors were doing this without having to think about it.

The very fact that you're here reading this book means you already have a winning mindset. It's innate, has evolved, and has been part of you forever. You have focus. It's just been exploited by the factory owner who is performing a magic trick. Everything you need has been right with you all along. Experiencing your winning mindset is not about adding new techniques. It's about seeing the truth and subtracting what's getting in the way.

Your Winning Tribe of Interdependency

The first tribes were based on the idea of dependency. Everyone contributed something, and it needed this culture of everyone working together to create enjoyable outcomes. They were all dependent on others for life. That's not the case anymore. Broadly speaking, we can all sustain ourselves in a tribe of one, but we all know we're not built for isolation.

If we're to make our contribution to the next generation, we need to evolve our ideas of the tribe and see that working together gets better results and that we can all bring our unique contributions to play to create something that none of us could achieve individually. Not because we just want our basic needs met, but because we want to create something that doesn't yet exist, that can enrich everyone's lives. This is different from dependency. This is called interdependency.

Observation shows that we tend to settle into a rhythm with the people we spend time with. My favourite idea on this theme is that we're the average of the five people we spend the most time with. I don't know if this is entirely true, but what I do know is that the basis for this is sound. Who you have in your tribe, the people who you spend the most time with, is important because there's a tendency to form a collective way of thinking and validating one another's perspectives. You may have heard of this referred to as "group-think", and it can either propel you or hold you back.

In the past, we spent significant amounts of time with our tribe collaborating and connecting. This helped the winning mindset flourish, and this is what we need to do today. Your authentic tribe will welcome you and be complementary, not competitive. This will give you less on your mind, and fewer distractions from the magic trick means less ego around winning.

Connecting with Your Inner Winning Mindset

Through this chapter, I've invited you to look within and realise that a winning mindset is not something you learn but rather something you realise. I want you to see that it's not emanating from some external place but something deep within each of us, and it's deeply personal.

As long as our basic needs are met, no amount of additional "stuff" is going to make our life more fulfilled. If the only reason you're continuing to put all your focus into "winning" at something that serves only the purpose of increasing the amount of "stuff" you own, you're overlooking the authentic path that is signposted from within. And this is the only path that truly leads to a fulfilled life.

When you have a good relationship with yourself and with your tribe, you have less on your mind, which allows you to focus. The less you have to carry, the lighter you are. The lighter you are, the easier you move, and you will adapt and then you will really win.

A winning mindset that lasts is not about tactics and techniques, but about understanding where your winning mindset really comes from. When you understand this, you can do the work that needs to be done because it reflects who you truly are. Your innate winning mindset is going to be fuelled by an authentic purpose that is intrinsically rewarding. It's going to be supported by a complementary tribe and fewer distractions. I want you to know, at the level of feeling, that when you realise your reason for being, and you embrace it without fear or comparison, you'll awaken that winning mindset. I want you to know that it's not about adding, but about taking away what's getting in the way of that. Misunderstanding this will hold you back from realising your potential.

A Strategy for Realising Your Inner Winning Mindset

Firstly, you need to take action. The people who succeed are those who do the work. Thinking about it isn't enough. You need courage, not confidence, to take action that at first seems counter intuitive (that's how the magic trick works).

You need to take a core lesson from evolution and focus on improvement not perfection. When we make comparisons, we tend to compare in a vacuum. We don't see the whole picture or the effort it took to create that outcome. We don't see what someone had to say 'no' to (what they had to give up) in order to be able to say 'yes' to something else (to get something).

It's a good idea to give yourself the gift of time and take yourself to a place where you can do this work. A place you can listen to yourself without all the distractions the world is hurling your way. Here are a few steps you can take toward doing this.

Step 1—Look Inside and See What's Already Within You

Reflect on these questions and take notes on what surfaces for you.

1. Think about a person you admire. Notice what makes them show up and perform day after day, and remain relentless against the odds. Consider where their mindset is coming from.

2. What did you love to do as a child? What themes do you notice and where is this pointing you?
3. Who are you being when you're at your best?
4. What are you doing when you lose track of time and forget to eat?
5. What's the legacy you want to leave, the story you want people to share about you?
6. What gives you energy and what takes it away?
7. Where do you get distracted and what's really behind that distraction (fear, comparison, etc.)?

Step 2—Create a Purpose-Driven Mission Statement for Yourself

A mission statement can take any form, and it can evolve over time as you change. My first mission statement took the form of a bulleted list of positive behaviours and contributions. For example, "I contribute more than I take". My current version is a short sentence. The format is less important than its message to you. It's my observation that the ones that work best incorporate a number of elements:

- A future state you'd like beyond yourself and something that has value beyond money
- Who you need to be and how you'll contribute to making that state a reality
- How you'll know you're making progress

Step 3—Make a List of All the Distractions You Need to Extract from Your Life

This is such a simple, yet hugely powerful exercise. Make a list of everything that is getting in your way and take action to remove each one from your life. This might be an iterative process. Seek help with this if you're struggling, but don't neglect this simple exercise that produces powerful results.

Summary of the Core Concepts

- You already have a winning mindset—you're just distracted and need to remove the distractions from your life.
- Your winning mindset is fuelled by something intrinsic, not extrinsic.
- You need a tribe that supports you, not one that competes with you.
- You're more capable than you realise.
- Three things you can do right now to be more productive, enjoy your existence, and realise your full potential are to (1) ask yourself reflective questions, (2) create a personal mission statement, and (3) list and eliminate distractions from your life.

About the Author

Robin Goldsbro is a guy with a vision for the future. A world full of people, doing exactly what they were born to do. Instead of work-life balance, people are living … for a living. He founded Level Seven with the goal of making this dream come true.

Before Level Seven, Robin had a corporate career where he challenged the status quo and was known for creating change. He dared people to think bigger and believe in themselves enough to take action. After realising this was what he was born to do, Robin left his job to follow the dream he'd been building for himself. That's how Level Seven came to be. Now it's dedicated to helping people experience a life with more joy, freedom, and purpose by doing what they love.

If you want to live for a living and have more life in your life—you can check Robin out at the following:

Email: robin@levelseven.org
Website: https://www.levelseven.coach
LinkedIn: LinkedIn.com/in/goldsbro
Facebook Life with more life community:
https://facebook.com/groups/305093070975049/

CHAPTER FOURTEEN

BE THE ARCHITECT OF YOUR HIGH-PERFORMANCE MINDSET

By Susan Hobson
Nat'l Hockey Champion, Leadership Mindset Coach
Toronto, Canada

Opportunities to find deeper powers within ourselves come when life seems most challenging.
—Joseph Campbell

What is the winning mindset?

The winning mindset is the mindset of a high performer—strategically hardwired beliefs that maximize your rate of growth, so you can unleash your highest performance potential sustainably and play your biggest impact game.

Architecting the winning, high-performance mindset all starts with stepping into pro-status as the expert in you, so you can cultivate a deep sense of knowing who you truly are, why you were designed the way you were, and why you experienced all that you have experienced on your journey thus far. With this, you can identify who you are meant to impact most or how you are meant to serve in this lifetime.

Stepping into pro-status in your self-leadership and self-mastery is a requisite starting point for any true high performer because it ensures that the mission you go on in your high-performance journey is strategically, intrinsically aligned with where you will be able to play your biggest impact game.

Doing so sets you up to perform optimally in your peak state of flow, resiliently, relentlessly and sustainably, no matter where you are, no matter what is happening around you.

It's extremely important, before going on your mission to win, to align yourself with the number one value that intrinsically drives the winning, high-performance mindset, which is max growth—realizing peak potential as a human being, so you can help other human beings to maximize theirs.

Where do you actually begin when you're ready to cultivate the winning mindset of a true high performer? As a high-performance leadership coach, I've seen this day in and day out in my practice throughout the last 15 years working with some of the highest-performing people on the planet—professional athletes, entrepreneurs leading start-ups, and C-suite executives and their leadership teams.

I wish I could say that they come whistling through my door, curious about how to strategically realize more of their performance potential. However, the harsh reality is that these busy, hustling, go-getters often don't slow down when things are "working" to learn how to make it all work even better. I often meet them for the first time when they are up against the painful glass ceiling in their growth (their results are flatlining) or in much more extreme fashion, when they are crashing into the brick wall going hundreds of miles an hour (in a tailspin, with their results plummeting).

The reality in the human experience, and especially in the experience of busy, hustling, ambitious people, is that it most often takes pain to act as the wake-up call to their untapped potential.

Not only do I see this first hand in my practice, but it's how I was lucky enough to first stumble across this game-changing mindset intel myself on my own high-performance journey.

Like many high performers, I realized at a very young age that I wanted to be the best. I woke up at eight years old and decided the way I was going to be my best was to start playing hockey. When I first started competing, I remember staring up at the glow stars on my ceiling at night, dreaming of playing in the NHL for the Boston Bruins. It didn't take me long before I started putting this dream of mine out there into my world. Immediately I started receiving feedback from my world that taught me to believe that, as a girl, I wasn't going to be capable of achieving it.

So, like any true high performer, I quickly pivoted my strategies and decided that I would, instead, set my sights on getting the best education I could out of my hockey talent (collegiate hockey was the pinnacle for women's hockey in the '80s, as we, women, weren't even in the Olympics yet). After talking to my parents, I knew this meant making it to the Ivy Leagues.

I started on my mission, determined to do whatever it took to make it there. I started to gather more feedback from my environment as to what I would need to do to get there. I learned to believe that I needed to get the best external results—get straight As, be on the top lineup, and get the most ice time—so I could score the most goals. Essentially, I learned to believe that I had to get to and stay at the front of the pack.

That's exactly what I did. At first, my strategies for controlling these external results "worked." At 14 years of age, I got recruited to and offered a full ride to one of the most elite boarding schools in all of New England. I knew that this meant I was well on my way, on my mission, one step closer to those Ivy gates.

Without hesitating, I answered the call to courage and adventure. I packed my bags, said goodbye to my family and friends, and moved from Toronto, Canada to the United States. I say that my strategies of putting tremendous amounts of pressure on myself to achieve perfect results "worked" at first, because although they earned me this once-in-a-lifetime opportunity, they were killing me on the inside. This was my first wake-up call, my first brick-wall moment. Overnight, I developed a life-threatening autoimmune disease my first year away at boarding school.

Nonetheless, I was determined and full of grit, so I found ways to pivot around these health obstacles, white knuckling it and staying on my mission. Silently, I continued to suffer, believing this was part of the sacrifice necessary to be the best. I was using the same broken deficit strategy of perfectionism, i.e., doing whatever I had to do to get the perfect external results. And again, it "worked." By the time I reached my senior year of high school, I had gotten recruited and was granted admission to the number one Ivy League school— Princeton University.

Victory, right? I had achieved my goal. I was in. Little did I know that was when I would have my second brick-wall moment. Only this time, it was all going to come crashing down around me. Overnight, I went from being a big fish in a small pond to being a little minnow in the ocean. I went from being one of the top hockey recruits in the world, scoring 100 points and being on the academic high honor roll my senior year, to being a bench rider my first year at Princeton and getting Cs and Ds in the classroom for the very first time in my life. And my father, who had been my biggest supporter, always in the stands cheering me on and validating my efforts, got diagnosed with terminal cancer and quickly passed away. Suddenly, I found myself in a complete and utter tailspin.

I had no idea who I was without these "perfect" external results. Where would my confidence and motivation come from if I couldn't get on the ice and score goals, or raise my hand in a classroom full of the world's smartest kids? This was a real crossroads moment for me, as it is for many of the clients who first walk through my door.

Many high-achieving people believe the best mindset strategy for peak performance is to seek to control the validation of their external results. After all, that's what most of us are conditioned to believe as kids competing in school and in sports. The problem is that it's a broken, unsustainable strategy that leads to suffering in the lives of the people who pursue excellence in this reckless way. When we believe we are only as good as our most recent results, it places our self-worth, self-confidence, and self-motivation outside of us, which is dangerous and completely unsustainable, especially the higher you climb in your performance ascension.

The problem here is that the higher you climb, the more the pressure builds, which leads to even more self-sacrifice, more anxiety in the nervous system, and a breakdown in our health and psychological wellbeing. This is where the wheels start to fall off the bus inevitably for us all.

Luckily for me, I found myself breaking down at a place and space on my journey where I was surrounded by resources that could teach me better mindset strategies. Most people don't realize this, but once you make it through the Ivy League gates, these places will do almost anything to ensure you make it out the other side. So, I got exposed to this high-level mindset intel and was shown how to architect the winning mindset of a true high performer.

As a high-level athlete, I knew I had to get into the gym and onto the ice to train my body, but what I didn't know was that to succeed sustainably and realize my peak performance potential, I also had to get into the mental gym and train my brain. I learned that 90 percent of performance is actually mental. I was shown how to make my strategies internally based, so no matter where I was at, no matter how much pressure I was under, I knew where to go inside of myself to manage my mindset, my nervous system, and, therefore, my performance.

I did this by aligning myself with what I now truly believe is what inspired my eight-year-old self to go on my high-performance journey in the first place, towards becoming my best. I learned that as an eight-year-old (and to all of us as children), being the best had nothing to do with being better than everybody else. Being the best really meant being *my* best, seeing what I was made of and celebrating what I had to my fullest. Challenging myself to realize max growth potential in a sustainable way.

Once I had successfully pivoted my mindset strategies off of the uncontrollable factors, i.e., seeking to control external results with perfectionism, I was able to deconstruct the limited beliefs that had been conditioned by my environment—beliefs like "You're only as good as your most recent results" and "Less-than-perfect results are failure." I had to re-architect empowering beliefs that were based on sources that were inside of me, so I could intrinsically validate the value I had to bring, rather than seeking that validation from others.

This was the turning point moment for me, just as it is for the clients I work with today, where I went from maladaptively trying to be some perfect false version of myself, to adaptively learning to make the goal progression—believing instead "the goal is for me to do the very best I can with what I have each and every day." Which, when you really think about it, is a goal that is in our control and one that we can always reach.

I was back on the road, back in alignment with my true sense of purpose (max, sustainable growth), and this time, with all the confidence and motivation I needed to perform optimally. Because the goal was to do my best, I now stood on a healthier, much stronger foundation of knowing who I was and seeing all that I was made of in my potential—all skills, talents, strengths, and attributes that made myself me—the gifts that made up my sweet spot and those which got me into a place like Princeton in the first place. I learned to believe that these things were always inside of me and that experiencing challenge and pressure from my environment was how I could actually enhance and increase my performance capacity (similar to how it enhanced my strength and fitness in the gym), and realize even more of my true performance potential, progressionally.

The results spoke for themselves. I went from bench rider of the century, getting Cs and Ds my first year, to being one of the leading scorers on the top lineup and on the National Dean's List by my second year. Now that I had re-hardwired my mindset with these intrinsically based strategies and empowering beliefs, I learned how to unlock my peak performance state (confident, motivated, and focused on the controllables).

Best of all, I went on after Princeton to realize my childhood dream of playing professional hockey. By the time I graduated from university, the National Women's Hockey League (NWHL) had formed, and I was offered one of two spots back in my hometown, on the Toronto Aeros, alongside six Olympians. We went on to win a National Championship and NWHL Cup, which sits today in the Hockey Hall of Fame. In other words, learning how to architect the winning mindset of a high performer helped me achieve the best results I had ever achieved and showed me how to unlock even more of my performance potential.

The pivot: focusing on the process of growth rather than the outcome of perfect results. The mindset strategy: it's all about progression, not perfection; feedback, not failure.

The best part is that this too was when I saw exactly why I had gone through all of these tremendously painful experiences so far upstream on my high-performance journey—so I could show people just like you how to unlock the same winning formula on their own high-performance journey. I knew this was what I was made to do; this is where I could add the most value to the world based on who I was, what I valued most, and all that I had experienced and learned along the way. I understood so clearly in this pivoting moment that this was why I experienced all I had experienced. This is where I learned how to turn my pain into purpose, which is how I play my biggest impact game in the world today, where I unlock peak levels of fulfilment, passion, and joy, and it's how you can start to find yours and play yours too.

About the Author

Susan Hobson is a high-performance leadership coach and founder/CEO of Elite High-Performance Inc. and host of the podcast *The Leadership Launchpad Project*. Susan's science-based high-performance coaching process was developed from her first-hand experience competing at some of the most competitive environments on the planet—Princeton and Harvard Universities and the National Women's Hockey League (NWHL).

Susan now leads a practice of high-performance mindset coaches based in the financial district of downtown Toronto, Canada. Susan has been leading the industry for 15 years, working with some of the world's highest-performing people and teams: professional athletes, C-suite executives, entrepreneurs, and many of the world's leading tech companies like Google. Her specialty is in the area of mindset strategy architecture, which essentially means that she teaches high performers how to think strategically, so they can play their biggest impact game. Your highest potential is her passion, and she's on a mission to change the way the game of life and business is being played forever.

For more information on how to work with Susan, one of her coaches, or to apply for one of her high-level masterminds, group coaching programs, or high-performance mindset coaching certifications, visit her website or find her on LinkedIn.

Email: susan@elitehighperformance.com
Website: www.elitehighperformance.com

CHAPTER FIFTEEN

FOR PEAK POTENTIAL, FOCUS ON WE, NOT JUST ME

By Nick Holton, PhD
Education and Performance Consultant
Philadelphia, Pennsylvania

I've studied expert performance at an elite level as much as anybody else alive, and a couple of things are very true across the board. One of them is that if you're at the top, one way or another it's because there were probably a handful of people who were phenomenal mentors to you.
—Steven Kotler, Flow Research Collective

I was born and raised in the suburbs of Grand Rapids, a mid-sized town in western Michigan. If you were a sports-loving Michigander during my adolescent years, which I very much was, it typically meant two things. First, that the Detroit Lions were abysmal year after year. Second, the Detroit Pistons were anything but. In fact, during the late '80s and early '90s, the Pistons teams, known as the "Bad Boys," became famous, or maybe notorious, for their aggressive, hard-nosed, and often dirty style of play.

In the first 22 years of my life, the Pistons won the NBA championship three times. During the 1989 season, the Bad Boys had to travel through two different teams with multiple perennial all-stars and top-50 players of all-time on their rosters. In the East, this was the Boston Celtics with Larry Bird, Robert Parrish, and Kevin McHale. In the finals, it was the Los Angeles

Lakers with Magic Johnson and James Worthy. For most people, these series were clear mismatches, but the Pistons were able to upset both teams that season en route to the title. They then repeated as champions in 1990, which included a play-off win over a young Michael Jordan. In a league that was becoming increasingly focused on individual super-stars the Pistons were writing a different narrative.

As if that weren't already an impressive feat, the 2003–2004 Pistons managed to outdo those teams from the '80s. That year, the Pistons had exactly zero players who would be considered top-50 all-time by any stretch of the imagination. Once again, the Pistons were able to overcome that perceived gap and make it to the NBA finals. There, they would again face the Lakers, and just like the first time around, LA was loaded with talent. Only this time the Lakers roster didn't just have two hall-of-famers. They had four. In those days, the Lakers were two years out from having just won three straight NBA championships, and during that particular year, their roster was made up of a young Kobe Bryant, Shaquille O'Neal, and two aging superstars in the form of Karl Malone and Gary Payton. By any objective measure, the Lakers were a team with vastly superior individual talent. Yet, not only did the Pistons end up winning the series; they did it in dominant fashion, winning four of the five games they played. Much like the "Bad Boys" of the late '80s, the 2003–2004 Pistons squad handled a team of hall-of-famers. So, what was the magic sauce that enabled these surprise successes?

The answer is a focus on the collective, what I refer to as the "we," instead of just the individual or the "me." This chapter is devoted to just a small portion of the vast array of research that demonstrates what Shawn Achor, consultant to many of Fortune's top 100 companies, refers to as "big potential." The notion that in order to truly achieve our greatest individual potentials, we need to operate with the mindset that we can't get there alone, and we should be curating and cultivating our ecosystems accordingly.

Mindset and Beliefs

Let's start with two fundamental components of high performance in any domain—optimism and self-efficacy.

Optimism, as shown in Clinical Psychological Review's 2010 article "Optimism" by researchers Carver, Scheier, and Segersrom, is our general belief that things can or will go well. Optimism is the belief that underpins virtually any type of growth or positive change. From learning and skill development, to navigating adversity, to accomplishing our boldest goals, it always starts with the belief that taking action in a certain direction might go well. So, it's worth having a go. Without this sense of optimism, we can convince ourselves that there is no use in trying to push forward. Which, in turn, can perpetuate a self-fulfilling cycle of what Seligman, in his article "Learned Helplessness" in the Annual Review of Medicine (1972), calls learned helplessness and failure. Armed with realistic optimism, we're more likely to have higher levels of wellbeing, to cope with and persist through challenges, and to have better physical health.

While an optimistic mindset is critical, it does have a sweet spot. Dr. Karen Reivich, professor at the University of Pennsylvania and consultant to the NBA's Oklahoma City Thunder, suggests that we need to be cautious not to fall into "Pollyannaism," meaning positive illusions created by what we call "unrealistic optimism" or just thinking things will work out. The sweet spot in optimism involves thinking positive outcomes are possible while understanding that it typically requires action on our part, not just wishful thinking.

That effort is where self-efficacy comes in. According to Friedman, Kane, and Cornfield (Social support and career optimism, 1998), self-efficacy is our belief in our own ability to take on a challenge, complete a task, or accomplish a goal. When we have high efficacy, it predicts that we'll take action, put in greater effort, and persist in that effort and action for longer amounts of time. Why? Because we believe success is possible. So, the brain's calculus lands on the conclusion that putting in the effort is worth it.

While each of these components of a winning mindset sound like exclusively "me" beliefs, in that they exist inside our own heads, they're actually tremendously susceptible to the influence of the people we surround ourselves with. For instance, studies in *Health Psychology* demonstrate that perceived social support often mediates the relationship between optimism and the impact on our self-esteem, coping mechanisms, wellbeing, and post-traumatic growth. Think about that—the ways you cope with challenges, with growth from trauma, with how well you feel and with your level of self-esteem, it all often comes down to the social support around you.

Likewise, social surroundings can have a dramatic impact on our self-efficacy too. In 1977 Stanford professor Albert Bandura published a seminal paper outlining four of the primary sources of self-efficacy. The second and third sources Bandura lists are *vicarious success* and *verbal persuasion*. "Vicarious success" refers to whether we're surrounded by or can see other people who have successfully taken on the particular challenge or task we're considering. If we have line of sight and can see ourselves in these people, we're more likely to believe it's possible for us to successfully navigate that task or challenge too. That's the basic process of inspiration. The third source, "verbal persuasion," refers to two elements: (1) self-talk, which can have dramatic effects on our neural structure and behaviors, and (2) other-talk, the language and messages we receive from the people around us. It means having people in our lives who help convince us that we can handle the challenges or tasks we need to take on.

If you're counting as you read this, you'll notice that half of these predictors of self-efficacy and our belief in ourselves actually come from other people. Various studies conducted since Bandura first published his paper have reinforced the significant impact social support can have on levels of self-efficacy. What we think about ourselves and how we take action are not just "me" endeavors; it pays to give attention to the "we," too.

Consider some common examples. Why do we look up to our heroes or idols when we're young, like I did with Isiah, Joe D., and Cobi Jones? They make us believe it's possible to reach those heights too. Any elite performer has likely had a good coach or mentor who built confidence and helped them to believe that through hard work and perseverance, they could accomplish their boldest goals. These sorts of experiences can be efficacy boosters, and all of them come from the actions of the people we surround ourselves with and allow to make up our worlds.

Resilience

Having people to look up to in our lives, and the optimistic and efficacious beliefs they help foster, are also critical components of resilience, the ability to navigate adversity. Any path to winning at the highest levels will inherently involve losing from time to time, whatever that might mean in the context. For my Pistons, they had to go through several defeats at the hands of the perennial powerhouses of the '80s. For Michael Jordan, it was getting cut from his high school basketball team. Walt Disney was fired from his first job for not being creative enough, and early in her career Serena Williams was overshadowed by her sister, Venus. More often than not, this is the typical trajectory for elite performers. We don't just skyrocket to the top and land in the winner's circle. The path to long-term success is much more jagged.

This brings us back to optimism and self-efficacy. If we're talking about the most elite performers in all of sport, in other words, the hall-of-famers, resilience is a requirement. To make the baseball hall of fame, hitters usually need to have a batting average above three hundred, which means throughout their careers they fail to get a hit as much as two-thirds of their at-bats. In the NBA, the greatest shooters of all time still have career averages at or below 50 percent in most cases. That means they miss more than half of the shots they take. Yet, the best keep swinging and shooting because they believe each attempt will go well (optimism) and have worked hard to refine their craft, which helps support the belief that they can make it go well (self-efficacy). That is resilient behavior.

Various lines of research on resilience make the case that social support is an integral part of resilient mindsets and actions. Some even argue that the relationship exists on a systems level, meaning that our own individual resilience is, in part, the result of the resilience of our friends, family, neighborhoods, and contexts. In a study of hundreds of college students, social support actually mediated the relationship between resilience and life-satisfaction. The relationship between stress and social support is so strong that scholars, like McGonigal, often argue for the inclusion of an additional stress response beyond fight, flight, or freeze; a response they call "tend and befriend." The stress response can actually prime the human body with oxytocin, encouraging us to reach out to get or give support during a difficult time.

If we want to more easily enable ourselves to overcome the inevitable adversities that accompany long-term success and living a good life, we'd be wise to surround ourselves with people we can count on for support and people we want to give support to in return. We're hardwired to do both.

Motivation and Purpose

The impact of our social surroundings is not limited to our beliefs, mindsets, and resilience. It extends to our motivation and behavior as well.

When we consider the motivation necessary to become elite in anything, we are generally going to find that winning motivation tends to be predominantly intrinsic. Full intrinsic motivation means that we feel a sense of volition to engage in a behavior because that behavior itself is a reward. We don't just play a game to win, a musical instrument to make money, or perform or make art to receive awards. We do them because they're enjoyable activities even without those external rewards. This is not to say that a winning mindset can't ever include extrinsic motivations such as winning or financial security. It simply means that, across most elite performers, you're going to see a motivational profile that is predominantly intrinsic. This sense of joy in the activity itself, often the process rather than the result, is ironically critical to good long-term performance. As shown by Kaufman in *Transcend* (2020), a lack of this intrinsic drive can lead to lower levels of persistence, performance, and productivity.

While that intrinsic joy is a great arrow to have in our quiver, Grant shows us that we can amplify the positive effects of intrinsic rewards when we pair them with prosocial motivation. What we commonly call a sense of purpose. While a litany of research exists on the topic of purpose in life, the general idea is that purpose is how we bring ourselves to something outside our own self-interest. It is, per Kaufman, a "need for an overarching aspiration that energizes one's efforts and provides a central source of meaning and significance in one's life." If meaning is a belief in or connection to something more significant than ourselves, purpose is our desire to contribute to it.

As you're probably guessing by now, our sense of meaning and purpose are very often connected to other people. It might be something local and simple, like taking care of our family, making our parents proud, or building a business that provides a community with good jobs and benefits. Purpose can also be grandiose, what Peter Diamandis and Steven Kotler in *Transcend* (2020) call a "massively transformative purpose." One through which we hope to have a transformative impact on a global problem or challenge like the environment, poverty, or famine.

These sorts of goals require a sense of belonging and connection to the people around us. Sometimes they're in our immediate vicinity, sometimes they're far away, but it all still centers around a basic essence of connection. That's an essential component of the jet fuel that is intrinsic motivation.

The neuroscience around the topic of purpose further supports how critical it is to peak performance. In my work for the Flow Research Collective (FRC), I coach professional athletes, state senators, C-suite executives and entrepreneurs, software engineers at some of the influential companies in the world, and many more individuals and teams looking to experience flow—the psychological and neurological state in which we both feel and perform our best. Flow entails being completely absorbed in what we're doing, losing a sense of self, experiencing time dilation, and dropping into "the zone." In this state, we become immensely more creative and productive, and get a release of a neurochemical cocktail, often made up of most or all of the so-called "happy chemicals." It feels good and it is good.

Flow also can be triggered by a sense of purpose. As Steven Kotler, director of FRC, puts it, once we've satisfied our own core needs, many of us start to consider how we can help our "tribe" or species do the same. When we gain this sense of purpose, we often see a flush of oxytocin in the brain, which, in addition to being one of those "happy chemicals," also enhances our focus, productivity, resilience, and our intrinsic motivation. This sense of purpose is so important that we actually place it at the very beginning of our training at FRC.

When it comes to a winning mindset and peak performance, intrinsic motivation is the fuel, and adding a focus on the greater good to it is the nitrous oxide that can give us the extra boost toward the winner's circle.

Habits

In his New York Times bestseller *Atomic Habits*, habit expert James Clear notes that our earliest habits are not built; they are learned through observation and imitation. This imitation piece is important to understand when it comes to thinking about how other people influence our habits.

Habits are the stuff of consistency. Often, they are behaviors that will in one form or another determine our destinies. Goals are simply targets. Habits are the processes that help us steer toward those targets. Clear goes on to demonstrate that many of us imitate others in ways that form habits (we primarily imitate "the close, the many, and the powerful"), rather than consciously making or breaking our own, a finding that should be alarming.

Consider some of the simplest examples. We know that sleep is key to active recovery, consistent experiences of flow, emotional regulation, energy levels, and the ability to focus and self-regulate. We should do what we can to control the process and environment of sleep. The hard part is, anyone with a partner or spouse (i.e., "the close") knows that our sleep is subject to the needs and desires of the person we share a bed with. They likely impact what time we go to sleep, what we do before we go to sleep, the temperature of the room, the feel of the mattress, etc.

You can see this sort of impact throughout your typical day or week too. Do you watch more TV when certain people are around? Do you eat or drink differently when you're out with friends or after you see a commercial ("the close" and "the powerful")? Do you mimic the people in your in-group ("the many")? How is that mimicry impacting your behaviors and outcomes? The key here is to avoid being blind to your habits and subtle behaviors. This means giving particularly close attention to whom you spend time with and how that time either moves you toward your goals or away from them.

Do not confuse the message here. Our relationships and sense of connection are among the most significant predictors of a good life, globally. The people in our life can have a tremendous impact on our mood, wellbeing, motivation, and more, just as we've seen throughout this chapter. All of that evidence points to the need for us to be very conscious of and intentional about our relationships. Not only so that we can deepen the ones that help us thrive, but so that we can also be aware of and adjust the ones that don't.

About the Author

Dr. Nick Holton is an author, speaker, consultant, and coach in the science of flourishing—a synergistic combination of wellbeing and high performance. Through his work for and collaboration with the Flow Research Collective, the Human Flourishing Program at Harvard's Institute for Quantitative Social Science, The Shipley School, and his own business, Eudaimonics, Nick has had the opportunity to train, coach, and speak internationally with professional and collegiate athletes, C-suite execs, entrepreneurs, organizations, and schools that are striving to cultivate the greatest angels of their nature and actualize their highest potentials. He is most passionate about re-envisioning societal systems in ways that prioritize and promote individual and collective flourishing, and ultimately lead to a better existence for humanity.

Email: nick@eudaimonics.org
Website: www.eudaimonics.org

CHAPTER SIXTEEN

EMBODYING THE ORDINARY
LEADS TO THE EXTRAORDINARY

By Richard Husseiny
Former Olympic Coach, Founder of The Conscious Life Collective
Brighton, England, United Kingdom

The most important question anyone can ask is: What myth am I living?
—Carl Jung

The Olympic Games are fascinating for so many reasons. For one, they bring together people with extraordinary skills that most of us can't even begin to imagine. My personal desire to work with these awe-inspiring people was fuelled by the wonder of what makes their feats possible. What I couldn't see, at the time, was how much the lessons I would learn coaching were going to support me through the toughest time of my life—when I gave end-of-life care to my mother.

Helping my mother near the end of her life was as much a privilege as it was a brutally life-changing experience. As I will show in this chapter, being in the presence of death is a profound teacher, one that has the potential to free us from our limitations. This was the catalyst for me to ask the big questions of life and set out on my path of personal mastery.

Witnessing the truly extraordinary in others and being personally stripped bare has revealed a profound truth to me. When talking about peak performance, there's a natural tendency to project towards someone who embodies those qualities. This highlights the idea that when seeking peak performance, one is in a place of lacking. My aim, here, is to show that you already have everything you need to achieve the extraordinary—whether that's in sport, in business, or in life.

You will be presented with a case that you don't need more of anything. It's the idea that all you need is to reconnect yourself back to your innate raw materials. These raw materials are the very ordinary qualities that underpin extraordinary human achievements, which you can utilise to your advantage in life.

Extraordinary achievements are just ordinary practices done extremely well. Every single one of us has unique magic within us, and that is needed more now than ever before. In this chapter I am going to share what I have learnt from working with some of the best performers on the planet.

Witnessing the Extraordinary

For reasons I am supremely grateful for, my coaching career formed around acrobatic and action sports. Witnessing people fly through the air for a job taught me what is meant by extraordinary. Yet it's not only what these athletes achieve on a snowboard or from a diving board, but how they experience their lives.

There are the more familiar aspects to their preparation that forms part of the foundation for success. Three examples of these are that they are process-driven, they get immediate feedback, and they have clear goals. "Process-driven" means they allow their focus only on what they can control. The weather and their competitors are not qualities they have any influence over at all. Therefore, the best in the world give no energy or time to them. Rather they put their focus on all aspects within their power to affect. They receive immediate feedback in their competitive life to understand what's working and what needs changing. Practice is not all there is to it. It's the practice of what is needed that unlocks progress. Clear goals are specifically about them knowing what they are doing within their plan, and most importantly they know why they are doing it. It all ties back into the process and allows them to have a clear mind when it matters.

These three examples form crucial pieces within a larger puzzle. I could write extensively on each of these, but they are not the stand-out qualities I want to share. The qualities I want to share are retuning your awareness and embracing mortal stakes.

Retuning Your Awareness

Action sport athletes push the boundaries of what's possible; therefore, for me to be witness to them discussing fear, panic, and how they deal with it, is liberating. If they survive without big crashes, then that's a good day. Winning matters, of course, but the real adversary is fear. They have a profound respect and connection for their environment, and they need to heed the warning signs of danger. Therefore, they have to be in tune with themselves and with nature—otherwise they can pay the highest price with their lives. But what does being in tune really mean?

Mindset suggests there is only a psychological approach to achieving peak performance. I agree that our mental constructs and views are a crucial part to how we experience our world. And yet the human condition is so much more expansive than what we perceive with our mind. When we really take a moment and sharpen our awareness of our inner world, we realise just how much noise is going on within our head. It's relentless and when left unattended, becomes a freight train of anxiety and clutter that significantly limits our physical and mental performance.

Without developing awareness, it's almost guaranteed that we will take our thoughts and emotions as our genuine state in the moment without question. We are at the mercy of them because we rely on them to drive our actions. But it doesn't have to be like this. The profound work by Dr. Lisa Feldman Barrett in recent years has redefined many outdated beliefs around the mind and emotions. At the heart of her work is that our brains are interpreting our senses first and turning those into the emotions and states that we experience. An emotion is simply an event where our whole brain is making meaning of internal sensations in our body, in relation to what's going on around us in the world.

What you consciously or unconsciously feel in your body influences what you see, hear, smell, taste, and touch. These bodily feelings are known as your interoception, your interior perception.

Our gut and heart are in a two-way communication with our brain. The gut produces 90 percent of the brain's serotonin neuro-chemical supply. Medical doctor Zach Bush has shown that for every ten-bits of information shared between the brain and gut, nine-bits travel upwards. The heart has over 40,000 neurons, which are the basic working units of the brain. The Heart Math Institute has shown that not only does the heart have its own intuitive intelligence, it also radiates an electromagnetic wave several feet outside of our body. When we feel emotions such as fear or anger, that wave is incoherent. When we feel love and gratitude, the wave is coherent. These objective markers have significant consequences on our breath pattern, heart rate, and nervous system.

Think back to a time when your gut instinct or your heart was giving off a clear signal to you. Did you listen or ignore it? This is an example of your body talking. Thoughts are the language of your mind, and your feelings are the language of your body. Being in tune means being able to perceive these signals and use them wisely.

Practicing the Ordinary

We are living in an "age of disembodiment", or disconnection from our body. Our culture, technology, and medicine have progressively made us into poor interoceptors. So being in tune means practicing awareness of these powerful signals in and around our body. The good news is that this is a skill that we all have the ability to reconnect with and master. And this is where the ordinary practices come in.

Practice 1

The first ordinary practice is to retrain where you habitually put your focus, moving away from your mind (thoughts) and into your body (feelings). A powerful way to do this is to use a pattern interrupt. This involves breaking a routine, habitual thought pattern, or behavioural pattern with a prompt. One of the most profound prompts for me personally has been to direct my awareness into a scan of my body by asking myself: "Does this inform me, or does it affect me?"

"Informed" means we determine the factual data we have from a situation that we can use to inform our action. Assumptions and guesses are not factual, yet our brain will enter automatically into their arena with a flurry of predictions.

"Affect" means that we notice what is happening within our body in relation to a situation. In a heightened emotional state, our breath rate quickens, our heart beats faster, and our nervous system gets us ready for action. An elevated heart rate does not mean anxiety, yet our brain potentially turns it into that emotional experience. That means that in this anxious state we can't respond, learn, or access well-considered decisions. We default to emotions, stored memories, breathing patterns, and reactions that are survival-based. This is how we handle things when a situation of stress overwhelms us. So, if we're feeling one way or another at our core metabolic being, it will influence our choices.

Monitoring your body helps you know when your physiology is changing and then empowers you to self-regulate to bring yourself into the now, away from the what-ifs and doubt. You will then be in a better physiological state to assess the information you are receiving, to then respond effectively rather than react emotionally.

Practice 2

The second ordinary practice is to develop a breath practice. It seems so counterintuitive to discuss and focus on our breathing. We do it every moment of every day of our lives. Yet what I've come to realise, from both a physiological perspective and an actual practice, is that taking control of my breath is one of the most profound practices I have access to.

Action sport athletes use breath control and mindfulness in the minutes before they drop into a huge jump or half-pipe. Not to be calm, but to be focused and clear. By understanding a little of what's happening in our amazing physiology, we can use those physiological knobs and levers as very easy and straightforward tools. These tools allow us to make profound changes to the way we experience life.

Dr. Andrew Hubberman describes fear as the sum of anxiety plus uncertainty. Uncertainty is in all of life. Anxiety is our physiological response to the unknown, and this is where we can influence with great effect. We are not limited to our stress fight, flight, or freeze responses. We can choose to interact with our autonomic nervous system, which is where breath comes in. By consciously controlling how we breathe, we can self-regulate and manage our internal state positively to initiate our best response when we encounter challenges, disagreements, and stressors. Furthermore, all chemistry in our body is regulated through how we breathe.

Breathing Tips and Nasal Breathing

Emotional State—nasal breathing helps bring on the parasympathetic response, which helps calm us down. When life is stressful, and you note that you are mouth breathing, try switching to nasal breathing and inhaling slowly and deeply.

Exercise Performance—at first, high-intensity exercise may feel more difficult with nasal breathing. The body needs to adapt to a different approach to the respiratory process, and if the body is accustomed to hyperventilating during exercise, nasal breathing may feel a bit slow at first. Things will shift. Be patient.

Exercise Recovery—switch to nasal breathing in between sets or during rest. Because nasal breathing is more efficient, recovery should be smoother.

Immune System—nasal breathing is a major line of defence against airborne pathogens. The mouth has no defence system. You may experience improvements with overall breathing and decreasing allergies or colds since breathing through the nose acts as a built-in air filter.

Practice 3

The third ordinary practice is to change your relationship with the mortal stakes that are built into the fabric of life. The moment you become aware of this fundamental quality of life, you can step into a place of empowerment, and life becomes a fun experiment.

Action-sport athletes have serious injury and their own death to comprehend as the ultimate price of what they do. This connection to their mortality leaves them with as much of a free spirit as I've seen anyone in my life. Their ability to overcome adversity is astounding. Their desire to put themselves back in harm's way after serious injury is inspiring. And they squeeze every drop of life available to them.

This is where grief ties back into this story. To be witness to a loved one at the end of life is as much a privilege as it is desperately painful. What is pushed away in our Western culture is warmly embraced in Eastern and indigenous cultures. It is the most ordinary of events as each and every one of us will experience our death moment. The extraordinary lies within those last breaths, which I got to witness with my mother.

To develop a relationship to your mortality doesn't mean you have to take up big wave surfing. A powerful practice is to spend five minutes a day contemplating the idea of your own limited time in this life. No other structure is needed, but if you want structure, many esoteric traditions will serve you well for guidance. My own practice has allowed me to be less fearful in life. I now say yes more often than I say no to opportunities that feel outside of my comfort zone. I embrace challenges that come my way with an understanding that life is finite, so I try to enjoy each experience. This is embodied within every part of me, rather than just a nervous voice in my head whilst the rest of me is gripped with fear.

Conclusion

Elite athletes push the boundaries of what's possible—yet they use techniques we all have access to, to manage fear associated with life, change, chasing dreams, and the ultimate fear of death. A question one of the Red Bull athletes I coached frequently asked is "Do you want to get to the end of your life and wish you'd lived the life you wanted rather than staying safe?"

So, ask yourself today—what do you want in life? Anything worth getting takes risk and the ability to step into fear. You have all the raw materials you need right now to live an extraordinary life. A winning mindset doesn't only have to exist in the elite athlete. It can exist in you and help you become more alive right now.

> *Don't ask yourself what the world needs; ask yourself*
> *what makes you come alive. And then go do that. Because*
> *what the world needs is people who have come alive.*
> —Howard Thurman

About the Author

For over 16 years, Richard Husseiny worked as a performance coach in high-performance sport, with some of the best organisations and athletes in the world—from Great Britain, USA, and China. This included supporting teams in preparation for two Summer Olympic Games (London 2012 and Rio 2016) and the 2018 Winter Olympics (Pyeongchang).

Richard is an experienced coach and speaker, and he founded The Conscious Life Collective. He is dedicated to helping people progress along the path to personal mastery. This is the process of inner work and outer action, in service of a flourishing world. He has developed a five-stage pathway to enable people to live and work purposefully towards a vision, in alignment with their values and in a state of constant learning about themselves and the reality in which they exist. Richard specialises in coaching topics including self-care, resiliency, leadership, and expanding awareness using states such as flow.

Email: richard@theconsciouslifecollective.com
Website: www.theconsciouslifecollective.com
YouTube: www.youtube.com/c/TheConsciousLifeCollective
Instagram: @theconsciouslifecollective
Facebook: Facebook.com/theconsciouslifecollective
LinkedIn: https://www.linkedin.com/in/richard-husseiny-msc-ascc-a18aa928/

CHAPTER SEVENTEEN

WAKE UP YOUR INNER CHAMPION

By Gavin Ingham.
Founder of #IAM10
London, England, United Kingdom

What differentiates a top performer from a merely good one? What enables one person to fly whilst another, seemingly with all of the same opportunities, fails to get airborne? Why does one team kick ass and another can't even get their boots on? Answering these questions has been my passion for over two decades and has helped me create my IAM10 system for high performance, which I have had the privilege of sharing with over 250,000 people on over 2,500 stages in over 40 countries.

I don't know you. I don't know your business. I don't know your personal life. I don't know what is important to you. But I do know that everyone has areas they need to work on. Areas that they would like to improve. Put simply, everyone wants to be more, do more, and have more. Even those who do not want to admit it!

Maybe your business and your career are flying, but you have put on some weight? Or maybe both of those are sorted, but your relationship with your nearest and dearest is under pressure? Or perhaps you feel great, and your relationships are fabulous, but your business and career have plateaued and you're stuck in a rut?

In this chapter, I will show you how you can take back control of your business and your life. I have helped thousands to achieve more, but it requires *you* to get started.

Many people never start the process of taking back control of their lives. They fail even to take baby steps towards this aim. They fail even to get to the airport, let alone getting on the plane, or getting the plane into the air. This is because most do not have the right mindset—they need a mindset shift before they can make the changes that they want.

It's time for that mindset shift.

There are three core mindsets that you need to adopt if you want to successfully implement change.

- The first is courage.
- The second is humility.
- The third is discipline.

Recently, I put on a bit of weight, and I decided to take up running again. My wife suggested the Couch to 5K program. If you have not come across it, the approach takes you from the couch to running five kilometres in under 30 minutes in nine weeks.

As I looked into the Couch to 5K program, my ego kicked in. I used to be a runner. I held school records. I was fit, and, in my head, I was still that 18-year-old athlete. I wasn't going to start by walking and slow jogging, all the while being "patronised" by some talking head, heckler!

I started to draw up my own plan based on my knowledge and motivation of yesteryear. I knew what to do. I knew better. Within two days of running, I had injured my calf muscle and was back on the couch. The whole thing was an unmitigated disaster.

I had to remind myself of what I teach my clients …

Have Courage

You need the courage to face up to reality as it is. Not how you want it to be. Not how you'd like it to be. But how it actually is. And that requires brutal honesty.

The first step of the #IAM10 process is to help you to look at how you are doing in *all* areas of your life. I had to face up to the fact that I was an overweight 52-year-old with a heart issue who had not run for years. I was the perfect "Couch to 5K" participant, not the athlete I saw myself as.

Have Humility

Humility is all about accepting what you see when you look at your situation. I needed to be able to take advice on how best to approach running from where I am now, not where I thought I was (or where I thought I should be).

When you want to make change, what matters is your ability to face the truth, take it onboard, and start from reality. As I always say, "You cannot launch a rocket from quicksand".

Have Discipline

Change requires commitment. It requires consistent action. It requires the ability to stay focused on simple actions that will deliver more of what you want in your life. This doesn't just happen. It is something that needs to be worked on and is where so many fail.

This mental shift sounds simple, but it is not. I ask people to rate themselves on a scale of one to ten for *courage, humility*, and *discipline*, and then ask them where they want to be. We then regularly check in with how they are doing as a reminder to keep a constant vigilance on maintaining the right mindset.

So, with *courage, humility*, and *discipline* in mind, let me give you some principles of high performance, a winning mindset, and getting more of what you want.

1. Champions Have Conviction

High performers have total *conviction*—in themselves, in their businesses, in their ability. They know that success starts on the inside. If you do not believe you can build the business of your dreams and create the lifestyle that you want whilst also staying fit and healthy and surrounding yourself with loving relationships, then you never will. *Conviction* is all about mindset. It is all about how you turn up on a daily basis.

I have asked about 200,000 people to envisage themselves operating at their best. Whether that is leading a team, making a sale, or making a presentation,

I ask them to visualise it and then answer this question: "What attributes do you display when you are at your best?"

The answers are surprisingly similar whether I am with a team of salespeople, a group of lawyers, or a board of directors. They say words like *motivated, focused, energetic, driven, responsible, goal-seeking, results-oriented, happy.*

I then ask them whether these are more attitudes or skills. People always conclude that they are more attitudes than skills; on average about 80% attitudes versus 20% skills.

Skills are obviously critically important; if you had all the motivation and none of the skills, you'd be a motivated muppet. Equally, without the right attitudes, skills are useless. Attitudes provide the energy and the drive to deliver on those skills. You can know what to do, you can have the tools to do it, and you can have the opportunity, but if you do not have the right mindset, you will either not do it at all or you will not do it well. Your attitude impacts your behaviours, and your behaviours impact your results.

It gets worse. Most people allow their results (and a whole load of other external factors) to impact the way they feel, thus creating an "outside in" motivation where they can literally "prove" they were right to be negative in the first place. High performers experience the highs and lows and bad results the same as everyone else. The difference is that they find a way to motivate themselves from the "inside out." They do not allow people, events, and circumstances to impact the way they feel. And often, the more critical the situation, the faster and more successful they are in getting back into the right state in comparison to average-to-good performers.

Bottom line, your mindset is critical and to get this right, you need inner *conviction.*

Questions to ask yourself:

- *What do I need to do to build and maintain my conviction?*
- *How can I be my best today and every day?*

2. Champions Have Clarity

Clarity is all about knowing what to do and when to do it. And knowing what not to do and when not to do it.

One of the core reasons champions achieve extraordinary results is because they have so much more *clarity* than average performers. Champions have *clarity* about what they want. They have *clarity* about how they are going to achieve it. They have *clarity* about what actions they need to take. They have *clarity* about what actions they are not going to take and what they are going to say no to.

Clarity is the secret weapon of high performers. They are capable of isolating the exact mindsets, systems, and habits they need to achieve exceptional results.

When I coach individuals, even incredibly successful people at the highest level, they are often lacking in *clarity*. I ask them to describe their visions and their 90-day goals and what comes back is often woolly. With woolly visions and goals, you are going to lack specificity in your behaviours.

Without *clarity* in how you need to behave, you are not going to achieve the results you desire. Let's face it, what you do daily defines you, the results you get and the journey you are on. You cannot act like a two-star leader and expect to lead like a five-star leader. Likewise, you cannot behave like an average parent and expect a superior relationship with your child. It just doesn't work like that.

As if all of this weren't enough to chew on, *conviction* and *clarity* are interconnected. When one is dragging, it impacts the others. When your *conviction* is down, your implementation of your plans will lack "va va voom", even if you do have *clarity*. Likewise, if you have all of the *conviction* in the world but no *clarity*, you will end up rushing around with no results, and this will start to eat away at your *conviction*.

Clarity is about simplicity. It is about making things easier for yourself. It is about narrowing your focus, so you know what you're going for, and so you know why and what you need to do to achieve it.

Take one area of your business or your life. Be as specific as you can. Flesh it out so you have complete *clarity*. Be absolutely specific. This needs to be binary, so afterwards there is no argument about whether you did or did not do it. Don't give yourself any wiggle room.

Questions to ask yourself:

- *What is the one most important thing I want to achieve in the next 90 days?*
- *What are the core (no more than three) actions I need to take daily to achieve this?*

3. Champions Have Consistency

Consistency is exactly what it says on the tin. It is how you behave habitually. Many people have *conviction*, they have *clarity*, but they just don't turn up *consistently* and do what they are supposed to do regularly enough. Champions are often no more motivated or skilled than anyone else. The one thing they are, though, is more consistent. They turn up and act like a champion, day in and day out; on good days and on bad days.

Leaders often tell me that they are not the sum of their behaviours. They say, "I am more than this".

My response is always: "You are what you do, not what you want to be or what you say you are."

It is not how you behave sometimes but how you behave consistently that determines the results you get and who you are as a person, a leader, and a friend. If you missed your sales targets last quarter, and you haven't changed any of your behaviours, you will likely miss them again this quarter. If your relationship with a dear one is patchy, and you haven't changed any of your behaviours, then it will likely get worse. If your fitness isn't what it should be, and you haven't changed any of your behaviours, then you will need to buy some elasticated waistband trousers!

This might sound harsh, but it is just reality. Your habitual behaviours—what you do consistently—determine the results you will get in any area of your life and your ultimate destination.

When it comes down to it, the enemy of high performance is chronic in-consistency. Many people know what to do. There are no prizes for knowing something. Doing it—that is the (not so) secret sauce.

For virtually everyone, the results we want lie on the far side of something that we don't want to do or, at least, something that we need to do when we'd rather be doing something else. To get over this, we need:

- A *big* vision that inspires us to take action (your "why" if you like).
- Time blocking (scheduled time) to focus without disruption on our most important actions
- A system of measuring, monitoring, and holding ourselves accountable.

As with both *conviction* and *clarity*, lacking *consistency* will impact the other two. You know what you need to do. It's not rocket science (most of the time).

So, when you don't do it, you start to lose *conviction* in yourself. And when you lose *conviction*, you lose *clarity*.

Questions to ask yourself:

- *What is my vision for my business and my life?*
- *When am I going to time block to protect my most important behaviours and start to build high-performance habits?*
- *How am I going to measure and monitor my results and hold myself accountable?*

And now it's over to you. What are you going to do about it? Success isn't complicated. In fact, it is simple. Despite this, many avoid doing what they need to do to get the results they want in their lives and their businesses.

Many people reading this chapter (and this book) will think, "That was a good book", stick it on their bookshelf, and move on. No action will be taken. Nothing will happen.

But a small percentage will act. They will think through the core points and decide that now is the time for change. They are the few who will be able to look back in a year or five years, and recognise this moment as the moment they woke up their inner champion and took back control of their business and their life.

Will you be one of them?

About the Author

Gavin Ingham is the founder of the #IAM10 system and helps individuals and organisations to take back control of their business and their lives in 90 days.

You can join a community of like-minded business owners, entrepreneurs, and leaders who want to achieve more than they ever thought possible here: www.iam10.com/community/

Gavin is also a speaker and coach, and would be delighted to talk with you about how your organisation can use #IAM10 to help your leaders to lead with conviction and build high-performing teams that fulfil their potential, embrace change, and grow sales.

Website: www.iam10.com

CHAPTER EIGHTEEN
BECOMING A HEROIC FATHER

By Luke Jensen
Founder and Head Coach, The Victory Mindset
Coronado, California

Well, every man has a religion; has something in heaven or earth which he will give up everything else for—something which absorbs him—which may be regarded by others as being useless—yet it is his dream, it is his lodestar, it is his master. That, whatever it is, seized upon me, made me its servant, slave—induced me to set aside the other ambitions a trail of glory in the heavens, which I followed, followed with a full heart ... When once I am convinced, I never let go.
—Walt Whitman

I was 23 years old when my father died. The day was Tuesday, August 21, 2007.

He was my hero. He kicked cancer's ass for ten years before it found its day to take him. As I was standing by his hospital bed, I realized that I had never truly explained to him how much he meant to me. Fortunately, I had the opportunity to do so before he passed. I told him how much I loved playing basketball with him, how much I admired his character, and how much I appreciated his presence. I promised him that I would carry on with strength and purpose in his memory, helping and serving as many people as possible, just like he had. His last breath came shortly after.

Fast forward to when I found myself on a dark, rainy road, 1,000 miles from home, coming to an abrupt stop on my bike. The bike was fine. It was me that broke down. Here I was, at 4:15 am, sitting outside of a liquor store, crying—weeping—and making myself late for work. My life purpose had gotten so far off track that I could barely take care of myself and my family, much less others. How did it go so wrong?

Grief, for one. My hero was gone, his passing the first of several people close to me all within a year. Grief can consume you when you let it (and sometimes even when you don't).

Second was failure, or at least the feeling that I was failing. My girlfriend (now wife) and I had moved from San Diego to Oregon, where I found an opportunity to follow my passion for both fitness and entrepreneurship by opening our own gym. We had one son and another on the way. When the business started to sink, so did my confidence. Soon, we were on welfare, risking homelessness.

I was doing the right things, but not taking the right approach and, thus, not getting the right results; working 18 hours a day with nothing to show. What upset me the most was that I was simultaneously breaking my promise to my father and blowing my responsibilities as a father myself.

In that morning moment on that empty road, a nervous breakdown led me to the idea behind my successful business today. The idea was The Victory Mindset, and it is for any father who wants to step up in business, in life, and above all, in the deeply meaningful role of being a dad. While my focus is on fathers, the principles can be used by anyone.

What Is Your Battle?

Everyone has a battle, and it doesn't necessarily need to be one of devastation or desperation. Maybe you're spending too much time at work and not enough time with your family, or you could be getting plenty of family time, with no clear direction for your career. Physical health is probably the most common battle for fathers. While the world has become more embracing of the "dad bod," whether it's actually attractive or healthy is questionable at best. Comparing yourself to others is another big one (especially if you have a dad bod and they don't).

Whatever it may be, the battle is where your journey begins. You're stressed, depressed, or simply not content. You want more for your kids, your family, and yourself. You want to go from struggling to strong; flab to flex; good to great; great to heroic.

What are you fighting for? What drives you? What's most important in your life? Identifying your battle is a series of soul-searching questions. Don't be afraid of it and don't be ashamed by it. You need that battle for motivation to get up and go be better. And if you think you don't have a battle, make one up—like how Michael Jordan would convince himself of disses that no one ever said just for fuel to beat them (both the disses and the people to whom he attributed them).

Humanity's number one job is to evolve. The battle activates your desire for your own evolution, which naturally influences and impacts those close to you as a father figure.

Who Is Your Villain?

In every battle, there is a villain. And in your battle, you are the villain to start. The villain will explain and excuse your faults. Your behavior, patterns, decisions, and actions feed the villain. For me, the villain was eating processed foods, drinking excessive alcohol, burying my feelings, constantly demeaning myself, not following through to my goals, and above all, failing at my life mission. I was constantly worried, anxious, bitter, and broken.

After months of living as the villain in the gloomy and rainy Northwest, you can see why I eventually had enough. I don't know why it happened at that time, that morning, at that intersection, but it did, and I'm thankful for it. Hopefully, your villain is a little less rampant than mine was. Either way, you're going to fight him.

How Will You Transform into a Superhero?

To beat the villain, you need to be better than mediocre. You need to be a hero. After all, that's what dads are—superheroes. Where the villain reacts, the heroic father anticipates. When the villain feels tired or scattered, the heroic father is energetic and focused. The villain fights for himself, while the heroic father has a greater purpose. The heroic father is a man of his word. I know my dad was a heroic father because when I lifted my chin after saying goodbye, I saw a room full of people grieving with me.

Listen, you're not going to become the heroic father overnight. You're going to have to live with the villain—and more importantly, fend off that villain—while you create, and learn to fulfill the identity of a heroic father. It's a process, and like any process, it's best followed in small steps.

100 Days of Victory

The program I lead fathers through today is the same one I made for myself while climbing out of my lowest low, when I made the decision to fight both my battle and my villain, so I could become, to my kids and wife, my own version of the heroic father that my dad was to me. It's called 100 Days of Victory, with "victory" standing for:

Vision

Without a vision, it's easy to be distracted and derailed. Vision is the beginning stage of self-fulfillment and purpose in life. It paves a path to success and helps us course correct if we're veering toward failure. Businesses, brands, celebrities, and recognized leaders constantly talk about their visions, but why don't everyday people do the same?

To have a clear vision, you need to detox and declutter. Clean up your diet, your home, your office, your closet—anywhere or anything messy, clean it up. Only then will you be able to see the moments, priorities, and experiences that define your vision.

Intensity

In the victory mindset, we call the detox-and-declutter phase the Victory Vortex. If it sounds intense, it is. To spark real lasting change, we have to attack with intensity. The first ten days are crucial. We go on a clean eating routine to reduce inflammation because the villain lives and thrives in an acidic environment. We also make an irritation list. What's bugging you and why haven't you fixed it? Now, go and fix it. No excuses. Fix it.

Intensity is the only way to break old patterns and make new ones. We add an element of intensity every ten days to keep the body and mind in battle mode. Otherwise, the momentum fades, and the villain will get his way. Vision without intensity can just as easily lead to laziness or denial.

Congruence

When you have a vision, you design your life to pursue and support that vision. The villain, however, loves to disrupt your intentions. He'll tell you that you can do it tomorrow, relax today, and accept who you are even if that person is not who you want to be. Intensity enables you to make decisions that are congruent with your vision because there's more at stake than your own interests. There are other people counting on you.

Can you hear it? Can you feel it? You're starting to think and talk like a superhero.

Training

The Greek philosopher Archilochus said, "We don't rise to the level of our expectations, we fall to the level of our training".

When you've been the villain for weeks, months, and years, you have to train yourself out of your villainous tendencies. Training your mind through exercises like meditation visualization, affirmation, and box breathing will help you rewire subconscious habits into conscious, deliberate, productive decisions.

Rebuilding your body may be part of the equation as well. My villain made me what they call skinny-fat—a notch below dad bod. Part of the identity change I wanted was to be fit and strong, which made me feel like the father who could conquer anything. I'm not saying fitness, physique, or a major body transformation need to be as important to you as they might be to myself and others, but exercise and healthy eating do need to be part of your training if you really want to feel your best.

Mental and physical wellness go hand in hand. Buy into one, and you're more likely to buy into the other. If you're the dad who just doesn't have any interest in the gym, start with the mental aspect. Your mind will soon crave the same improvement for your body.

Ownership

The villain will blame others for your incongruent acts. You need a few beers because your clients stress you out. You can't pack a healthy lunch because there's so much traffic in the morning, and you don't have the time. You didn't work out because your wife asked you to pick up the kids from school. Yes, the villain will even blame your wife! And your kids!

Recognize that no one owes you anything, nor can they stop you from anything. You are the owner of your decisions. Ownership isn't pressure; it's power. When you take ownership, you begin to take back your life from the villain.

Relationships

You can be the strongest, most successful badass on the planet, and yet you will only be as happy and healthy as the people around you. Establish and manage your relationships in line with your purpose. Keep dudes who are bad dads around you, and you will become one yourself. Choose friends, colleagues, and business partners with strong, honest values, and you will be in good company to maintain your vision. Keep no one around you, and the isolation will eventually catch up.

Being a solid father, much less a superhero father, isn't easy. You need your extended family. You need friends. You need to build personal connections within your professional network so that your work enriches your life rather than detracting from it. One of the things heroic fathers love about the 100 Days of Victory program is that they're on the journey with other fathers who share the same experience and often become buds for life.

Your Blueprint

All of the above leads to your blueprint, and on a larger scale, your legacy. What are 50 accomplishments you want to achieve in life? One hundred things you want your kids to know? What work can you do in your community to make it a better place not just for your kids and family, but for others too?

Lastly, heroes often have codes. Do you have a code? If not, here might be a great place to start.

The Heroic Father Code

A heroic father strengthens and trains his mind daily.
A heroic father strengthens and trains his body daily.
A heroic father surrounds himself and his family with positive role models.
A heroic father takes massive action toward his personal goals.

A heroic father lives a life of contribution.

A heroic father gives more of himself than he expects to receive from others.

A heroic father is the leader of his life story.

A heroic father creates meaningful moments for his family.

A heroic father stays true to his word.

A heroic father is fully engaged with the person who is right in front of him.

You've learned plenty about and accepted plenty from the villain. It's time to focus on being the superhero you know you can be. With your blueprint in hand and heart, go forward with setting heroic goals. Live life on your track and your terms while being fully present for all of the special moments, occasions, and milestones that fatherhood brings.

About the Author

Luke Jensen is the founder and head coach of The Victory Mindset, a personal growth program focused on helping ordinary dads reinvent themselves to become heroic fathers and achieve their life, family, and business goals.

Being a young father of two boys, a husband, and a business-owner, Luke struggled managing it all. As a result, his relationships suffered. He was burnt out and stressed out. He felt weak, tired, and his business nearly failed. But he was able to take control and turn it around. Now, his mission is to inspire and equip heroic fathers through a framework of accountability, strategy, discipline, and training.

The Victory Mindset encompasses mental wellness, mindfulness, physical health, fitness, nutrition, and more to achieve each heroic father's own unique definition of success. Learn more at the victory mindset website.

Email: victorymindsetcoaching@gmail.com

Website: www.thevictorymindset.com

CHAPTER NINETEEN

WINNING MINDSET FOR PARENTS OF YOUNG ATHLETES

By Kirsten Jones
Peak Performance and Sports Parenting Coach
Los Angeles, California

*The only six words your young athlete needs to hear from
you after a game is, "I love to watch you play."*
—Anonymous

Meet one of my son's former teammates, Jake. He's the 14-year-old kid over there who walks as if he's 85, bent over like a question mark. That's his father, Tom, the one whose eyes get all glassy-eyed when I ask him why he thinks it happened—why a teenager with all the potential in the world wound up with a pars stress fracture in his back.

"Bad parenting," Tom says. "We never should have signed him up for two club sports, soccer and basketball, that involved far too many hours a week of games and training."

That's a pretty harsh self-evaluation, and honorable, in its honesty. But in my seven years as a sports-and-life coach, I've dealt with hundreds of young people and their parents, and when things go wrong, it's usually not because of bad parenting. It's because of lost-perspective parenting. Snow-plow parenting. Drone parenting. FOMO (fear of missing out) parenting. Unrealistic parenting. Parenting as if you suddenly found yourself in a youth sports jungle that resembles nothing of the "rec-ball" days you remembered from your youth.

Hey, we're not all Indiana Jones. Besides being a peak performance coach, I'm also a mom of three young athletes, one of whom recently reached a life-long goal to become a Division 1 basketball player. Anyone who's heard my #RaisingAthletes podcasts or heard me speak, knows that when it comes to hacking our way through the ever-changing youth sports jungle, I've fallen into a few sports-parenting traps myself. Like when my daughter made a highly competitive volleyball team but didn't get to play. (Man, it is so hard to sit on the sidelines and watch your kid not get subbed in the entire travel tournament.) Or the time our oldest child lost in the state high school boys basketball quarterfinals to a team they had beaten earlier in the season in triple overtime. As a parent, listening to your child quietly weep from the backseat in the car ride home just guts you. You know there is nothing you can do to fix their pain.

I could go on. There are too many moments to count. But in short, we're in this together, baby. I'm here to help!

Most parents want what's best for their children, but we just get caught up in the king-of-the-mountain game. And then bad things happen to good families.

Take Jake, with his stress fracture. He was a talented soccer player from an early age. With size, speed, natural athleticism, and an off-the-charts athletic IQ, he was like the Wayne Gretzky of youth soccer. He didn't run to where the ball was, he ran to where it *was going to be.* Tom, his father, grew up playing and loving soccer in his native South Africa. All he wanted was for his son to share his passion for the game.

In 2016, at the age of 13, Jake was moving on from AYSO (rec soccer) to a highly touted soccer club in Southern California. But in addition to playing club soccer, Jake loved basketball and played on a middle school and a club team. His parents knew little about basketball but could see that their son had passion for the sport. They also realized that because he hit puberty early, he had the size and physicality to be great; he dominated the pre-pubescent late-bloomers in hoops too.

How could they *not* encourage such talent? So they did. Weekends became a blur, the family driving from this practice to that game, from this sport to that sport. Jake's schedule often looked like this:

Friday   5 pm 6–7 pm   Soccer practice

Saturday	8 am	Basketball practice
	10 am	Soccer game
	1 pm	Soccer game
	4 pm	Soccer game
Sunday	9 am	Basketball game
	11 am	Soccer game
	1 pm	Basketball game

And this was just the weekend. During the week, multiple practices and conditioning sessions sucked time from the family. School, practice, games, rinse, repeat. Free time? What was that?

Despite the frenetic schedule, Tom was thrilled that Jake was having fun and getting lots of playing time—he always started and was hardly subbed out—so both parents supported the challenge of Jake juggling both sports while managing to keep his grades up without breaking a sweat.

Then, seemingly without advanced warning, the payment came due. In a summer basketball game prior to his freshman year, Jake went up for a rebound and his back seized up so badly the pain dropped him to his knees. He couldn't walk. He was later diagnosed with a pars stress fracture in his back. Stress fractures are caused by "monotonous and repetitive loading of the back," a code phrase for "overuse." Youth are particularly prone to this because their bone structure isn't fully developed yet. When you combine hours of play each day for six or seven days a week, little rest, and hard-working growth plates, you end up with chronic injury.

Youth sports participation has dramatically increased over the last two decades, according to the National Youth Sports Health and Safety Institute. Approximately 45 million children aged six to18 participate in some form of organized athletics. If that's not particularly alarming, this is: roughly half of all injuries evaluated in pediatric sports medicine clinics are associated with one thing—overuse. Kids like Jake and fathers like Tom who didn't know when to say "when."

"Jake loved every minute of it," Tom told me, "but right now he's absolutely miserable, and we feel incredibly guilty for not making better choices for his health because he wasn't old enough to understand the potential risks." He paused. "I'd like a do-over. I know I wouldn't make those same mistakes again."

How Yesterday Changed Today

Question One: how did we get here—to this place where youth sports, which are inherently supposed to be fun and teach us an array of life lessons, have become a source of relentless pressure, heartache, and disappointment?

To the place where our children's backs crumble because of overuse—and the bond that drew a father and son together shatters like glass?

To the place where the average 15-year-old competitive athlete will be involved in eight to ten workouts a week?

To the place where 70 percent of children are dropping out of sports by age 13?

To the place where youth sports is now a $20+ billion industry, exceeding the amount of money generated by the NFL. One in five US families spends more than $12,000 a year on youth sports?

This is not the youth sports we Generation X-ers all fondly recall from our childhoods, where we all played at least two or three different sports, our parents were barely involved, and very few of us gave even a second thought about playing past high school.

Question Two: how do we get *out* of this jungle?

To the place where sports are fun, kids look forward to participating instead of dreading it?

To the place where sports help our children become healthier adults who are more likely to be active, suffer less anxiety, and are better suited to handle stress throughout life?

To the place where everything isn't about selling one's soul to the devil of win-win-win and everyone getting a trophy?

To the place where there's some sort of practical compromise between "D1 or bust" and "just roll out the ball and let them kick it around"?

If you're asking yourself those two questions, you've come to the right place for answers, as I'm all about finding that sweet spot between sports as part of a young person's life and sports *as* their life. About raising kids who are not only passionate about life on the court or field, but curious about life beyond the chalk lines. About teaching your kids that it's a competitive world—without being the disgruntled parent who, to shame a baseball coach for not playing their kid, hires a skywriter to buzz the stadium with a "Coach Sucks" banner. (Yes, that actually did happen.)

How did we get to this point? How did we lose perspective? Because we Generation-X parents have become the proverbial frog in the pot, slowly boiling to death because of benign neglect—instead of heeding the warnings from raised-to-be-a-star types like Andre Agassi, Tiger Woods, and Todd Marinovich. Back in the 1980s, we Gen-Xers were so mesmerized by their successes that years later, when we became parents, we failed to realize the price those athletes paid for that success.

We didn't learn from the past. Instead, parents started to ask what it would take to get their child to an elite level. And how did these child prodigies manage to do it at such a young age? They wondered what would happen if more focused time and attention were placed on nurturing their child's sports "career"—as if they were business associates, not kids. While parents of previous generations didn't give their kids' athletic futures a second thought, this new generation of parents saw a possibility rarely witnessed: creating future stars. College scholarships. Prestigious universities. Fame. Fortune. The possibilities danced in the minds of parents who wondered, "Can I, too, raise a Serena Williams?"

And because we didn't learn from the past, that's why we'd be foolish to not try to understand it. Let's take a moment to look back. Generally, here's how it unfolded:

Growing up in the 1970s and 80s, the rage of fashion was painter pants, puffy vests, NIKE Cortez running shoes, and heavily permed haircuts with enough Aqua Net to hold your feathered Shaun Cassidy shag in place. In 1981, Music Television (MTV) appeared on the big boxes in our living rooms.

Simultaneously, a parental shift was rippling across the country, even if few noticed at the time—and some never noticed it, period. Three major sociological developments led to significant changes in the way people parented. The trifecta of youth-sports craziness triggered a decline in recreation (rec) youth sports over the next 20 years, the vacuum of which was filled by the professionalization of kids' leagues that looked nothing like their predecessors.

Three Factors That Changed Youth Sports

First, family life changed dramatically. By the early 1970s, women began joining the workforce, and by the 1980s, two-income families were common. Among married women ages 24 to 44, 26 percent worked outside of the home in the 1950s. By the mid-1980s, this number had grown to 67 percent. Dads were gone all day. Moms were gone all day. And so a new problem arose: what were the kids supposed to do after school and on weekends so that they wouldn't be left unattended? (Hint: sports.)

Second, children in the United States began falling behind on the global academic front. The 1983 National Commission on Excellence in Education report, famously titled "A Nation at Risk," touched off a wave of local, state, and federal reform efforts. Parents started to panic that their children were falling behind academically. How would parents solve this gap? (Hint: getting more involved in their children's academics.) This would lead to a parental shift that involved Mom and Dad spending more time doing homework with (for?) their kids, hiring tutors, and starting to micro-manage their children's academic lives. Their obsession with that naturally carried over to their children's sports worlds too.

Third, in 1981, six-year-old Adam John Walsh was abducted and murdered in Hollywood, Florida. His severed head was found in a drainage canal. His death attracted national attention and led to the 1983 television film *Adam*, seen by 38 million people in its original airing. Parents began worrying that their children would no longer be safe playing in their neighborhoods unsupervised until dark; the days of letting kids basically create their own fun were over, replaced by adult-led programs, teams, leagues, organizations, and clubs—the operative phrase being "adult-led."

"Create your own fun" was out. Structure was in. "Be on your own" was out. Parental involvement was in.

These three cultural shifts—mothers joining the workforce, parents doubling down to make their kids academic wizards, and the fear of child abduction—made the landscape ripe for a sea of change involving children, period. And on September 7, 1979, something debuted that would give that sea change a sports twist: Entertainment and Sports Programming Network launched. Like a flat-screened Pied Piper, ESPN burst on the scene with round-the-clock sports, there to fill the vacuum of kids who, in earlier times, would have simply "gone outside and played."

Suddenly, athletes were front and center on televisions across America. Youth sports prodigies who may have gone unnoticed in previous years were running, throwing, tackling, flipping, shooting, swinging, and spiking their ways into the imaginations of kids from Malibu to Maine. Hockey's Gretzky, tennis's Andre Agassi, golf's Tiger Woods, and gymnastics' Nadia Comaneci—such young superstars were, seemingly overnight, part of our children's lives. And part of our lives as parents.

Light bulbs began turning on in the minds of parents all over the country: "Our kid could be the next Gretzky, Agassi, Woods, Comaneci!"—pick your prodigy. Subconsciously, parents began thinking, "What better way to keep my child safe, supervised and focused?" They also began realizing that this wasn't going to happen without a major commitment of time, effort, money, and "aggressive involvement," much of which, of course, would prove counterproductive.

They didn't have to look far for inspiration. In the early 1970s, former Iranian boxer-turned-Las-Vegas-tennis-pro Emmanuel (Mike) Agassi, decided his fourth child would become a world-class tennis player. Unaware of any formula to mastery but determined to see one of his children succeed where he had failed as an Olympic boxer (1948 and 1952), Mike put a plan in place to create a tennis prodigy.

Legend has it that he actually taped a ping pong paddle to Andre's hand while he lay in the crib. In 1977, when Andre was seven years old, the ball machine—nicknamed "the dragon" by his dad—had become "abject horror" to the young boy.

"Nothing sends my father into a rage like hitting a ball into the net," he wrote in *Open: An Autobiography*. "He foams at the mouth … My arm feels like it's going to fall off. I want to ask: How much longer, Pops? But I don't ask. I hit as hard as I can, then slightly harder …. My father says that if I hit 2,500 balls each day, I'll hit 17,500 balls each week, and at the end of one year I'll have hit nearly one million balls. He believes in math. Numbers, he says, don't lie. A child who hits one million balls each year will be unbeatable."

Andre remembers standing on the tennis court in their family's backyard, a court his father built by hand himself. He didn't have an inch to move, the entire court covered in fuzzy yellow balls. He had spent the previous three hours in the 100-plus degree Vegas summer heat trying to beat the dragon.

At 13, he was shipped off to Nick Bollettieri's Tennis Academy in Bradenton, Florida, though he didn't want to leave Las Vegas or his friends or family. But, ultimately, the commitment paid off. Agassi became an eight-time Grand Slam champion, won an Olympic gold medal in 1996, and amassed total tennis earnings of close to $200 million.

K. Anders Ericsson, a Swedish psychologist at Florida State University, argued in his 1990 book, *Toward a General Theory of Expertise,* that anyone who puts in 10,000 hours of practice at any activity (chess, darts, or, yes, sports) could become an expert. And there was no shortage of parents willing to test the theory.

"Robo Quarterback"

Take the Marinovich family of Orange County, California. Marv and his son Todd were football's equivalent of Mike and Andre Agassi. In 1988, *Sports Illustrated* dubbed Todd America's first "test-tube athlete." When Todd was one month old, Marv was already working on his son's physical conditioning. He stretched his hamstrings. Taught him to do push-ups. Kept a football in his crib 24/7.

As a toddler, Todd was placed on a strict diet. When he went to birthday parties as a kid, he would take his own cake and ice cream to avoid sugar and refined white flour. He would eat homemade catsup, prepared with honey. No Big Macs. No Oreos. No deviating from Dad's plan.

Eventually, Marv brought in a team of 13 individuals to work on every aspect of Todd's physical condition—speed, agility, strength, flexibility, quickness, body control, endurance, nutrition. He found one to improve Todd's peripheral vision. He enlisted a throwing coach, a motion coach, and a psychologist.

"I'm a tyrant," Marv told *Sports Illustrated*. "But I think you have to be to succeed."

His son's athletic career was mixed. As a redshirt freshman in 1989, he became the starting quarterback at USC and was chosen as the country's freshman of the year. Two years later, he entered the NFL because of a fallout with Coach Larry Smith and an arrest for cocaine; he signed with the Los Angeles Raiders. But three years later, he was already out of the NFL, largely because of his inability to kick drugs. Since then, he's been in and out of prison, most recently in 2018—at age 47.

If the demands put on Agassi and Marinovich by their fathers inspired some other parents to set the bar high for their sports-oriented children, they also raise questions: is it worth it? How much is too much? How do you find balance? Can you raise athletically successful children without turning them into "projects" or "experiments?" And, finally, is it possible to inspire your athletically oriented children to be the best they can be without becoming, as a parent, "a tyrant"?

Andre and his wife, Stephanie Graf, a tennis legend in her own right and a survivor of a parenting tyrant herself, went on to have two children of their own. Because of the grueling childhood's they'd had, they agreed not to encourage their children to play tennis but rather choose whatever activity appealed to them.

A few years after Andre's retirement from tennis, his aging dad confessed to him that if he could do it all over again, he wouldn't have made him play tennis, either. "I'd make you play baseball or golf. You can play for longer and make a lot more money."

If you are a parent raising an athlete (or three) and are struggling with the balance of how to support them in learning the lessons you feel you learned from youth sports, there is a way to do it so that when the proverbial ball stops bouncing for your child, they not only grow to be a better team player and collaborator, but are more empathetic, more dialed into what it means to win and lose, and most critically are willing to stand back up, dust themselves off, and try again when they get knocked down. You've got this!

About the Author

Kirsten Jones, a Hall of Fame D1 volleyball player from The College of William and Mary and 14-year NIKE executive, is now a motivational speaker, writer, and peak performance coach. Her clients include teen athletes (and their parents), where she helps them learn how to reach their goals and release their limitations. She co-hosts the #RaisingAthletes podcast with Susie Walton on iTunes and is working on her first parenting book about raising empowered athletes. Kirsten and her husband are raising three athletes themselves (ages 20, 17, and 14) in Los Angeles and have found joy in working out at home together as a family. Please sign up to receive updates and hear the podcast on Kirsten's website.

Email: kirjones@me.com
Website: www.kirstenjonesinc.com

CHAPTER TWENTY

THE AUDACITY TO WIN. RISING ABOVE IMPOSTER SYNDROME

By Kristie Kennedy
Image Confidence Coach, TEDx Speaker
Tallahassee, Florida

The butterfly is beautiful because the caterpillar is brave.
—Unknown

As a young girl and only child, I grew up in a highly volatile environment. My dad had an alcohol and drug addiction. Four decades later, I can still remember the night he punched a hole in the bathroom door trying to get to my mother. Those were pivotal moments that would shape my internal convictions. Anytime he and my mother would fight, I'd run to the next-door neighbor's house to escape the pain of what I was about to see.

As I matured it wasn't long before I was emulating the same toxic behaviors. In all honesty, when I began experiencing my own unique pain, I was unaware of how to heal it, speak about it, and be free of it. As a result of my unhealthy coping mechanisms, I became someone I never desire to be again. The dark thoughts of destruction were leading me into a scalding hot desert of despair.

I remember sitting in class during my senior year in college and the professor quoted Dr. Martin Luther King, Jr., "Nothing pains some people more than having to think." This was my lightbulb moment. In the middle of the crossroad, I finally realized that my negative thought patterns were charting a course of misery. For most of my life up until that point, I was petrified of public speaking. The opportunity to raise my hand and hear my thoughts out loud still brings me to tears. The instructor asked a question, and when I responded, it felt wrong as two left feet.

One of my favorite affirmations is "Use your voice even if it trembles." I discovered, on that day, that there is no perfect way. It is okay to miss the mark. There's always a challenge to overcome. As I sat in the back of the class weeping from the joy bubbling up, the prison door was opened, and I was breaking out of the chains of limited thinking. I will never forget this defining day that has fueled the transformational work I am honored to facilitate. I celebrate the dexterity to catch my falling heart before it hits the ground and the tenderness to mend its brokenness should it be ripped into a million tiny parts.

I've had innumerable hurdles to overcome, especially in business. In 2015, I remember turning a pink slip into Queenfidence Image Consulting. Two days before I received the news, I'd written in my journal, "I am not happy at work. I want to live out my dreams." What a powerful reminder of "Be careful of what you ask for"!

In my past experiences of launching a business, the outcome was not successful. I was playing it safe in my eight to five job, and I knew it. I always felt overworked and underpaid. Who was I to start another business with zero traditional education in that area? The worst subject in all of my school years was math. I remember failing the math portion of the college exit exam at least seven times. They extended mercy and rewarded my tenacity with a free pass. Persistence pays! I knew that it would be imperative to have a bodacious belief to soar above whatever curve balls were heading my way. Over the course of six years, I designed 20 vision boards and six vision books to ensure I was a skilled sniper ready for any negative thinking.

The National Science Foundation reported that the average person thinks about 12 to 60,000 thoughts per day. Of those thoughts, 80 percent are negative and 95 percent are repetitive as a broken record. If you are not deliberate about disrupting your internal beliefs, the dysfunctional cycle will continue. The saying is true, "What you allow, will continue."

According to Wikipedia, "imposter syndrome" is a psychological pattern in which an individual *doubts their skills, talents or accomplishments* and has a *persistent internalized* fear of being exposed as a fraud. Oxford Languages stated that "imposter syndrome" is the persistent *inability to believe* that one's success is deserved or has been legitimately achieved as a result of one's own efforts or skills. Harvard Business Review explains it as "a collection of *feelings of inadequacy* and a sense of intellectual fraudulence that persist despite evident success." Very Well Mind says, "It's an internal experience of believing that you are *not as competent as others perceive* you to be."

At the root of imposter syndrome, you will find countless anxieties ranging from fear of evaluation, fear of not being as capable as others, fear of failure, fear of not having an answer, fear of disappointing others, or fear of making the wrong decision. Albert Einstein, one of history's brightest minds wrote, "The exaggerated esteem in which my life work is held makes me very ill. I feel compelled to think of myself as an involuntary swindler."

Recently, as I was leading a fragile soul through her insecurities. The person I was dealing with was exhausted from the walls erected around her heart and mind. She desired to be more vulnerable with her peers. Inspired in the moment, I asked, "What would you like to add to your wall of protection, a door or a window?" She said, "A little window." I proceeded to tread lightly, "If you were to open it and share one truth you are comfortable revealing, what would it be?"

Deep sigh. "I'm lonely."

Personal development is the continuous interior and exterior renovation of self. We often want to speed through transformation. Yet the beauty of our personal evolution becomes more breathtaking with every dare we boldly accept in the face of fear.

> *Some moments make you feel big. Some moments make you feel small. A precious few make you feel both.*
> —Unknown

There are numerous famous people who have secretly struggled with imposter syndrome. John Steinbeck won a Pulitzer Prize for *The Grapes of Wrath*, and a Nobel Prize in literature in 1962 decades after his death. In his journal he wrote, "I am not a writer. I've been fooling myself and other people."

I highlight these internal thoughts of others, who even though they succeeded wonderfully in their respective fields, didn't believe they were good enough. They didn't have a winning mindset, and they are not alone. Imposter syndrome isn't only reserved for the famous; it is very prevalent in people from all walks of life. But there is something we can do about it.

I've discovered seven confidence-keys to rise above the disempowering beliefs we call imposter syndrome.

- *Awareness*—powerful presence begins with acute self-awareness. In your fragility lies fortified strength and the power to realign on the inside.
- *Acceptance*—embrace the willingness to release what was and welcome all that is to come.
- *Acknowledgement*—vulnerability dismantles the ego and allows you to own your truth by standing in transparency.
- *Authenticity*—you are distinct by design and never have to live in someone else's shadow for fear of shining your light.
- *Audacity*—nothing massive ever occurred by being passive. Dare to play by the rules you write.
- *Appreciation*—harness the power of gratitude and the spaciousness of abundance until the mountains of frustration surrender.
- *Action*—radical results are the by-product of relentless execution in the face of excuses.

The willingness to lead with a limp can unlock the doors to exponential potential. Oprah Winfrey stated, "When you undervalue what you do, people will undervalue who you are." Imagine the power to transcend beyond inconceivable heights despite the seemingly insurmountable obstacles.

The Hyperion, also known as "The High One," is a Redwood tree in California and is one of the tallest trees on earth, out of three trillion trees. It is estimated to be 380 feet tall, which would be the equivalent of a 35-story skyscraper. This statuesque tree is full of majesty and might. A unique characteristic is that the tannin content of the wood protects it from diseases and the thick bark shields it from the hottest fires. An interesting note in this harmonious song of praise is that the roots can range from two to 12 feet. This can appear shallow in comparison to the great oak whose roots span much wider. Nature teaches us how to turn a disadvantage into a prime opportunity to triumph over any weakness. The Redwood tree family leverages the strength of other trees and connects its roots with neighboring Redwood trees to create a force of resistance against the strongest winds.

There are times when we need someone else to hold the light for us while we venture into the dark cellars of our subconscious to ferret out our fear.
—Sue Patton Thoele

I recall a thought-provoking image coaching session where a client asked me a soul piercing question. "Why am I this way?" In response, I told her, "The answer is going to require courage to gaze deep within and unearth what lies beneath the surface."

Could it be ... you've muted your voice because you don't value the message?

Could it be ... you hide in the shadow because you don't value standing in the light?

Could it be ... you refuse to ask for help because you don't value a supportive community?

Could it be ... you choose to play small because you don't value embracing the fullness of your brilliance?

Could it be ... you erect invisible walls of isolation because you don't value the exhilaration of loving others deeply?

Could it be ... you blame the world for a life of challenge because you don't value the investment personal growth demand?

Could it be ... you stare at closed doors because you don't value the limitless possibilities waiting on the other side of them?

Could it be ... you rarely take breaks to rejuvenate because you don't value the vessel transporting you to divine destiny?

Could it be ... you squander countless opportunities because you don't value the freedom of imperfection?

There were many possibilities for my client's desire for change, and at least she was searching for a solution, a way to change, a way to tap into her winning mindset.

I dare you to explore your entire life with a brand-new set of eyes, understanding that internal vision is more potent than external sight. Infinite potential is built on the foundation of imagination. Risk aversion is merely a diversion designed to prevent you from experiencing an immersion of limitlessness. The next step awaits your unflinching courage. In the words of Horace Mann, "Seek not greatness, but seek truth and you will find both."

Imagine ...

The courage to act.

The confidence to lead.
The chance to win.

About the Author

Kristie Kennedy, The Image Confidence Expert, is a TEDx Audacious Leadership keynote speaker and authentic lifestyle author. As the owner of Queenfidence Global Image Consulting, her electrifying inspirational gift empowers women with confidence and clarity keys to succeed in the face of adversity. She specializes in four areas of peak performance: mindset mastery, massive momentum, magnetic messaging, and potential maximization. Kristie's evocative teaching style elevates your self-perception from stuck to unstoppable, invisible to invincible, and timid to tenacious. Her bodacious belief is a testament that you can shift from mediocrity to magnificence one daring action step at a time.

Email: kristie@queenfidence.com
Website: www.queenfidence.com

CHAPTER TWENTY-ONE

THE INNER LEADER AND PEAK ENERGY PERFORMANCE

By Jody Kennett
ICF Leadership Coach, Peak Energy Performance
Vancouver, Canada

You have power over your mind, not outside events.
Realize this, and you will find strength.
—Marcus Aurelius

There I was, warming up in the early morning on a cold, but clear November day with nerves in my gut knowing a full marathon distance was before me. I was secretly contemplating if an exit strategy to get out of it existed. My commitment for this race had been like no other because somehow, I got it in my mind that it would be a great idea to run a marathon in honor of two very important men in my life that had passed away; one being my dad who inspired me to run and the other a 12-year-long personal training client named George who loved running. I was running for them and possibly to distract or re-channel my grief into something I felt was positive and which would give me focus.

Wait a second, are we not talking about winning here? And if so, why am I bringing up loss when we are focused on how to have a winning mindset and peak performance? The answer is, if you can create a winning mindset amidst loss, struggle, and failure, you truly have the mindset of a winner. Performance is won in the mind first. Often, the focus on winning is on the outcome and what we need to do in order to win, but what if winning has nothing to do with the external "doings" outside of us and everything to do with our internal world, our inner leader, and the inner game?

It is these three inner dynamics that make a champion. They have everything to do with who we are being to ourselves, with our goal, and in our lives. Yet many of us get pulled solely to the outer, external world of doing and outcomes.

There was another reason this marathon was like no other I had done before. I had set another goal for myself which was to set a personal best record. Of course, this gets driven by a time marker, and then the entire training is marked for a specific pace, time, and volume. Indeed, there is an extraordinary amount of physical energy output training for a marathon, especially if you are like me and detest speed and hill training days; however, none of this energy output would be happening at all if it was not for the energy input from the mind.

It was the vision of running for them, the commitment I made to myself to make this race a personal best, and the energy of its significance and meaning that pushed me to train in the rain, do numerous speed track workouts, and even hill repeat intervals. I mean, really, who in their right mind repeats a hill they just climbed at maximum speed with lactic acid filling their legs to a heavy fatigue telling the body to stop? Someone with a set mind is who!

You see peak performance has often been limited to people's output, and it has been believed that it is one's results that create performance. Yet, the output would not even exist and is only driven by the input of the energy we put into our body, mind, emotions, and environment. Let that sink in for a moment, as there would be no output and the entire drive or motivation that creates performance is first made possible from an energy input. Whether that input be a thought, emotion, fuel, rest, or from someone's environment.

This is exactly why I created Peak Energy 4 Performance because performance is fueled by the energy of our mind, body, emotions, and environment. There is a fifth factor in Peak Energy 4 Performance, and it is having a spiritual energy, health, or practice. Yes, this fifth factor may just have been in play energizing my marathon all through the training and on race day.

The marathon was an out-and-back route, so you end up running back the exact route you ran to the halfway-turnaround point. It was just before and at this midway point, that a spark of curiosity and possibility lit up inside me. You see, a male runner who was already running back and had just come from the turnaround, gave me a suspicious, fun smile that piqued my interest as to what it could mean. Then as I rounded the bend and saw my brother and mom and a few other women, my brother informed me, I was in third place for the women. Are you kidding me?

My standing in the race was the farthest from my mind. I wasn't even considering that I would place in this race perhaps because, in years past, I had trained with a fierce, light-weight, competitive runner who was faster and leaner, and I knew I did not have her kill(her) instincts. Top female runners or athletes of any sport are "wired" differently, well different from me anyways. Oh yeah, finding out I may be in third gave me a surge of excitement and bewilderment, and the thought, "Oh crap, now I need to maintain because there is a new incentive, one that will help me cross the finish line, not just as a winner in completing a marathon, but now to perhaps place in the top three!"

Non-runners often marvel at the physical feat of a marathon, and yet runners will say it is just as much, if not more, a mental game. I believe this is true for every big goal or challenge every one of us is facing. The inner world of our thoughts, our mind, and emotions is creating an environment every day that either sets us up to win or lose. It is an inner game because we have an opponent. The opponent is the critic, the doubter, the "I am not enough," "I am afraid," "Keep me safe" from judgement, and the side of our brain that focuses on the negative voice and thoughts that limit who we can be.

You have an inner leader that creates your inner world of thoughts and emotions who is your only hope to win the inner game against the automatic, conditioned, preprogrammed, and reigning champion, the "limiter"—your limiting mind.

I have created mindset quotes to focus the mind. One of my favorites is "Play to the possible," not your past, not the probable, and not even your perceived potential, but to what is possible.

Whether you are in the middle of a marathon exhausted and only half done or climbing your very own Mount Everest in your life, your inner leader needs to be trained and be the only voice you give airtime to if you are to win and perform at your peak. Your inner leader knows your weaknesses, knows when and where you are most vulnerable, knows your excuses, and knows what you need to succeed and be at your best.

If you do not conquer self, you will be conquered by self.
—Napoleon Hill

This brings us to the first peak performance tip which is to cultivate your inner leader who is somewhat of a self-manager, self-leader, and self-coach. Let me give you an example here. I know I can sometimes underestimate myself and also not set my expectations high enough. Left to my nature, these under-estimations would stay status quo and limit me and my life, but enter in my inner leader who is aware of these and that badass is not going to let me get away with underestimating myself and it will expect more!

Your inner leader will step in to keep your focus, heighten your resolve, and fight for what you want with everything you have. It will do this at the very point the challenge feels most difficult, and the mindset is fatigued by obstacles that have taken all your energy to endure.

My inner leader stepped in at the first two water stations after the midway point where I was following and gradually catching the woman in second place. As Wayne Dyer says, "It's never crowded on the extra mile," which in this race meant very few people were where we were and all I was left with was my own inner world and mind chatter as I paced behind woman number two whom we will call Serious Socks. My focus was on her compression socks and running attire, which to the naked eye spelled out a very serious technical runner.

Really, I was going to allow a pair of long socks that give pressure to the calves limit me or intimidate what was possible for me? It didn't matter how ridiculous it sounded; the seed was planted.

"I don't have those socks on. She is way more technical. She is scientific, and I am not. She has an advantage I don't. Don't expect too much, Jody, just do your best. Try to just keep pacing behind her. I'm not like her; I'm in over my head here. Don't push yourself too hard … remember why you are here. You're not like these women, Jody, you don't want it bad enough."

By the second water station, Serious Socks and I were both grabbing some much-needed replenishment, and I tried to catch her attention and be sportsmanlike and to show how non kill(her) my instinct was; she was having nothing to do with me, not even a friendly gesture.

My inner leader kicked in and as per what I know works for me, I did not rest too long and kept going leaving Serious Socks behind at the water station. My inner world dialogue changed to self-management and self-coach.

"Scan your body, you're feeling good … Keep your pace … Check in on hydration and electrolytes … Track your time from last replenishment. You're doing great, Jode, and now you are in second. Manage your pace to one you can sustain, but one where you are not letting up. Lastly, wow, you passed Serious Socks."

The inner world we create with our self-talk, perceptions, experiences, beliefs, self-doubts, and fears produces an environment and the world we are living in. My first inner dialogue there was the "limiter" talking, and luckily it pretty quickly shifted to a winning mindset coaching me to perform at my peak.

Sometimes as a runner, entrepreneur, and woman leader in business, my body leads my mind to a winning mindset, but more often it is my mind leading my body and life to possibilities. Both were at play here in passing Serious Socks.

Cultivating an inner world that breeds a winning mindset is peak performance tip number two. How do you create an inner world and a winning mindset? It is simple:

1. Choose the lens through which you view yourself, your world, and your future.
   This means you either view yourself as a winner and champion, or not. You see a world of possibilities or obstacles. An amazing future or a grim one.
2. Uproot the weeds of self-limiting beliefs that keep you stuck, unhappy, or underperforming to your true potential. Challenge old beliefs and test them for fact or fiction, truth or lie, and choose what you want to believe.
3. Self-talk will take you all the way to success or lead you to sorrow. As one of my mentors, Judith E Glaser, says, "Words create worlds." Choose your words wisely and speak success into yourself always.
4. Self-manage and use self-leadership to quiet the critic, doubt, and fear that will rise in all of us when we do something new, are challenged beyond our current capacity, or when we compare or compete.

There was a space where I did not see any other runners in front of me and what felt like a long time without a water station. This space with no distractions had me thinking about my dad and my client George. Were they with me? Were they in heaven telling jokes? I was thinking about how grateful I was for having known them while at the same time making sure I didn't get too emotional because it would make it hard to breathe while running.

All of a sudden, I see someone in the distance off the gravel running path on the grass. It was far enough away, I could not quite see the whole picture, but I knew whoever it was, they were not in good shape. As I placed every tired foot in front of me in a robotic rhythm, I was now close enough to see the woman in first place off to the side in the grass, which could only be described as squatting to relieve herself. No, I did not make up a nickname for her as my heart went out to her.

However, as I passed because I had just been thinking about the two men I was running for, I couldn't help but wonder in a playful way if they had anything to do with that. Your mind goes to mysterious, playful places when you have over three hours of straight running; in a way, you entertain yourself, use your imagination, and in this instance, I was curious about the possibility of their spiritual presence being with me as I ran the marathon. Nonetheless, I was now in first place or so I calculated from what they told me at the turn-around. No way! Unbelievable! ... And yet it currently was believable because it was happening.

The inner game is always in play because of the way our brains work towards safety, belonging, acceptance, ego, fear, doubt, and the critic who is ever present telling us, we are not enough or not good enough. If your "limiter" is always in game mode, influencing your behaviors, mindset, and performance, you need a competitor with a winning mindset who is always active and the champion of your inner game.

This is peak performance tip number three: the inner game is always in play, and you must conquer the inner game before you can win the outer game. What you put in your mind, in your thoughts, and give voice to, will win; it will either be the "limiter" by default or the "champion" winning mindset and attitude by choice. The input of self-talk, self-beliefs, and self-love is one of the most important elements to peak performance.

After passing runner number one, I knew there was still a good distance left to try and keep my lead. This is the point where there is not a lot of gas left, and you almost feel you can't push any harder. I looked down at my watch and knew I may not make my personal best time if I didn't pick up my pace. Not knowing how long I would need to endure and not having a lot to give, I gave it everything I could for as long as I could, never looking back.

All of a sudden, I hear footsteps behind me pacing fast and puffing hard, the kind you know are sprinting to the finish. They flew past me, and as I looked closer, it was a male runner with really long legs or so I told myself.

Then, I rounded a corner which became my last and the loud speaker muffled, yet clear said, " …and here comes our first female runner to cross the finish line."

Disbelief and adrenaline kicked in, and just as my dad taught me to always look good crossing the finish line, I gave it one more push with everything I had left in me to sprint as fast as I could across the finish line. My brother and mom were off to the side with excitement and support only a family could endure, and all I remember is hearing the words of confirmation that I was indeed the first female finisher that day.

I did get a personal best that day, won first place, and qualified for Boston, but I had won something far greater: my inner leader led me from loss to triumph, from grief to greatness, from pain to purpose, and from limited to unlimited.

When we engage our inner leader, inner world, and inner game, we cultivate a winning mindset. Albert Einstein said, "Everything is energy." Thoughts are energy. Peak performance depends on our energy input. I don't know if they were there that day, but a spiritual energy definitely influenced my performance.

About the Author

Jody Kennett is an ICF-certified leadership, health, and life coach. She is the creator of Peak Energy 4 Performance where she elevates people to peak performance by energizing their body, mind, emotions, and environment. Her experience in health began with the science of the human body in kinesiology at SFU where she then became an ACE Medical Exercise Specialist and personal trainer. After learning the science of the human body, she became fascinated in the science of our brain, obtaining a certification in C-IQ, Conversational Intelligence, which is the neuroscience of communication. Her career then led her into coaching bridging science with the art of transforming human behavior for personal and professional growth.

As a peak performance coach, Jody created Peak Energy 4 Performance to address the increasing problem of fatigue, burnout, and overwhelm by focusing on energy input for optimal health, wellbeing, and performance.

Email: jody@jodykennett.ca
Website: www.jodykennett.ca
LinkedIn Profile: https://www.linkedin.com/in/jodykennett/
LinkedIn Business: https://www.linkedin.com/company/elevare-leaders-and-health
Instagram: @jodykennett3
Facebook: https://www.facebook.com/jodykennett3

CHAPTER TWENTY-TWO
MENTAL FLEXIBILITY: BEND OR BREAK

By Karen Machuca
Founder of Better Me Karen LLC, Neuro-Coach, Speaker
Boynton Beach, Florida

*The Law of Requisite Variety: The part or person that
is most flexible will control the system.*
—NLP Principle

Imagine being a palm tree in a fierce storm. Hurricane gales are coming at you with devastating force. High winds are pulling out trees by their roots and demolishing buildings while you sway back and forth, threatened with every gust of its intensity. Unprotected from an unpredictable tempest destroying everything around you. When the calm comes, and the sun finally shines through, and everything around you is wrecked, your tree is the only one that still stands. Perhaps, a little bent from the wear and tear of the torrential assault, maybe missing a few palm fronds, but still the last one standing.

You must be wondering, "Why is being able to bend like a tree so relevant to my life? What exactly is flexibility, and how will it make a difference in my success?" Being inflexible is like having no peripheral vision and only seeing what is in right front of you. Not because you can't explore what's around you, but because you are so rigid in your thinking that you refuse to move your head and enjoy a better view. When you limit your perspective, you close yourself off to others, limit your options, and stop educating yourself. If you believe that nobody knows better than you, you stop listening.

Once you gravitate towards mental or cognitive flexibility, and better understand how being flexible can help you adjust to new situations with confidence and grace, it will change how others see you and, more importantly, change how you live your life. Suppose you are willing to stretch your mind and your attitudes. In that case, it will make a positive difference in your personal and your professional relationships, and open your world to endless possibilities.

When you think about flexibility as "something I do" and not "who I am," you realize that you can make lasting positive changes that may open up opportunities for some relaxation, laughter, and happiness. You must be wondering: if flexibility is good, why is it so hard for some people to change?

According to experts, the average toddler hears the word "no" or a form of "no" an astonishing 400 times per day. Most times without explanation. We are programmed to know the rules and stick to them with little or no room for flexibility from a very young age. We are often so stuck in our beliefs that we limit ourselves from finding solutions. Some of our views are inherited and never questioned. They are so ingrained in our unconscious that they become an automatic response.

The irony is that inflexible people prefer to stick to their plan even when it is clear that it's not working. There are numerous reasons that hinder a person from changing their strategy, including:

- Seeing flexibility as a sign of weakness
- Being unwilling to give others credit
- Fearing the unknown
- Seeing feedback as criticism
- Being unmotivated
- Feeling vulnerable

In contrast, cognitive rigidity is the consequence of a lack of mental flexibility. If you cannot change behaviors or beliefs even though they are ineffective in reaching your goals, your rigidity will negatively affect your daily life. Suppose you are unwilling to find alternate solutions or strategies by adapting your way of thinking. In that case, you will feel unnecessarily stuck in a situation that could have been easily avoided if you allowed yourself to be more open-minded and creative.

Wisdom requires a flexible and open mind. Mental flexibility refers to our ability and willingness to adapt our thought patterns to new situations in less regimented ways, ultimately creating a more resilient and productive mindset. It demands honesty about yourself that admits you don't know it all and are willing to learn from others. It means you openly embrace new concepts and understand the importance of shifting your perspective, adjusting, and pivoting to achieve your goals. In your personal or professional life, the person with the most flexibility is always ahead of the game.

Some of us lead at work, church, or home. We have to work together to get things done. Teamwork is crucial in the professional arena. But if you refuse to acknowledge a colleague's opinion or a new way of doing things, you are stopping yourself from finding efficient solutions. If you refuse to change your practices at home, even if you know you are not making your partner happy, you will continue to put your relationship at risk because you would rather be "right" than compromise. How will that serve you?

The professional world moves quickly. If you have cognitive flexibility, you will feel energized by change, applaud innovation, and quickly adapt to the unknown. You will be open to learning new skills and be better able to study multiple concepts simultaneously. Practicing flexibility in the business world gives you the advantage of efficiently dealing with rapidly changing markets, resourcefully managing complex workloads, and meeting clients' constantly shifting needs. It is a quality that is attractive to employers. If you show the employer you are flexible and willing to change the route as needed, you will be a valuable candidate. Employees with a relaxed attitude are eager and able to pivot and tailor their objectives to reaching the company mission. Leaders who practice flexibility are more apt to respect their employees' needs, creating a more accommodating work environment and optimizing performance.

Flexibility attracts opportunities for another level of growth. If you can open your mind to change and view the world from another perspective, it gives you options you may have never considered. Capturing that there are different dimensions of reality and understanding that someone else's may be different from your own will help you better tolerate errors and transitions. This type of thinking opens the door to empathy and compassion for others. It activates your problem-solving skills, opening your mind to new ideas that pile onto one another and strengthen your ability to see past what is directly in front of you. Don't you want to be seen as the "solution finder"?

Flexibility fosters learning, encouraging multi-dimensional thinking, which allows you to leverage intelligence assets to effectively deal with change, solve complex problems faster, and effectively structure and use incoming information efficiently.

Being flexible in the workplace not only encourages teamwork and collaboration; it gives you the upper hand by inadvertently promoting you as a leader, one who is confident enough to nurture the new ideas, opinions, and strategies of your co-workers to get the job done.

The flexible person lives a much more peaceful life, with less anxiety and fear associated with change and the unknown. It relieves you of the need to always be correct and all-knowing. It allows you to fall and make mistakes, learn from them, get up, and bring the best of yourself to each new situation.

Mental shifting is the main component in cognitive flexibility and is so closely related that they are often referred to as the same concept. We use each almost constantly in our daily lives. However, cognitive flexibility refers to the ability to adapt to a change while mental shifting is the process that makes it possible to adapt to the change.

An example of cognitive flexibility: your wife asks you for a divorce. Cognitive flexibility would be the ability to reflect on the reasons why she would have asked for one—your ability to put yourself in her shoes and think about how you could have done things differently. You are examining how to change your behavior, not to repeat it in your next relationship.

An example of mental shifting: your ride to work calls you at the last minute to tell you he's not going to work today. Your car is in the shop, and you work 45 minutes away. The process of shifting your thinking from the original plan to alternate solutions is mental shifting. "Can I make it in time if I take the bus? Should I call Uber? Should I ask my neighbor to drive me? Maybe my car is ready?"

Practicing flexibility could mean the difference between marriage and divorce in your personal life. Or a healthy and loving relationship with your children, and none at all. Not to mention your ability to make and keep friends for the long term. If you are rigid in your opinions and quick to judge others' decisions because you refuse to see their point of view, it can probably be traced back to how you were raised and your generational beliefs. It takes practice to break inherited patterns, and you can set small goals for mental stretching. Here are ten brain exercises to help you put this knowledge into practice.

1. Accept your behavior history and mindfully practice changing it.
2. Question your thoughts about things you have always believed to be accurate.
3. Substitute negative or rigid thoughts and phrases with positive ones.
4. Break a routine. Figure out a new way of doing things to reach your goals.
5. Identify places where you can compromise and reward yourself for it.
6. Practice physical flexibility by doing yoga or Pilates.
7. Think before automatically saying no to a new idea. A good trigger for this is to take a deep breath and hold it for three seconds, then exhale for five seconds while you consider the best answer.
8. Practice not being in charge. Trust others to make a decision.
9. Be spontaneous. Don't plan.
10. Step out of your comfort zone by trying a new experience or activity.

Cognitive Flexibility and the Brain

There is an area located in the front part of the brain called the anterior cingulate gyrus (ACG). When the ACG is working properly, it is easier to adapt to change and transition, and you are better able to shift your attention and refocus. When it is not correctly functioning, because it is working too hard, and there is too much activity in the ACG, there is more cognitive rigidity, which is focusing on things not going as expected, and inflexible thinking.

Psychiatrist and brain disorder specialist Dr. Daniel Amen recommends natural solutions to calm an overactive ACG, boost serotonin, and help you go with the flow, including the following:

- Supplements: 5-HTP, saffron, and omega-3 fatty acids (especially ones that are higher in DHA than EPA) are the most helpful supplements to boost serotonin and calm the ACG.
- Diet: many people unknowingly trigger cognitive inflexibility or mood problems by eating diets that are low in l-tryptophan, an amino acid. For example, eating a high-protein, low-carbohydrate diet, which is popular these days, typically worsens ACG problems. L-tryptophan

is a relatively small amino acid. When you eat a high-protein diet, the larger amino acids compete more successfully to get into the brain, causing lower brain serotonin levels and more negative emotional reactiveness. Eating complex carbohydrates, such as sweet potatoes and garbanzo beans, are a healthy way to boost serotonin. Brain serotonin levels can also be raised by eating foods rich in l-tryptophan, such as chicken, turkey, salmon, beef, nut butter, eggs, and green peas.

Evaluating Your Flexibility

It's simple to see how being open-minded can be helpful to all of those unyielding and closed-minded people you know, but does it apply to you? It's easy to believe you are an expert in the workings of your own mind. After all, there's no other person who spends more time with you or knows better how you think than yourself.

Our foundational beliefs go unexamined because we lack the perspective from which to evaluate them fairly. The false narratives we create about ourselves help us perpetuate confidence that, if questioned, can open the door to new self-awareness. Are you willing to acknowledge that no matter how sure you are of your viewpoint or opinion, there is a possibility that you may be wrong or there may be a better way? How many times has your partner or friend pointed out a characteristic or habit hindering your relationship or the outcome of your intended result?

If you get that uncomfortable feeling when someone disagrees with you or when things don't go as expected, it may be time for self-examination. Start by laying the groundwork for honest discernment and genuine insight. It's that revolutionary, "Now I see" moment that will allow a new mindset that will transform your behavior.

Do you want to be like the tree that cracks in half or is pulled out by its roots because it would not yield? Learn to bend, like the palm tree. Be flexible with a supple, winning mindset, and live a life with minimum stress and maximum strength. Being able to pivot and sway with new situations is a sign of resilience, self-assurance, and competence, and will lead to a healthier and more peaceful life.

About the Author

Karen Machuca, aka "Better Me Karen," found her passion through pivot and flexibility, becoming a neuro-coach after spending over 20 years in the airline industry. She is a certified trainer and coach in NLP, and has certifications in brain health, and CBT. Karen loves helping others explore their potential, find clarity, and reach goals through life-changing coaching.

Karen describes herself as an eternal learner and enthusiastic sharer of life lessons. Her most significant teachings are based on her experience as a perfectly imperfect daughter, wife, mother, and grandmother. She embraces the true essence of life as she travels the world and finds beauty wherever she goes. Karen is also an author and motivational speaker sharing inspirational messages globally.

You can take a peek at Karen's encouraging lessons on her website.

Website: www.bettermekaren.com
Facebook: www.facebook.com/bettermekaren
Instagram: @bettermekaren
LinkedIn: www.linkedin.com/in/karenmachuca/

CHAPTER TWENTY-THREE
REACHING YOUR GOALS: THE FRAMEWORK

By Dr. Tim Mann, PT, DPT, OCS, MTC, CSCS, Cert-CMFA
Owner, Hybrid Fitness & Physio, Sports Physical Therapist
Puyallup, Washington

Everyone has a plan until they get punched in the mouth.
—Mike Tyson

Nothing is impossible.

We've all heard this phrase, but do you believe it? Can you really accomplish anything that you want, no matter what limitations or obstacles stand in your way? The real answer is—it depends. Being successful is a matter of degree and requires being ruthlessly honest with yourself above all else.

I'll give you an example. Can someone who has had a catastrophic injury return to a sport they love? Almost certainly. Can they do it without sacrifice, perform at the level they once did, and have an easy time of it? Almost certainly not. I have helped countless individuals who were told they would not be able to run, walk, lift weights, or perform any number of activities to do so again.

Achieving a goal requires the application of a specific framework, which can be applied almost universally. There may be those who can get away with skipping steps, due to natural ability, social or economic advantages, or other factors. But success leaves clues, and for optimal performance, these clues only need to be followed. Following this framework can help to make things simple, but it does not guarantee to make them easy. If something was easy, everyone would do it. We often choose our goals in spite of them being difficult, and at times *because* they are difficult to achieve. In the face of such difficulty, you need a plan.

Establish Your Mindset

What do you want to do? What does success look like for you? What does winning mean to you? This isn't some abstract visualization exercise; you need to be crystal clear in what you want, in concrete and measurable terms. Presumably, this is a big goal. This framework can take a very long time to work through if you want something massive. It's not necessarily something you need to go through for every goal you have, but it is scalable to pretty much anything.

Have you got your goal clear in your mind? Good, now commit it to a record of some sort. Write it down, so you have something to refer back to when the going gets tough, or you're not sure of your next step. Your mindset must be both a bullet and bulletproof, which requires the ability to not only keep on target, but not be knocked off course.

In short, make a goal. Then, keep the goal the goal. Be very clear with yourself about what you are willing to sacrifice, spend, miss out on, or lose in the pursuit of this goal. Quitting is much easier when unforeseen circumstances arise, so try to consider all the possibilities and know what lines you are willing to cross, what you're willing to give up, to miss out on, and to put yourself through.

What you're willing to commit isn't set in stone. Over enough time, people change. Their priorities change, and there's nothing wrong with that. Sometimes something we wanted with all our heart just isn't the thing we want anymore. This is true of material possessions, relationships, and intangibles, such as status. But if, one day, you wake up, and you don't want your goal anymore, you'll be able to honestly self-reflect and know that you truly don't, rather than know that you rationalized giving up to yourself because you didn't have a plan, didn't have the means, or simply got stuck and overwhelmed by the work involved.

Find Your Why

Here is where you have to be truly honest with yourself. Why do you want the thing you want?

Are you after money?

Fame and repute?

Achievement or recognition?

Are you following in someone's footsteps?

Or, do you just have a burning desire to do something great, and you honestly can't tell yourself why?

All of these are acceptable answers, but this question needs to have an answer. If you want to build a nonprofit organization from the ground up, find the love of your life, start a charity, open a restaurant, or run a marathon, you need to know what drives you towards this achievement.

If you are doing something for reasons that won't hold up under pressure, or worse yet, you don't have a reason, then you're asking for trouble. If someone asks you for your why, you should have one, and you should believe it.

Get the Appropriate Assistance

Trying to figure out how to do something, even something you love, can be a long and difficult process filled with trial and error. While there is something to be said for learning from your mistakes, learning from *someone else's* mistakes is not only less painful, it's much faster.

As I said earlier, success leaves clues. Someone out there has done what you are trying to do, or at least some version of it. Finding that person brings you that much closer to your goal. If you're trying to be the next Michael Jordan, wouldn't it make sense to go talk to Michael Jordan? Obviously, it's not quite that simple. Sometimes the people we seek to emulate are not accessible to us. Sometimes they're not even the right person for us to be talking to. Maybe it would be better to find Phil Jackson, not Michael Jordan; or, maybe it would work best to find a local mindset coach who understands basketball.

In any event, you need to find a way to walk in the footprints of success. Whether that's reading up on a subject, finding a mentor, observing someone's performance, or just starting with a web search, taking the time to do your research is never time lost in the long run. Learning not only what to do, but what not to do, can speed up your development process when moving towards your goal and save you far more time than trying to figure it out for yourself.

Now, a word about coaching. Find a good coach, mentor, Sherpa guide, etc. Do not be afraid to pay them for their services. In the first step you decided what you wanted and what you were willing to sacrifice or spend to get there. You also decided that this is something you truly want and found your reason. So, consider any costs incurred in this phase as investment in yourself and your ultimate destination, which is never wasted money or wasted time.

Develop and Prioritize Your Sub-Goals

This is where the shift begins from planning to strategy. The big picture becomes several smaller ones, and it's time to dial in on how to get from where we currently are to the end goal by planning the stops along the way.

These should be sequential, so they must be followed in order. They should be interdependent, so that they can't be skipped. And they should be achievable in a reasonable amount of time, so it's difficult to get "stuck" on one goal.

These qualities not only help fight distraction, they feed an ongoing sense of purpose and accomplishment. Starting your own multimillion-dollar company is an inspiring vision, and one to keep in the back of your mind at all times. But if you let it live in the front of your mind, it can be crushing in its enormity. The ability to believe in yourself and think big is an admirable (and necessary) quality. It's likely the reason you bought this book.

That's why a goal of "get your website up and running" can be more fulfilling in the short term. Not to mention, if you need a website to start attracting customers, it quickly becomes clear that this is the next thing that needs to happen. In addition to that, if the website needs to be up and running by the end of the month, this helps you to find the most efficient way to get it done (or to find someone to do it for you), rather than spending the afternoon agonizing over what color the tile will be in your corporate bathroom.

When you get that website running, it's the shot of dopamine you need to *keep moving forward*. It's a win, a victory, and moves you on to the next step. Monotony is the enemy, and it's easy to get bored or overwhelmed when a task is too big. In the words of Zig Ziglar, "People often say that motivation doesn't last. Well, neither does bathing—that's why we recommend it daily."

So, make sure you break down what you're doing in a way that lets you see fairly regular rewards for your hard work, because there's more of that coming your way.

Build a Game Plan

The shift from strategy to tactics is a subtle but important one. If strategy is the sum of all the stops along the way to your goal, tactics are the individual footsteps that need to be taken. They are more concrete, operate in a shorter time frame, and can potentially be carried out by someone other than yourself. At this level, the final vision is still important, but the pieces can be completed by someone who hasn't seen it.

In other words, if I'm building my dream house, the person who delivers the wood for the framing is an essential part of the process. If that wood doesn't arrive, the house is not getting built. However, that person does not need to know the entire blueprint for the house. In fact, they don't even need to know what I'm building.

At this level, things can vary wildly depending on the level of your ultimate goal. If you do happen to be building your dream home, then the scenario applies perfectly. If you're trying to learn to play the guitar, not so much. But you still need to get your strings and picks, keep your instrument in tune, and have someone to tell you whether or not your rendition of "Stairway to Heaven" is sounding better.

In this scenario, your downstairs neighbor might give you some unexpected feedback, but all the more reason to have a conversation and let them know when you're going to be practicing. In other words, try to control as many variables as you can, so you can keep the goal the goal, and move on to the next milestone.

Execute

This is the smallest, most granular level of the larger framework. It's also the hardest. Mike Tyson once said, "Everyone has a plan until they get punched in the mouth." Assuming that you're not trying to be a professional boxer, the metaphorical punch in the mouth comes when the inspiring, lofty planning stage ends and the real work begins. When we're no longer just thinking big, and we have to *do the big thing.* The problem is that often the thing can be boring, uncomfortable, tedious, difficult, and just not all that fun. It becomes the day-to-day execution of your plan—the "grind."

This is again where it all comes down to mindset. In order to get things done at this level, you either need to keep your eyes on the prize and have iron willpower, or you need to make the behavior in question an automatic one.

Willpower can certainly be trained and developed, and should be, but there's no reason to work hard and not smart. In fact, there's really no reason not to work hard *and* smart.

If you can establish a routine to get your desired execution done on a regular basis, without having to force yourself, then the proverbial boulder rolls downhill instead of up. This again may take some trial and error, and honest self-reflection. But the payoff is when you do get punched in the mouth, you probably saw that punch coming, and you can still pick yourself up and keep swinging.

Do you *really* have a better session in the gym after a day of work, or does this actually give you a higher likelihood of skipping your workout? Would you be better served working out in the morning and going into your day with that particular box already checked, even though you don't *want* to get up earlier?

Do you *really* get more work done on your novel at the coffee shop, or does it just make you feel more like an author to write in a cafe? Or maybe there are too many distractions at home, and you actually *do* have better focus in a different place. But then couldn't the library be more suitable, and cheaper?

Are you spending hours updating your calendar and rearranging your workspace because you just don't want to start calling sales prospects? Can you start with emailing them, or even stopping by in person? Maybe you really, truly do have to force yourself to make those phone calls. In that case, it's a good thing you already established a reasonable rate of growth for your small business, and you know *exactly* how many of those dreaded calls you need to make every week. That way, you can just get them over with and move on to something else.

Remember those sub-goals are not only interdependent, they're sequential. Therefore, there's really no way you can move on to the next thing until you've done the first thing. Which means if you're doing something that is neither the first or next thing, you're doing some other thing. In other words, you're procrastinating, and you've made it *really* hard to tell yourself otherwise.

Sure, it's bad in that you have to face the fact that you're avoiding something and be honest about it. Then you have to do something about it. But it's good in the fact that you can make it really hard to get in your own way when it comes to progress towards your goal. As unappetizing as the current task can be, you already have some pretty concrete knowledge of how to do it (from your mentor and your game plan), how much of it you need to do (from your sub-goals), and why you need to do it (your ultimate goal, and what you love about reaching it). So, yes, you still have to do the little dirty, unenjoyable tasks that get you to the next (hopefully) less dirty and less unenjoyable task, but you can also zoom out and visualize how much closer to your dream that task puts you. It might not be much fun, but you've laid out the framework to ensure that, yes, it absolutely does need to be done.

So, do it. Then do the next thing on your list. Now use those two things to show yourself that you're making forward progress. Then use your ultimate goal to look at the progress you've been making with your hard work, be it a lot, or a little. Check in on your tactics, be honest with yourself, and change them if you're not being successful. Get some more guidance if you need it.

If you're feeling stuck, you can always check in on your why and revisit what you said you were willing to sacrifice to achieve this goal. Do you still believe it, and does it still fit? Does it still motivate you enough to keep going?

If not, you need to put yourself back into your original mindset, all the way back when you started this process. Find that place where you were, weeks, months, maybe years ago. If the willingness is still there, then steel yourself and keep moving forward.

At this point you essentially have the choice to either scale down your goal, or scale up your desire. There's no shame in this. If you look at the big picture and see that you really don't want this anymore, *it makes so much more sense to quit than to keep going forward with the wrong priorities.* If this is the case, by all means, select a new goal. Just make sure to have a crystal-clear goal that you're focused on. Find your why again, re-establish your winning mindset, strategy, tactics, and your framework.

Then ... keep going.

About the Author

Dr. Tim Mann is a high-achieving health professional, bridging the gap between rehabilitation and performance. He is the owner and founder of Hybrid Fitness & Physio, a company dedicated to not only helping people recover from injury, but becoming stronger, healthier, and more resilient human beings. He graduated from St. Catherine University with a doctorate in physical therapy, and since then has relentlessly pursued excellence in not only the treatment of orthopedic and musculoskeletal conditions, but strength and conditioning, health and wellness, nutrition, and behavior change. He specializes in treating athletes, individuals with persistent pain, as well as anyone who wants to embrace a healthy lifestyle.

If you've ever been told that you couldn't achieve something, Dr. Mann believes that sentiment reflects much less upon your actual abilities, and more upon someone else's impression of how hard and how long you're willing to work. Helping people find that out for themselves is the core philosophy of his practice.

Email: hybrid.fitness.wa@gmail.com
Website: www.hybridfitnessphysio.com

CHAPTER TWENTY-FOUR

INNER VOICE CONTROL: A CRITICAL COMPONENT OF SUCCESS

By David Motto
Founder of Apifany LLC, Performance Coach, Speaker
Oakland, California

Like anyone showing up for an important job interview, presentation, or competition, Jonathan arrived at his audition after months of preparation. He would have 15 minutes to prove he had the skills to be accepted into a university music program. As the faculty member auditioning Jonathan, I was on the other side of his future. I would say yes or no.

From my perspective, auditions were predictable. The auditionee arrives. We talk briefly. They perform. I assess their abilities. I tell them they'll hear the results soon. They leave. The next person arrives. For the person auditioning, the situation is anything but predictable. They control how well they perform, but not my decision. Luckily, Jonathan felt confident about his abilities.

When it was time for him to start, Jonathan picked up his instrument, took a deep breath, and ... froze in place. His voice barely audible, he looked at me and said, "I was a Marine in Iraq, and I'm more nervous right now than I was going into combat."

I was speechless—and totally unprepared for the effect Jonathan's words would have on me. Turns out, more than Jonathan's future was affected that day. So was mine. His words changed the course of my life's work.

Knowing What You Can (And Can't) Control

What went wrong for Jonathan? Somehow, his fight-or-flight response was triggered. His feelings around performing at an audition suddenly felt like an actual life-or-death experience. Enduring the disorienting fight-or-flight response in stressful situations often relates to thinking about things outside our control. In Jonathan's situation, he worried about my opinion of him and how his performance that day would affect his future.

If you create a winning mindset, you'll react differently than Jonathan. Whether you're a leader, performer, or athlete, you'll focus on what you *can* control rather than on what you can't.

You cannot control:

- The outcome
- Environmental factors like temperature, outside noise, distractions
- Whether you get the job, make the sale, get the funding
- Whether your audience likes you or your content
- Whether you win the game, competition, or event
- You can control:
- Showing up as your best self
- Preparing at a world-class level
- Mastering the skills needed to compete
- Executing your craft through repeatable, practiced routines
- Delivering your personal best at the right time
- Regulating your thoughts, emotions, and reactions

This second list contains the essence of the winning mindset: focusing internally and putting yourself in a frame of mind where you have the best chance to succeed. You need to recognize what you *can* control and concentrate your efforts there.

Success Requires Skill and Mindset

Before Jonathan's audition, I spent my time helping musicians develop their craft to an elite level, so they had a shot at making a living performing. I focused on skill development, practice regimens, and repetition.

After his audition, my life completely changed. I became obsessed with world-class strategies that not only lead to elite-level skills, but also allow people to use those skills when it most matters—on stage, in competition, in front of decision-makers. It's one thing to be at your best when no one's watching. It's completely different to achieve a personal best when your future depends on one attempt at getting it right.

I've spent 25 years exploring and researching high-level performance. Out of hundreds of insights, I'll share my two most important with you:

- Skill and mindset are *both* needed for success.
- This combination of skill and mindset applies to *every* field of human endeavor.

These insights changed my career. I could no longer work solely with musicians. I felt compelled to help anyone who had ambitious goals, including athletes, public speakers, and entrepreneurs. I now coach corporate leaders and teams whose ideas might transform their organizations and society.

I help my clients combine technical skills, mental acumen, and emotional readiness. I provide formulas for instilling confidence, control, and clarity, and share three pieces of advice to ensure my clients' orientation is geared toward their ideal future:

- Talent and high-level skills alone give you some success, but not world-class success.
- Mental focus and emotional resilience alone also give you some success, but won't carry you to your ultimate goal.
- Success at the highest levels always combines elite-level skill with a winning mindset.

To Create a Winning Mindset, I Help You "Set Your Mind"

Creating a winning mindset does not happen automatically or with a single attempt. You must actively work to "set your mind." Many strategies exist for setting your mind to create a winning mindset. My favorites include:

- *Visualization*: a multi-sensory process where you see and feel yourself achieving your outcome.
- *Rituals*: repeatable actions you always perform just before engaging in your task.
- *Positive Framing*: using positive language to describe what you *do* want rather than what you do *not* want.
- *Distraction Practice*: running through your skill with everything going wrong around you—while focusing exclusively on your execution.
- *SMARTER Goals*: setting highly focused goals and including motivational tools that help you succeed.

These strategies help you make positive decisions about your thinking and mindset. The most important strategy I can teach you, though, is inner voice control. No matter which winning mindset strategies you try, inner voice control will be an integral part of the process.

Inner Voice Control

We all engage in self-talk and have two inner voices. There's you. And, there's that other inner voice talking at you. You can't silence, delete, or eliminate that other voice. It's part of the human condition. In terms of creating a winning mindset for peak performance, though, you can control your inner voice to gain advantage. While there are several approaches to controlling self-talk, let's focus on three:

- Acknowledging your inner voice
- Neutralizing your inner critic
- Utilizing a motivational mantra

Strategy #1: Acknowledge Your Inner Voice

The first strategy for inner voice control is acknowledging your inner voice. Whether you perceive your self-talk only occasionally or are overwhelmed by it, acknowledging your inner voice is a crucial step in creating a winning mindset. Part of this acknowledgement is recognizing the default mode of your inner voice to determine if it supports your quest for achieving your goals. Whenever you perceive your inner voice, ask yourself:

- Does this voice sound rational or like a three-year old throwing a tantrum?
- Is my inner voice helpful, propelling me toward my most ambitious goals, or does it put me down and question my motivations and capabilities?
- If this were the voice of a real person, would I want to be friends with them, or would I avoid them at all costs?

As you think about your answers to these questions, you will likely spot trends and patterns. Perhaps your inner voice pops up when you're under stress, contemplating something new, or considering an important decision. Recognizing these trends will benefit you in the next inner voice control strategy.

Strategy #2: Neutralize Your Inner Critic

Once you're acknowledging your inner voice, be on the lookout for a certain version of the inner voice that questions your motives and says you're not good enough. This version has its own name: the "inner critic." The inner critic can be particularly damaging to a winning mindset. The inner critic stops you from trying and prevents you from ever experiencing peak performance.

While you can't silence or eliminate the inner critic, I can help you master a powerful process that replaces it. With practice, you'll be able to use this process quickly, consistently, and effectively. I call this process the Inner Critic Neutralizer. It's composed of three steps:

- Notice exactly what your inner critic is saying.
- Reframe the inner critic's words, eliminating negative language and anything that is incorrect or untrue.
- Restate the thought in a detached, factual way.

This third step introduces another version of your inner voice: the "inner correspondent." The inner correspondent acts like an objective journalist reporting just the facts: who, what, when, where, how much. The inner correspondent exists to neutralize damaging words from the inner critic, so you remain calm, focused, and willing to work toward your goals. Let's compare the inner critic to the inner correspondent with two examples:

Example 1: A manager trying a new, group decision-making process

o   *Inner Critic*: I never seem to get this right. It's not working. What's wrong with me?
o   *Inner Correspondent:* I got this right twice last week and three times this week. Out of the ten times I've tried this, five have gone well. It's currently working half the time.

The manager needs to decide whether to continue this potentially successful strategy. His inner critic could easily convince him to impulsively abandon it. His inner correspondent removes his panic and enables a thoughtful decision.

Example 2: A corporate vice president pitching to senior executives

o   *Inner Critic*: What if they hate my presentation? Do I really want to go out there? This audience expects a lot. I'm not ready!
o   *Inner Correspondent*: I've interviewed 16 people about my content and spent three weeks preparing my slides and practicing my pitch. My idea will save my company time and money. I control myself, not my audience. I will make the presentation today at 4:00 p.m.

This presenter's inner critic could paralyze her and prevent her from being inspiring and persuasive. Her inner correspondent subdues the negative emotions and allows her to be at her best when it counts.

The inner critic neutralizer is a powerful tool for creating a mindset that leads to peak performance. By employing your inner correspondent, you set an even playing field for yourself. It's an easy choice to make: let the inner critic get the best of you and stop you in your tracks, or neutralize the inner critic and get on with your life.

Strategy #3: Utilize a Motivational Mantra

Make sure you're deploying the first two strategies—acknowledging *and* neutralizing your inner critic—before you move on to my third strategy: the motivational mantra. Motivational mantras are among the most important mental strategies for achieving peak performance. A mantra is a word or phrase that you repeat to yourself whenever you need to calm your mind and focus your mental, emotional, and physical efforts toward your goal. Your mantra replaces the self-criticism of the inner critic with a deeply personal, powerful message that you design to stay motivated and on track. There are multiple times to deploy your mantra:

- During your daily practice of building your skills and knowledge
- Just before entering a high-stress experience
- In the heat of battle—during the high-stakes situation

Your mantra will be highly effective if it captures a key element of what drives you toward achieving success. For most people, understanding that drive starts with the inner critic's insights into what stops you. Here are the steps needed to start with your inner critic and end up with a mantra that helps you replace the inner critic's message:

1. Find a recurring theme in the inner critic's words.
2. Define the opposite of that theme.
3. Brainstorm names and visual representations for your positive theme. Like a branding exercise, choose the strongest idea.
4. Hone your idea to a word or phrase that sounds and feels right.

This final step is crucial. Your mantra must impact you viscerally. You'll know when you've landed on the right one.

Here are examples of mantra work I've done with coaching clients:

Example 1: A successful, highly-regarded corporate leader

1. *Theme from Inner Critic*: You always over-analyze and lose out on chances because you move too slowly.
2. *Opposite*: Move quickly, swiftly, and efficiently.

3. *Branding Brainstorm*: Cheetah, shark, bullet, quasar, lightning. Lightning! Yes, that's it!
4. *Hone It*: Lightning energy. Flash of energy. Bright and bold. Light up the skies. Yes! "Light up the skies."

This corporate leader now starts every meeting, presentation, and discussion by silently repeating his mantra: "Light up the skies." It's powerful, action-oriented, and works for both in-person and virtual situations.

Example 2: A long-distance, collegiate runner

1. *Theme from Inner Critic*: You're going to hit the wall. You won't win. Why are you trying?
2. *Opposite*: Keep going through the wall so I can win.
3. *Branding Brainstorm*: Squeeze through. Go over. Go around. Break through. Destroy. Yes! Destroy the wall!
4. *Hone It*: Destroy. Dynamite. Tumbling bricks. Jericho. Yes! "Jericho."

Is running a race still painful for this runner? Yes. Does she expect to hit the wall? Yes. Her mantra doesn't stop the wall from occurring, but "Jericho" gives her the visual imagery and strength to conquer the wall.

Your motivational mantra replaces the words of the inner critic before the inner critic can begin its damaging commentary. Your mantra becomes a powerful tool for setting your mind for peak performance.

Success Starts with Inner Voice Control

Understanding that you'll need a winning mindset *and* high-level skills prepares you for the journey to peak performance. Creating a winning mindset requires active participation to "set your mind." Give yourself time for this process, and you'll be rewarded with the confidence needed to achieve your goals.

Inner voice control involves a combination of acknowledging, neutralizing, and replacing your inner critic. All three stages are permanent components of a winning mindset—even in the rarefied circles of elite-level success.

Imagine if Jonathan had known these strategies. Instead of freezing in place and failing his audition, what a different future he would have created! He would have acknowledged the themes of his inner critic—from his days both as a Marine and as a musician. He would have conjured a positive goal that directly opposed those themes. He would have been armed with a deeply personal and effective mantra to shield him from the agonies of his fight-or-flight response. He would have shown me, and the world, his personal best.

Now imagine if you employ these same strategies as you prepare for your next high-stakes, high-stress activity. By combining inner voice control with the right skillset, you'll significantly improve your chance of experiencing peak performance and achieving the success you desire.

About the Author

Performance coach David Motto helps individuals and teams achieve their most ambitious goals, communicate to create trust, and inspire the world with their ideas. He is the founder of Apifany, LLC, a Silicon Valley-based coaching and consulting firm with a global clientele. Apifany's services include executive coaching, leadership communication training, and presentation effectiveness. Apifany also works to align leadership teams around values-based, purpose-driven visions that drive exceptional organizational outcomes. David focuses his individual coaching clients on achieving meaningful goals, performing well in high-pressure environments, and sustaining mental and emotional states that drive successful results. He has developed a process for creating and delivering high-value, highly-engaging presentations, and has designed a learning system for mastering advanced skills in any field of human endeavor, ten minutes at a time. The essence of David's work is getting people from where they are to where they want to be—efficiently and effectively.

Email: david@apifany.com
Websites: www.apifany.com; www.davidmotto.com
LinkedIn: www.linkedin.com/in/davidmotto/

CHAPTER TWENTY-FIVE
IF I'M GOING TO GET SHOT, TODAY'S THE DAY

By Steven Nathenson, ME, MODL, PCC
Former FBI Special Agent, Leadership Coach, Speaker
Pittsburgh, Pennsylvania

Everything can be taken from a man but one thing: the last of the human freedoms—to choose one's attitude in any given set of circumstances, to choose one's own way.
—Viktor E. Frankl

As the soft, melodic tones of my alarm gradually grew louder, I knew it was time to get up. However, I hadn't needed my alarm on this morning. I was already wide-awake thinking about what lay ahead. Today, I was going to make an arrest, but it wasn't just any arrest, it was one that scared me. On this morning, I was already awake because I was thinking: "If I am going to get shot, today is the day."

It Starts in Our Minds Long Before We Take Action

While there's an inherent risk with making any arrest—a chance that walking out your front door that day may be for the last time—this arrest felt different. I knew with certainty the person I was going to arrest had guns, did not want to go to jail, and I was going to be right in the thick of it if anything "broke bad." On this arrest, it was my responsibility to hold the ballistic shield, up close and personal, right in front of the arrestee's door. In other words, when we knocked and announced, I was going to be inches away from the person we were arresting, responsible for not only my safety, but also the safety of each of my fellow FBI Special Agents behind me. It was a heavy weight on my mind, and literally upon my shoulders. The thought of getting shot played over and over in my mind, filling me with fear.

Part of becoming a Special Agent with the FBI is to accept your own mortality. Early on at the FBI Academy, potential new agents undergo a "gut" check. For the first time for many, it brings out the reality that being an FBI Special Agent means that one day, our lives may come to an end—that we are willingly entering a profession which will put us in harm's way each and every day. This "gut" check is meant to be just that—a forced look inward to see if we are truly willing to serve in a capacity that may take our lives.

On this morning, for the first time in my career, I felt like there was a very good chance I may not be coming back home that night. I had come face-to-face with my own mortality, harkening back to the "gut" check I had gone through at the FBI Academy, staring the possibility of my death in its face. Looking at it, feeling it, sensing it … there wasn't even a moment of doubt about what I was going to do. I was going on that arrest willingly, without hesitation, putting my life on the line regardless of my misgivings. Misgivings that, nonetheless, left me in a very precarious spot.

I knew if I let my fear consume me, I could end up creating a self-fulfilling prophecy. My fear could make me jittery. Being jittery could make me jumpy. And, being jumpy could cause me to react in a way that could result in people getting hurt, or even worse, killed. I realized that going into this arrest, I had a very important choice to make. I could either let my fear get the better of me, or I could embrace what would allow me to react appropriately to anything that might happen during the arrest.

On this morning, I had to ask myself the same question many of my clients have since asked me:

"How do I overcome fear in the moment?"

The answer is that it's a process that starts in our minds long before we take action, long before being *in the moment.*

At the core of what I do with my clients is an exploration of their mentality to uncover and address any hurdles that stand in the way of achieving what they want. To do this, we undergo a process called G.R.I.T. — Give,

Recognize, Implement, Time*. As it relates to what I was facing this morning, I had to first understand my fear before I could overcome it.

G.R.I.T. Tip #1—Name Your Fear

Once we know and understand what we need to overcome, it is a lot easier for us to do so.

Flipping the Script

Driving to the arrest, the typically jam-packed freeway was empty, leaving me alone in my car with only fear for company. The darkness of the night physically surrounded me while the darkness of getting shot swirled in my mind. As my mind wandered, I began to not only think about getting shot, but also that I did not want to get shot. I wanted to go home after the arrest. I wanted to live!

As my headlights bounced off of the lane reflectors in the road, another possibility illuminated before me—that I might not get shot today. I began to think about how that could happen. One option was the person we were going to arrest might not shoot at us at all. While that was the best-case scenario, I could not control the arrestee's actions. However, I could control mine and began to think about that instead.

I thought about how I was going to approach the arrest location, visualizing how I was going to position myself and the ballistic shield I would carry, where my eyes would focus, what I would listen for, and how I would drown out any unnecessary noise. As I thought, I created a clear picture of what I wanted to happen and how I *could* make that happen. For now, my mind was focused on what I wanted rather than what I feared.

In order to think about *not* doing something, we first have to think about doing it. In other words, if I say to myself: "Don't be afraid," I have to first think about being afraid. Instead, if I flip the script and say to myself: "Be calm," I've now focused on how I want to behave rather than my fear.

G.R.I.T. Tip #2—Focus on What You Want

Focusing on what we want to happen rather than what we are fearful of happening naturally makes us more successful.

Looking Outside the Tunnel

As my fellow FBI Special Agents and I prepared to make the arrest, my fear reared its ugly head again. The closer the arrest came, the more real the possibility of getting shot became. I couldn't help but think about all the different ways that could happen. Getting shot while approaching the door, getting shot through the door, getting shot after the door was opened—all I could picture was getting shot.

My mind was singularly focused on what I did not want to happen, and my fear was winning out. As the time for the arrest loomed ever closer, I knew I'd soon have to decide if I was going to let fear win, or if I was going to overcome it. Only I was capable of knowing, and only I was capable of deciding.

Breathing deeply and steadying myself, I focused on what I *wanted* to happen. As I did, I broke free of the tunnel vision my fear had created and was reminded that this was not my first arrest, nor was I a new FBI Special Agent learning the ins-and-outs of the job. I had undergone extensive and intensive training at the FBI Academy and had been a part of many arrests before. Not once had I ever failed to react appropriately to any situation that had arisen. Knowing this gave me the confidence that I was not only capable of going home that night, I was also capable of reacting appropriately to any adverse action by the person we were about to arrest.

As we departed, I knew I was capable of overcoming my fear because I had done it many times before. In that moment, a shift happened. I no longer allowed my fear to control me. Rather, I was filled with a calmness that allowed me to break free of my constraints and shift my perspective. While I had never been shot at before, the possibility of it was very real. If it happened, I would recall what I had already been through and react the way I knew I was capable of—the way my body and mind had been trained to do.

When facing our fear, we tend to get tunnel vision—singularly focusing on what lies ahead of us, forgetting everything we have already accomplished.

G.R.I.T. Tip #3—Look to Your Past for Confidence

Our past experiences hold the keys to successfully facing our fear and overcoming it.

Knowing Our Purpose

Advancing towards the door, my heart pounding in my chest, my senses kicked into overdrive. In this heightened state of awareness, I was consumed by the notion that my life was no longer my own. I was living to serve a greater purpose—to do right when no one is looking, be honest at all times, and uphold and hold people accountable to the rule of law. This purpose is the bond that connects every FBI Special Agent—past, present, and future—no matter if they've met or not. It is also what gave me the strength to walk out my door earlier that morning.

As we continued inching forward, I realized I was also living to protect those I served with—my brothers and sisters in blue. This instilled a fire within me to fight to my very last breath, boosting my strength and becoming more steadfast with every step. Drawing closer to our final position, getting ready to make the arrest, I knew I would shortly have to rely on this strength once again to overcome my fear one final time.

I have seen loss. In one example, we lost two FBI Special Agents in a shootout as they were executing a search warrant on a crimes-against-children investigation. I never met them … I didn't have to. Their deaths affected me as deeply as if they had served alongside me.

As I watched members of the armed services carefully and diligently fold the flag that had been draped over the casket for one of the fallen FBI Special Agents during their funeral, I thought about how they *had* walked out their front door for the last time. They had *not* gone home. And now their family, left behind, had to live in a world without them. They *made* the ultimate sacrifice in service of a purpose greater than themselves.

Near the end of the service, a radio operator called out for the fallen FBI Special Agent. Hearing no reply, they called out a second time only to receive a deafening silence in return once again. Afterwards, the radio operator declared the fallen FBI Special Agent to be officially off duty, and we, those who remained, would pick up the torch and continue to protect and serve in honor of them, giving them permission to finally rest in peace.

At any moment in my career, having worked crimes against children cases, it could have been me the radio operator was calling out for instead. Knowing this, the fallen FBI Special Agent's sacrifice, and the purpose we both served, the lingering quiet of the radio operator's final remarks caused an uncontrollable river of tears to pour out of my eyes from the deepest depths of my soul.

G.R.I.T. Tip #4—Identify Your Purpose

We're not talking about a "surface level" purpose here. We're talking about a deeply seated, to the very fiber of your being, purpose—the kind that inherently motivates us and rights the ship when we wane.

Harnessing Our Mentality in the Moment

Knock, knock, knock! "FBI! Open the door!"

This was it! Standing steadfast, expecting the door to open at any moment, I needed to make my choice. I knew I was capable of reacting the way I wanted to, the question was—would I?

Knock, knock, knock! "FBI! Open the door!"

Hearing my fellow FBI Special Agent's voice announce our presence, feeding off of their energy as I stood stoically, holding my ballistic shield, gun out at the ready, I was engulfed by my very purpose, as if radiating from every fiber of my being. I was there to protect my fellow FBI Special Agents. I was there to ensure they went home to their loved ones at the end of the day. I was there to serve justice. It was the final piece of the puzzle. In that moment, I embraced my purpose. I became calm, knowing I was fully capable, having been there many times before, and I focused on how I wanted to be. Keenly honing my focus on the door, I was ready to react calmly and appropriately to any situation which may arise.

The door opened and the person we were there to arrest appeared. Staring with laser-like focus, watching how the person we were arresting responded, I calmly and instinctively behaved the way I had been trained to do. I did not jump. I did not stumble. And, my fear of being shot seemed like a distant memory as I focused on the here and now, knowing what I was responsible for, knowing I was capable of doing it, and knowing why I was doing it.

If I had let my fear consume me during the arrest, it could have led to a bad situation—one that could have led to not only myself getting hurt or killed, but also my fellow FBI Special Agents and the person we were there to arrest being hurt or killed. Being physically surrounded by my fellow FBI Special Agents served as a very tangible reminder of why I had to overcome my fear.

G.R.I.T. Tip #5—Create a Reminder

When we are *in the moment*, a reminder can elicit what we want to embody, the confidence to do so, and the purpose for doing it, so we can overcome our fear and behave how we want to. Common reminders include images, loved ones, mantras, and physical cues (such as snapping a wristband).

Each and every one of us is capable of overcoming our fear and achieving what we want in life. That ability is, and will always be, within us.

> *If we never ask, we'll never know. If we never try, we*
> *never will. Be the movement in your life.*
> —Steven Nathenson

About the Author

Steven Nathenson helps leaders master their mindset to increase their focus, confidence, and performance while motivating others to do the same. As a leadership development coach and former FBI Special Agent, Steven's proven training and coaching programs help leaders and their teams thrive while overcoming challenges and achieving ambitious results.

Steven is also the CEO and founder of Strive For More, a world-class coaching and speaking organization. He holds master's degrees in mechanical engineering and organizational development and leadership. He has received two United States patents, five awards for his investigative work, been named an IRONMAN All World Athlete, and competed in triathlon at the national level. To date, he has coached athletes, students, and leaders of all levels in seven countries.

To learn more about Steven and G.R.I.T. — Give, Recognize, Implement, Time, please visit Steven's website.

Email: steve@striveformore.com
Website: www.striveformore.com

CHAPTER TWENTY-SIX

MAKING YOUR DREAMS A REALITY

By Anastasia Pavlatou
Rowing Coach and Athlete
Athens, Greece

Every journey begins with a single step.
—Lao Tsu

Dreams without action remain in our imagination. Athletes have to define and protect their future dreams. By drafting a plan, athletes are able to define how they will be able to fulfill their dreams, which in the future, will become goals. The key point is to start the journey with the first step.

A target is just a success you intend to achieve, but a goal is the result or achievement toward which effort is directed. Athletes intend to reach goals. When athletes set their goals, they have to try hard and stay dedicated to what they aim at. This chapter is about my coaching athletes, but the same principles for target and goal setting apply to people in any situation in business or life.

Setting Your Personal Targets and Goals

In order to win, athletes have to set goals, and specifically to write them down because in doing so, subconsciously, the goals get imprinted and become more perceptible, making athletes have a stronger commitment to them. But, how can these goals motivate athletes to keep up their effort? One of the basic factors that actuates athletes is the positive emotions that are associated with their goals. Consequently, excitement could be one of the emotions that motivates athletes to work hard to achieve their goals. Negative feelings, such as disappointment, fatigue, pain, tedium, and failure, do not inspire athletes. Goals have to be inspired by positive feelings that are able to overcome the negative ones.

The process of setting goals helps athletes to understand where they stand, set their destination, and lastly provide them with the navigation tools they need to find out where they want to go by narrowing their efforts to specific areas and avoiding being distracted by anything that will hamper their progress. By understanding this, athletes can improve their performance (performance = motivation x skill x environment) and adopt a strategy, which will lead them to success. Setting and fulfilling a target has a powerful emotional vibration and pushes athletes to continue struggling for greater performances and results. Ideal targets are those that pave the way for action. Therefore, ideal targets are those which force athletes to fulfil new performance requirements and whose fulfilment brings them closer to the final goal.

Subsequently, it is crucial for athletes to define specific targets, so as to establish their vision. When athletes manage to set specific targets based on their abilities, they stand a good chance of fulfilling them. On the other hand, if athletes get influenced by other people's targets, they do not strive as much, and it is more difficult for them to reach their goal. Athletes must make it clear—to themselves and their coaches—what they want to achieve. When the target is general and vague, it is very hard to accomplish it. Avoid setting indefinite and broad goals. The more specific the targets, the more motivating and committing the athletes become.

Furthermore, athletes' targets have to be measurable and objective. In the field of economics, it is said that whatever is countable is achievable, so targets have to be measurable in order to be feasible. Targets are measurable only if they can be quantified and, consequently, measure athletes' progress. Athletes must chart and document their progress. In that way, they will be able to know how close to their target they are.

Thirdly, targets should be attainable. An attainable target is one that athletes can achieve. Primarily, athletes have to set targets that are challenging but realistic as well as ones that help them gain confidence. Targets do not need to be easily attainable but should require hard work to be achieved. The increase in the difficulty of a target is what motivates and satisfies athletes more. Therefore, targets, apart from being attainable, have to be action-oriented. When a target is action-oriented, the motivation is greater because the indication of what athletes want is clear. Trying to reach something that is unattainable will probably lead to disappointment and low self-confidence, so keeping goals attainable is important.

Additionally, athletes have to set a logical number of realistic targets or targets that can be achieved after hard work since athletes will have improved their performance in the meantime. When athletes set too many targets, it is impossible for them to achieve them. By saying "realistic" targets, I mean those that can be achieved after hard work because athletes will have improved their performance in the meantime. Deficiency of incentives, confidence, and motivation occurs when athletes are not capable of achieving all the targets and goals they have set. Athletes should set some limitations and dedicate themselves to hard work to fulfil their targets and consequently their goals.

Ideally, athletes, in cooperation with their coaches, have to set deadlines for their goals and time-limits for the targets. Making a personal plan could be a good idea and is highly motivating. It is necessary that athletes write down their targets and goals, so they can monitor them regularly in order to certify their completion.

Coach- and Athlete-Set Targets

"Coach"—this word means a lot. A coach should be capable not only of leading athletes to peak performance but also of picking up their pieces after a failure. A coach plays many roles in an athlete's life, including that of an educator, a trainer, a teacher, a psychologist, an instructor … Coaches should regularly refresh and improve all these roles, so athletes can trust and confide in them.

First and foremost, coaches are responsible for making athletes find pleasure and enjoyment in the sport. Even with a winning mindset, winning is not always the target! Sometimes the obsession to win medals creates stress and reduces motivation and causes athletes to set targets that are their coach's desires. Coaches must be supportive of their athletes' decisions because athletes are the ones who determine what they desire. Nevertheless, coaches are indispensable because they push athletes to keep trying, and they do not let their athletes' dreams vanish into thin air. Commitment is what leads to success for both. When athletes manage to devote themselves to their targets, their efforts are greater and the results are better.

Moreover, coaches have to teach athletes the meaning of satisfaction. Every time athletes try to get better, the feeling of satisfaction appears. Self-confidence increases when athletes are satisfied with their personal improvement. For that reason, self-confidence affects a great percentage of an athlete's performance.

A coach is a versatile person and consequently a teacher. Coaches have to know their athletes not only as athletes of a sport but as people too! That being the case, coaches should individuate the personality of each athlete and respect them. Likewise, athletes should respect their coaches and their decisions. A coach's decisions should be established according to their athlete's personality; otherwise, it is difficult for them to be effective.

The relationship between athletes and coaches, as far as targets are concerned, is of high importance. There must be cooperation and the targets of coaches should not tamper their athletes'. Writing down the targets gives both athletes and coaches the ability to monitor their progress. In consequence, the monitoring of progress contributes to the assessment and the improvement of athletes' performance and constitutes the means for the fulfilment of targets.

Undoubtedly, athletes and coaches have to make a target plan for both short- and long-term targets, which they are going to follow with the aim of fulfilling the athletes' goals. Every step should be examined thoroughly. Obviously, short-term targets are of higher importance compared to long-term targets and goals, and they should be accomplished first. Short-term targets are achievable in a short period, are less difficult to achieve, are easily controlled, and, if not achieved, the feeling of disappointment is minor compared to that of not fulfilling a long-term target or goal. Additionally, short-term goals are viable, give pleasure and direction, and serve as the base for long-term targets and goals. The result of specific short-term targets is that athletes are more motivated, dedicated, and satisfied because they feel that they succeed regularly. Lastly, the possibilities of giving up because of failure to meet short-term goals are rare, so every obstacle is encountered as a challenge. Long-term goals require setting strategic short-term targets.

Facing Negative Feelings

Anxiety, fear, stress, nervousness, weakness, and other negative feelings are among the feelings that most athletes experience during their athletic performances. Negative feelings are considered obstacles in sport life. Obstacles which affect the physical and emotional health of athletes. Both are very important and interesting, and can be responsible for relinquishing athletes' efforts. "Danger" is lurking!

As it has already been mentioned, the first step before athletes reach the top is to set their targets. Define what winning means. However, the second important step is to define and understand the many bad feelings that lead them to bad performance.

Self-awareness is a very useful tool. The ability of athletes to understand themselves is an essential requirement for sporting excellence. It is critical to understand that athletes are humans first, so they have their beliefs, values, behaviors, and characteristics. If athletes manage to understand themselves better, they will manage to understand what they have to change and why. In that way, they will change their mindset, replacing negative thoughts with positive ones.

Self-esteem is another factor that contributes to peak performance. If athletes are confident and realistic about their abilities, then they will have a positive and good performance. By increasing the degree of an athlete's self-esteem, their performance will be better too. Fear, doubts, and negative thoughts are signs of distraction and, consequently, of low self-esteem. If athletes are not concentrated on what they strive for, they will not be able to do well. While athletes are performing, their mind should be void of distracting thoughts and focused on their target.

Another important factor contributing to high performance is self-confidence. From the moment athletes set targets, they are able to raise their levels of confidence, and they are ready to get over their fears. It would be advisable for athletes to reach an optimum level of self-confidence while they compete because it will give them the ability to withstand greater levels of stress. How can athletes improve their self-confidence? Willingness, determination, self-control, and concentration are necessary elements.

Several steps can be taken to avoid extreme manifestation of negative feelings and deficient sport performance. Athletes should prepare themselves both mentally and physically prior to a race, for example, in training sessions. When athletes follow certain positive, invigorating routines and rituals in their training, either mentally or physically, then it is easier to adopt the same procedures in a race to instill them with confidence and focus.

Visualization is a powerful strategy to lead athletes closer to their targets and goals. Visualization functions as a preparatory tool for what athletes are going to confront, both physically and mentally. It is a relaxing method because they visualize their race or event as a film. When athletes are able to imagine a great performance, a successful strategy, or even an alternative scenario, and simultaneously recall emotions and feelings of success, enjoyment, and focus, then, when the big day arrives, they will perform more effectively and with less anxiety. The action of repeated imagery raises athlete's confidence and, subsequently, efficiency. Visualization brings athletes absolute concentration by allowing them to focus and relax, which then puts them a step closer to completing their dream.

Despite the fact that athletes have the leading role, a coach is necessary to regulate athletes'' feelings and emotions. Athletes should learn to perform independently, but coaches have to improve athletes' psychology by developing an elite mindset. It will be advantageous if athletes trust their coach. Anxiety and constant thoughts of fear and distress can consume a lot of athletes' energy, so coaches have to boost athletes' mental performance to create a winning mindset. A deficiency in emotional energy could lead to inadequate physical abilities. Coaches should also teach athletes to think positively, focus on their self-confidence, and perceive failure as a positive feedback.

A coach should play a supportive role to athletes' wins and failures alike, both of which constitute an integral part of sports life. Most athletes hate to fail, but they need to comprehend failure. Failure should lead to learning and growth. Athletes who are not afraid of failure and are optimistic can motivate all the positive powers, which will lead them to greater results and later to success. Athletes should be responsible, understand their failure, and try to turn it into success. When athletes are capable of identifying their failure and analyzing it, then they will be more efficient to turn a failure into a process that will show them the road to success. It is commonly accepted that athletes who reach peak performance sink into the oblivion of failure. For this reason, it is critical that athletes learn to process failure in order to come out on the other side stronger and more resilient.

Furthermore, coaches have to help athletes stay focused. When athletes feel disappointed if they have a failure or a bad moment, they lose their concentration and their motivation. Athletes have to concentrate on what they can control because everything else is unpredictable. They should concentrate on the difficulties they can actually work with and try to perceive the challenges as opportunities of improvement. Athletes should not allow challenges to act solely as reasons for depression and disappointment. On the contrary, such challenges should be seen as chances to become better. Indeed, not all the difficulties are insurmountable. The brain is the most important tool for survival. The state of mind of an athlete is their most important factor to reach peak performance. Many times, it is difficult to direct the mind, but it is necessary and possible.

For an athlete to reach peak performance, the support of a coach is indispensable, but also it is crucial for the athlete to be able to regulate their negative feelings and thoughts. Smile and feel happy and satisfied, and then growth and achievement will come. Even if athletes fail, it is not the end of the world. There are many opportunities that come from failure. Try to avoid negative thoughts and struggle for the best despite any huge pressure. Try to relax and compete without caring about the result.

Evaluation Assessment

The last necessary step before reaching peak performance is the ability of athletes and coaches to assess athletes' performances. With the help of their coach and the right knowledge and the necessary skills, athletes should assess and evaluate their sport performances, as well as review their goals regularly.

The most important thing is what athletes and coaches do after a race. It is necessary to review the race and comment on their performance and reactions before and during the race. Then, focus on the things that prevented them from being efficient. Finally, with the support of their coach, make a draft that will mimic the conditions of a race.

Coaches should not stop providing athletes with the relevant feedback and should regularly compare athletes' goals with actual progress. Feedback is a very useful method that motivates athletes to continue chasing their goals throughout the year. Analyses of athletes' performances and the correction of errors helps them to improve, but coaches should avoid comparing one athlete with others. Sometimes the comparison with other athletes makes an athlete feel less satisfied, with less motivation and more stress.

Support from Family Environment

The ideal environment for an athlete is when a positive mood prevails because, in such an environment, athletes can have high-quality preparation for great performance. Athletes should try to keep positive people in their lives. Positive people need to be present. Especially those who come from their families. Athletes need "good teams" around them. They need people who share the same vision as them.

A supportive environment is necessary. A very simple method is for an athlete to inform their family and friends about the goals they are setting and the importance of those targets, so family and friends can encourage them to progress towards their goals. Athletes need people who will encourage them to exceed any limits they might place on themselves.

Family is a key factor, vital to an athlete's life. A family is able to partially raise an athlete's self-confidence. This kind of confidence may help athletes succeed in high-pressure races. For anyone without the possibility of family, they create their own "family" of friends and coaches who can provide positive support. After all, it is extremely difficult for anyone to become a top-performer alone. Athletes should allow others to become their support, to celebrate their wins, and to console them in any losses as they develop a winning mindset that is able to accept wins as a reward for sticking with their goals and accept losses as experiences to sharpen their focus and determination, so they are even stronger when they try again. With persistence in setting targets, facing feelings, and embracing support from coaches and family, it is possible for anyone to turn dreams into goals and goals into reality.

About the Author

Anastasia Pavlatou studied at the Technological Educational Institute of Larissa, Business Administration, and she did her MSc at the University of Peloponnese in sports management (direction management). Her thesis was the study of pre-race stress in rowing athletes. She has also attended Rowing Coaches School and is a certified rowing C-class coach. She has completed FISA's level 1 and 2 coaching course (FISA International Coaching Academy). Anastasia is also certified in indoor rowing level 1. Furthermore, she has a fitness trainer certification.

Anastasia is an athlete and a coach of the Rowing Club of Greece, which is an Athenian team. She has taken part and won medals in several races as an athlete, both in single and double sculls. She has won medals in the Rowing National Championships and Indoor Rowing National Championships. She has also taken part in World Rowing Coastal Championships and in World Rowing Masters Regattas. As a coach, she trains the junior and master's athletes who have won medals in National Rowing Championships and Indoor Rowing National Championships.

Email: pavlatounat@gmail.com
LinkedIn: https://www.linkedin.com/in/anastasiapavlatou/
Instagram: @natasapavlatou

CHAPTER TWENTY-SEVEN

PROGRAM DELTA: DATA-DRIVEN RESULTS FOR PERFORMANCE

By Bryan Sauder
EDGE Physical Development, Strength Coach
St. Louis, Missouri

You can't fire a cannon from a canoe!
—Charles Poliquin

As a strength and conditioning consultant for 18-plus years, I've carefully curated and tested ways to bring optimal function and performance to just about anyone. I've started to call it Program Delta. Essentially, this is a "change" in the way the fitness and performance community is currently thinking. Program Delta consists of four easily adoptable modalities that many people have already tried, used, and otherwise discarded over the years due to not following the "recipe." You see, if you have all the right ingredients for a specific recipe, but are unable to properly coordinate them together, you will get a less-than-optimal outcome. This is where having an experienced coach to organize these modalities will provide the ultimate experience to optimize your performance in any aspect of life, career, or health, which is essential to the process. World-class coaches use a multi-dimensional approach to create peak performance in a client-athlete-patient's life.

I've worked in high-performance, body composition, prehab-rehab, functional medicine, and technology at different times of my career. What I've learned is they all are methods that are beneficial to different people. For the most part, every client I've helped over my career has needed a different approach to optimize their function and performance. After carefully choosing my educators on all of these topics and putting them into practice, I created Program Delta as a niche product for performers in all areas of life. If you are interested in optimizing your output in any area of life, keep reading. First, I'll tell my story about how, at almost 40 years old with four children, I feel and perform at the best I ever have in my life. Then, I'll introduce how to incorporate these methods into a proper "recipe" for you and your life.

I am a 39-year-old performance coach with a beautiful wife and four children. My children's ages are almost ten, five, and I have twin three-year-olds. As you can guess, I have my hands full. I also run my training and consulting company, EDGE Physical Development. Lucky for me, I have been able to work and learn from the greatest minds in training, functional medicine, soft-tissue, and technology throughout my career. Without all these stops along the way, I would have never been able to keep my head above water. Business problems, family problems, and personal problems all have come and gone over the last 13 years. I am forever grateful I learned so much from my mentors. They have given me some real solutions to deal with these problems as well as how to keep my body and mind functioning properly to be able to absorb and then conquer these issues. This is why I created Program Delta, essentially to help people having issues find a plan and change their life.

If I, as a minimally athletic, skinny young man, can use (1) weight training, (2) nutrition, (3) soft-tissue protocols, and (4) technology to optimize my life, anyone can. The key to these four parts of the program lies in understanding that none of them by themselves is a silver bullet. Carefully managing these parts will consistently elevate other aspects of the program when life gets in the way. For example, if you are on vacation and don't have access to weights, the other three components are important to keep your body and mind optimized. Or if you happen to have a tough week with food and bodywork, the weights and technology will work concurrently to bring you back on track. Program Delta's main components are explained below, and I'll show how they are designed to optimize your life and get you to a winning mindset and peak performance. Let's dig in.

Weight Training

In my opinion, weight training is the foundation to optimal function and performance for the majority of people. It encompasses all that the human body and brain needs and asks for—stress, adaptation, recovery, and the ability to do it over and over again. There are many training styles and camps on how to use weights to optimize the body and mind. As I've said, I've been in many different worlds from athletic high performance, body composition, to injury prehab and rehab, and "health." The problem with most people who weight train is they have no goals, or their goals have no substance, meaning actionable steps. It is important to learn how to even set a goal—be it reasonable or not—so there is a starting point and maybe a few checkpoints on the way to the goal. Many people show or tell me what they are doing with their program, and it typically has no clear goal in mind. So, results typically are less than optimal.

I see the weight training aspect of Program Delta as a great opportunity for working with a highly qualified coach. Seek this out! It is very important to have trust in the coach and the weight training process to get you where you want to be.

Nutrition and Functional Medicine

Most people inside and outside of human function and performance know that nutrition has probably a 75 to 90 percent influence on how our bodies feel and perform. Not fueling our bodies with the right nutrients is a problem in society today. The ability to make sure your body gets the right fuel, nutrients, hydration, and signals to function, not only properly, but to optimize performance, is an undertaking many do not know how to navigate. I have trained under the top functional medicine doctors who have taught me how to support clients in the area of nutrition within my scope of practice. These experts have helped me educate my clients on nutrition, supplementation, and other performance-enhancing protocols—the backbone to increased human function and performance.

You might ask, "How can functional medicine help me if I have never heard of it?" Functional medicine is the study of getting to the root cause of health issues (instead of addressing the symptoms). When you address the source of down-stream mental, physical, and psychological problems, you concurrently fix many other issues. Essentially, killing two birds with one stone. The problem is most people don't want to put in the work, or they want a magic pill to fix numerous issues at once. The reality is that for positive effects from nutrition and functional medicine, a bit of research and follow through is very important.

Performance Therapy

ALTIS's performance therapy is a methodology that compounds knowledge of movement sciences and sports medicine in an effort to better understand and enhance health and performance. It is not a system or technique, and it does not replace other forms of therapy. The successful performance therapist is able to see movement, feel tissue, and affect change.

During my career, many different methods to address flexibility, mobility, stability, and muscle fluidity have come and gone. Static stretching, dynamic stretching, foam rolling, massage, and on and on have been a staple to make you a better performing and functioning human. They all have their merits, but typically they do not address the core issue within human anatomy and physiology. In many cases, the inflexibility or "tightness" of your body is a manifestation of weakness somewhere else in your body and/or a neurological inhibition somewhere. Getting to the cause of your inflexibility or weakness is the key to restoring proper range of motion, and the ability to do the activities you're eager to do.

Having specific and tested protocols to address these imbalances of the nervous and muscular system is a key to Program Delta. With the help of technology and science from some of my business partners, it incorporates just the right amount of bodywork, the correct way, and in the proper manner. As with anything, you want to grow in, these specific protocols will need to be done not just once, but throughout your life.

Data

There is a plethora of technology and applications that have been created over the last decade that have addressed biometric data and how to manage it. From sleep apps to wearables, the market has many to choose from, in fact, a bit too many for the average person to decide which one is best. Having used and vetted much of the technology out there, I have concluded what I think is and will be the future of personal health and performance monitoring. I use these two different monitoring systems for my clients and family: Oura Ring and Omegawave.

Oura Ring is a very simple tool to monitor sleep and the sympathetic/parasympathetic balance needed for ultimate performance and function. It is a ring you wear that has an accompanying app that records all of the info for you. Oura uses HRV (heart-rate variability) readings and sleep metrics to determine physiological performance. It also allows you to keep track of your data throughout the year(s). This data will help you get a better understanding of how your body is functioning and reacting to stress in your life. This is the easiest to use, but still takes a backseat to the next product I support.

Omegawave is a strap-based monitoring device that in four minutes, at rest, records your state of physiological readiness (sympathetic/parasympathetic tone) which is the ability to shift from a state of stress to one of recovery. It is the only non-invasive readiness technology to assess both the brain and heart. It records detailed biological data on the central nervous system (DC-EEG), cardiac system (HRV) and metabolic system (ATP). Omegawave remains the only technology on the market that is capable of performing a full physiological assessment that informs you how to train optimally today.

As you've seen, I put weight training as the first, and in my opinion, the base of the other components. There are numerous benefits that weight training can provide solely but, combined with functional medicine, it can elevate your performance in many parts of life. I lobby for weights earlier in the recipe because it is a method that can be curated to anyone. The nutritional piece is a very delicate situation considering all the different issues people consistently have with their health. Disease, digestion issues, personal preferences, and such—all these can throw a wrench in the recommendations at any given time. The nutritional component takes the longest to get the basics right for most people. Constant iterations with a qualified practitioner will deliver optimal results.

The last two modalities are the icing on the cake and will take your performance to the next level. Most people do not have a thorough plan for addressing previous injuries/performance inhibitions, and this can lead to injury and/or stagnation with performance. Having a professional set up a plan and implement it with you can be one of the best investments one can make. Doing this will add that edge many people are looking for while trying to figure out how to win at achieving their goals.

To dive into performance therapy correctly, a thorough structural assessment needs to be done by a qualified practitioner. Then, with that information, a very specific soft tissue protocol will elevate your body's ability to perform. This combination of weights, nutrition, and combined nervous system/soft-tissue work will help to turn you into a performance champion.

The data piece is being vetted across the board all over the world with more companies jumping in the mix. The great thing about the patented data that Omegawave (OW) brings to the table is to not only track data but to make recommendations from that data. This is where it stands out. Numerous professional organizations use OW to make real-time decisions on what load and volume to use with a particular athlete or team. This technology can now be in the consumer's hands. You can test yourself in the morning or a bit before your training session, and the data will provide information on what systems to not work (which, in my opinion, is better than knowing which systems to train), and how and what to train on a specific day.

Now that you have a roadmap of what pieces to use to produce optimal performing humans who have learned to expect high-performance results, Program Delta will be an unbelievable resource to many who are seeking the edge to become a high performer in any field. While traits like focus and dedication are important, we're in a world where high-performers need to find new and innovative ways to continue to be at the top of their game to win. Products like Omegawave and strategies like Program Delta are increasingly important for cutting-edge peak performers.

About the Author

Bryan Sauder partners with individuals and organizations to discover and implement next-level human performance strategy solutions that lead to positive ROI outcomes.

With over 18 years of coaching and human performance development expertise and 16-plus years in nutrition and supplementation, he's amassed a vast toolbox of practical people and performance-related solutions. Bryan has focused these strengths into equipping, advising, encouraging, and challenging others to unleash their potential and make a difference in their lives.

Working in partnership with CEOs, athletes, and highly driven individuals, Bryan challenges these executives and athletes to discover the roadblocks that hold them back, advises them through the process of solution-creation and implementation, and takes their knowledge and performance to the next level.

For more information on how Bryan curates all of the modalities together into an optimal performing recipe, you can email him or check out his website.

Email: coachsauder@outlook.com
Website: www.edgepd.store

CHAPTER TWENTY-EIGHT
CREATE SUCCESS WITH EASE

By Alaina Schwartz, JD
Business and Mindset Coach
New York, New York

Those who flow as life flows know they need no other force.
—Lao Tzu

We are all born for greatness, to fulfill a purpose. We get to choose whether we express it and to what degree. Learning to tap into flow states will help ensure your greatness is realized.

I understand high performers. Growing up, my parents motivated me to perform at peak levels through fear tactics and punishment. I learned to identify my worth with my accomplishments. I was loved when I was successful, so I became more successful.

I was a lawyer in the music industry for 18 years in New York City. I built a multiple six-figure law practice. My career culminated as the Executive Vice President of the largest independent music company in the world. Thing is, I never wanted to be a lawyer. It was my parent's agenda.

I kept thinking if I were more successful, I'd finally be happy. Except, I was miserable and became very physically ill. Not living my purpose and pushing myself to work 60- to 80-hour weeks in a career I hated finally took its toll on my body. I developed autoimmune diseases and couldn't hold pregnancies. This was the two-by-four that hit me across my head from the Universe that I needed to wake myself up.

I actually walked away from it all, having no idea what I was going to do next. I slammed into a "dark night of the soul." Some might call it a midlife crisis, but it can happen at any age and usually births your purpose. All the structures of my life collapsed. I left my mid six-figure career, the prestige, my identity as a lawyer, being the primary income earner in my family. My marriage fell apart. I moved out of Manhattan to Upstate New York, knowing no one and losing much of my community. Finally, my deep financial runway ran out, and I went into massive debt.

To get myself out of the living hell I was in, I discovered tools and techniques that helped me rewire my brain. I learned how to eliminate the limiting beliefs which were creating my suffering, how Universal law works to create our reality, and how to move into flow states at will.

I became a business and mindset coach/mentor and blended my years of experience as a business strategist with principles that help align a person's energetic frequency to create an invincible mindset and peak states of performance.

Almost every high achiever I've worked with drives themselves to prove they really are good enough (often to parents, but always to themselves). Yeah, they're highly accomplished, but rarely do they feel satisfied and fulfilled. There's still an emptiness inside of them, a void they're trying to fill through their next accomplishment. It is a never-ending cycle of chasing satisfaction through achievement.

There's a much easier way. A way that creates deep satisfaction and fulfillment, and allows you to express the true greatness inside of you.

Getting into the Zone—Moving in Flow

I'm sure you have all heard about athletes getting into the zone. When athletes train and immerse themselves and hyper-focus, they reach zone states. You may have experienced a flow state at some point too. States where it feels like everything is going right. There's a fluidity between your body and mind. Your senses are heightened, and you have a deep sense of clarity. There's effortless momentum. Time seems to stand still. You feel like you're on fire and nothing could go wrong. Sometimes it lasts an hour, sometimes days.

This state of flow is accessible to everyone, in whatever you're doing. And unlike what Csikszentmihalyi says about it being attainable during intense and challenging activities, you can cultivate flow even in passive and relaxing times too.

So what would it be like to have flow states as your new normal?

You can! It is possible. Just like going to the gym to build muscle, you can cultivate flow.

When operating at peak states of performance, you move in flow. I believe a winning mindset is removing resistance to flow, as flow is our natural state. Winning is not the finale, but being in the moment, without regard to the end result. There's still effort, but it isn't hustle and grind. There's an easy, graceful feeling to it. It births inspiration, creativity, and access to higher levels of intelligence, resources, synchronicities, and opportunities seem to just present themselves, generating inspired and intelligent action. You *know* what to do.

You don't have to run 20 miles every day to get into flow to make your life easier, more impactful, satisfying, and fulfilling. All you have to do is train your mind.

The Cause of Hustle and Grind

While there's a time for hustle, hustle is the inverse of flow. So, if you're hustling, grinding, or stressed, it's almost impossible to get into flow.

As a former lawyer, I get hustle and grind. It was my usual state. Yet when I look at the major successes I had in my lawyering days and as a coach, all of them came from being in flow. Incredible clients and opportunities seemingly magically appeared. I wasn't trying, I was energetically aligned. Times where I trusted that everything would work out, even if I couldn't see the evidence at the moment. The opportunities came to me because I got out of my own way.

Seventy percent of people are in some state of stress daily. We are the only animals that create stress from our thoughts alone. Think about it; if a rabbit outruns a fox, it moves from fight, flight, or freeze, from its sympathetic nervous system to a state of relaxation (its parasympathetic nervous system) within 20 minutes. The rabbit has moved on and doesn't stay in its sympathetic nervous system by reliving the experience.

With humans, on the other hand, it might go something like this: later that day, you tell a loved one, "You'll never believe what happened to me. I almost got eaten by a fox." Later that week, a friend asks how you're doing, and you retell the story. A year, two years, ten years later, you're still retelling that same story of the trauma you experienced when you almost got eaten by that fox.

Your brain doesn't know the difference between something that's imagined and what is real. Every time you tell that story, your brain thinks you're reliving the experience. You've created a well-worn path in your brain's neural circuitry. Now multiply that by the thousands of negative experiences or things that aren't working in your life, and you've hard-wired your brain, so your tomorrow looks almost identical to yesterday. You're essentially operating from your sympathetic nervous system much of the time. Yet flow states happen from your parasympathetic nervous system.

Earlier I said that 70 percent of people are in stress, created by their thoughts alone. What causes this stress?

Your beliefs create your thoughts and everything you experience in your life. Your beliefs were initially created during the period when you were in your mother's womb until about seven years old. Your brain wasn't fully formed yet, and theta was the predominant brain wave—the brain wave of hypnosis (highly suggestible). You were essentially a subconscious mind, as your conscious mind was not formed yet, with no ability to reject the input you were hearing and observing. You were being programmed by your environment, parents, teachers, society, and the media. Every time you had an experience, you gave a meaning to that experience. Maybe Mom and Dad were arguing about money, and the meaning that you gave that experience was that money was bad or hard to make. We are meaning-making machines.

Beliefs are just decisions you keep on repeating that you made about life and yourself. Those beliefs get hardwired into your brain and create your thoughts. And your brain is like a database, an archive of all the meanings you gave past experiences. So the next time you experience something that feels similar to a past experience, your mind searches the database and ascribes the same meaning you gave the past experience to the current experience. And— *presto*—you've just found evidence to support and reinforce your belief, even though the belief isn't true.

Your thoughts create your feelings. You have a whole pharmacy in your body, so when you have feelings, you release a chemical cocktail. Stress hormones are addictive (i.e., when you feel stressed, overwhelmed, frustrated, angry, etc., your body releases cortisol, adrenaline, etc.). You now have a habit (literally), and your feelings become habituated. So your body wants you to keep repeating the same feelings, by thinking and doing the same things again and again, so it can get another hit of the cocktail! How crazy is that? It's easy to see why it's hard to change habits.

Your feelings dictate the action you take and any reactions you have. As a result, your action-plan has probably looked more like a reaction plan. For example, if you're afraid you'll be rejected because you think you don't have enough experience, even though that hasn't happened, you may not apply for the speaking engagement you really want.

Your action or inaction dictates your results. You're overlaying the meaning you gave past experiences, creating the same thoughts, which keep you focused on the same feelings, so you're taking the same action, and you get more of the same experiences—your future has become your predictable past. Instead of living 80 years, you're living the same year 80 times, just like *Groundhog Day* with Bill Murray!

Creating Mastery

When you apply mastery tools *consistently*, you will break the habit of your beliefs, thoughts, and feelings, and install new empowering beliefs, thoughts and feelings in their place. *You* get to decide what your future looks like.

Those new neural neurosynaptic connections don't become hardwired until there's a repetition of firing and wiring them together. It's like trailblazing a new path in a field of tall grass. If you only go over the path a few times, the grass bounces right back up. *Consistency and repetition are key* ... Otherwise, those new neural pathways for the new empowering beliefs get pruned, and you'll keep repeating the same patterns over and over again. You're here for something different, right?

Research has shown that it takes 66 days to create a new habit. Ask yourself, "What do I really want?" Is it worth doing it for 66 days? Or how about 90 or even 120 days to get it? Of course, it is worth it, or you wouldn't be reading this.

Now ask yourself, "Am I willing to spend less than an hour a day for 66 days to get that thing I really want?" If you're not, then it's clear it's not your priority; otherwise, you'd focus on what it takes. Allow yourself to be uncomfortable and commit. If you are not willing to commit—and it *is* a choice—then you won't build the muscle to create flow states at will. If you don't use the tools consistently, the foundation doesn't get built, and the new neural pathways don't get wired. *Consistency* creates mastery.

Moving into Flow

Flow states happen from the inside out. It requires you to change your state of being (comprised of thoughts and emotions), shift your habits, cultivate self-love and self-care, and alter your environment. You actually become a different person—the truer, more authentic you—rather than an identity construct created by your limiting beliefs, patterns, and lens of perception.

When you really know who you are, why you're here, and how important you are to the whole, you feel deep self-love. You then transcend limiting thoughts that keep you in the stress response. And move in harmony with the Universe. Here's how you can do this:

1. Set clear intentions. You can't have what you want unless you know what you want. So get clear on what you want. Tap into your intuition to get clear. Clear intentions equal clear results.

2. Be kind to yourself. Shut down the itty-bitty shitty committee in your head that speaks badly about you. Do mindset practices daily that neutralize your limiting beliefs (EFT, Inner Child Reparenting work, RIM, Gestalt, hire a mindset coach, see Power Hour below). Choose more empowering thoughts. Treat yourself with the same kindness, love, and compassion you would treat your BFF (best friends forever).

3. Change your habits. The first thing most people do when they wake up is check their phone (go down the email or social media rabbit hole), go to the bathroom, check their phone in the bathroom again, make coffee, shower, etc. You're programming your mind to have the same day as yesterday because you're going through the same (e)motions. Do something different!

Don't check your phone for 30 to 60 minutes upon waking. Instead, before your feet hit the floor to get out of bed, focus on three things you are grateful for (really *feel* the gratitude). We've all heard so much about the benefits of gratitude. You cannot be in gratitude and some form of suffering (anxiety, depression, anger, frustration, etc.) at the same time. Gratitude moves you into your parasympathetic nervous system.

Start a Power Hour—if you don't have an hour in the morning, then start with 20 minutes. You can decide what fits into your Power Hour. I suggest meditation, journaling (ideas, inspiration, gratitude for things in your life now and future things you want in the present tense as if they've already happened), then listening to or reading something uplifting. Divide the time equally.

Exercise regularly—movement is key and causes the release of feel-good hormones!

Feed your mind positive, uplifting food. Stop tuning into media that focuses on negativity (news, social media, violent programs, etc.) by going on a low or no media/news diet. Limit the amount of time you spend on social media. If you feel you must know what's going on, then eliminate negative posts or people from your feed, set a timer, or put on a song or two, and be done with social media when the song is up. Find positive news outlets. Low vibration media makes *you* low vibration. Maintaining consistent flow states requires raising your vibration.

Think, act, and behave like a peak performer, like a winner. Are you interested in creating a seven-figure company? How would a seven-figure business owner feel, solve problems, spend their time or money? Practice feeling-izations (visualization with feeling) daily, so you're living into the feeling of your goal achieved (add it to your Power Hour).

Eliminate lack-language. Language is a prayer you speak out to the Universe. Words are energy. You create your reality as you speak. Words are things and also a reflection of your subconscious programming. When you speak lack-language, you receive more lack in your lived experience. "Should," "Need," "Try," "Can't," "I can't afford," and "Have to" in particular. They're all disempowering, scarcity language. Ditch lack-language.

4. *Self-care is not a luxury, it's a necessity.* It's not about bubble baths although it can be. It's about ensuring that you fuel your tank daily, so it doesn't run out of gas. Your car stops running on empty. So do you. Build a life you don't need a vacation from. Do something every day that fuels your soul. Self-care is a form of self-love.

5. *Recognize that mistakes and failures are "missed takes,"* providing only feedback, data, and information. Take the insight, implement it, and move on. It's not personal or about you. "Failures" happen on the way to success, they're not moving you in the opposite direction, unless you miss the gold nuggets. Most highly successful people experience more failures than success, but their successes are greater, and they meet "failures" with resilience. Fail forward and fail fast to learn, implement and iterate.

6. *Eliminate toxic people from your* life. Categorize people into three minute, three hour and three day people. Three minute people are unsupportive or negative people, often draining your energy. Three hour people are people who support you, lift you up and leave you feeling more empowered after being with them. Eliminate those who are three-minute people from your life where possible. Make sure you spend the appropriate time with the right people and minimize the time with three-minute people if you can't eliminate them completely.

7. *Focus on what you can control.* The only thing you can control are your thoughts. So it's pointless to focus on things out of your control. However, the magic is that your thoughts create your emotions, both of which determine your results. So you control your results by changing your thoughts. When you create *mastery* of your thoughts and emotions, you master your life.

I could write a chapter on each of the seven points above. What I've provided is just enough for you to get started. Follow the prescription, and you'll be well on your way to tapping into flow states at will. Remember, it requires repetition, consistency, and persistence. Coupled with commitment, it means all that you desire, and more, is possible for you with *ease*. Game on!

About the Author

Alaina Schwartz is a speaker, author, and business and mindset mentor. At 14, Alaina suffered a traumatic brain injury, and her mother was told she'd have permanent brain damage. Her mother retrained Alaina's brain to a full recovery. Today, we call that neuroplasticity. Then, after 18 years as an attorney in the music industry and the Executive VP of the largest independent music company, she lost everything. Her personal life completely unraveled. She became hyper-focused on rebuilding her life and rewiring her brain again for success and fulfillment. She has created multiple six-figure companies, and a beautiful life since. As a business and mindset coach, she uses those experiences and her training as the foundation of her work with entrepreneurs, helping them scale their income and impact working 20 plus hours a week less. Alaina's mission is to help people be who they truly are so they can live their purpose and potential.

Email: support@alainaschwartz.com
Website: www.alainaschwartz.com
LinkedIn: https://www.linkedin.com/in/alainaschwartz/

CHAPTER TWENTY-NINE

HOW TOP PERFORMERS ACHIEVE EXTRA-ORDINARY RESULTS

By Dr. Natalia S. Seybold
Executive Development and Transformation Coach
Gold Beach, Oregon

"It would be great to get your opinion, after all, you and your team are the gold standard."

This comment from a colleague caught our attention since we too felt humbled by the level of talent we had just encountered within the ranks of our organization. This comment was directed at Roland's team. Roland and his team were well-known for their advancements in medical imaging and women's health. Roland's team had just introduced the ultrasound product line to our group of 50 portfolio managers and shared the strategic cadence his team used to execute their innovation plan. Behind the technical roadmaps, we saw their genuine care for people, unparalleled expertise in the industry, and unrelenting desire to improve the human experience. From portable ultrasound units designed for remote and underserved communities to 3D sonogram printing for vision-impaired parents, their dedication to research and advancing medical technology was immediately clear.

Driven by this desire to continuously improve, optimize, or enhance the world around them, they had set strategic goals and meticulously planned each step of their mission. Being fully immersed in their environment, they could sense shifting trends and undercurrents, and make decisions that were informed by reality, not just a balance sheet. They held an intrinsic set of values which they used to guide every decision and tradeoff. They were consistent, congruent, self-aware, and authentic. They sought out, and solved, complex problems, building upon one another's success year after year. Together, the synergy, progress, and outcomes they achieved went well beyond the annual bottom line.

They advanced the capabilities of their entire industry into a meaningful, sustainable, and profitable future. The impact they left was long-lasting and often described as "the gold standard," which inspired others to think differently and achieve greater results themselves. This team demonstrated many of the traits common to top performers. In the stories shared below, we'll look at some more commonly shared attributes of top performers with winning mindsets.

A Distinct Style of Leadership

Top performers are extremely talented yet grounded in a sense of purpose and respect. They are not "on their best behavior," nor are they testing out the next best practice or habit to get that promotion at work or to win a new client. Instead, they hold more altruistic values at the core of their being, through which every decision, action, or behavior is automatically filtered. They attract and encourage the same from others and maintain a culture firmly grounded in care and respect for people, and grounded in harmonious and inclusive relationships.

Being autodidactic, top performers invest their time in learning, reflecting, and continuously seeking out opportunities to work alongside peers and solve complex issues. This creates more refinement in their knowledge, skills, and strategy. Their impact is felt, not just in their companies, but also within their communities.

Let's continue to look into some common traits I've witnessed among top-performing leaders.

People Come First

Top performers take every action with consideration for the wellbeing of their people. When Matt, a senior executive responsible for the operations of a

100-year-old, multi-billion-dollar factory, saw the early signs of a recession, he moved quickly to adjust inventory and add new services.

Matt explained simply, "Men like Owen and me don't wait around or go silently into the night and wait for the industry to turn around. We are responsible for this entire community. We won't let it get to the point where we have to decide who gets laid off." He beamed with pride when he talked about the people in his company and their long-standing reputation as top engineers. He never missed an opportunity to share that the current shift leader was the granddaughter of the first female machine engineer who started her career in the same company when it was founded in 1902.

Matt kept the work at the company simple, safe, and rewarding, and developed habits that helped his team to be proactive and flexible. Their responsibility extended beyond physical safety and operations into the psychological and financial wellbeing of their entire community. Ever-present, Matt invited a sense of belonging and empowerment by relating to everyone equally and authentically, taking the time to build others, and refusing to be (or let others fall) a victim of circumstance.

Leaders like Matt see the world around them as a reflection of their own decisions and behaviors. Their way of being resulted in a harmonious, uplifting environment that engaged everyone around them in deeper levels of trust, rapport, and loyalty.

Together in Achievement

Top performers have a clear definition of success that is customer-oriented. This commitment to customer success is behind the design of their products, services, and business models. Every tradeoff or decision considers the impact to the customer's bottom line: did we make or save the customer time or money? What is the true value provided?

"It's common sense," Nora, CTO of a global health information technology provider explained, "If we let our customers fail, who will be left to purchase?" Her approach demonstrated holistic, long-term thinking, and valued economic inclusion of the entire sphere, from supplier to customer and everyone in between. It was embedded into the structure and operations of her company, where she personally mentored each account representative to help customers identify risk, prevent loss, and recover from a financial setback, all pro bono.

Today, hundreds of community hospitals and medical centers across the United States overcame the threat of bankruptcy and remain open to serve the public because of one company's dedication to the success of their community. This propensity to care beyond their own success, together with unmatched expertise and focused execution, are the hallmarks of a top-performing team.

Raising the Bar

The habit of continuously improving how they create value is one of the secrets top-performing companies use to lead in the marketplace. On the outside looking in, we see the robust innovation strategy and highly creative teams that are behind the products and services offered by these companies. Complex value derivatives, multi-channel pricing strategies, and cost models guide what goes into a value-based product design. But a deeper sense of empathy through which an acute understanding of unspoken or unmet needs emerges and takes the creativity of top performers to the next level. These entrepreneurs are genuinely troubled by unmet need or unnecessary suffering in a way that they cannot help but to solve. They seek out opportunities to improve upon what is currently acceptable in the industry, whether by competitors or themselves, and in so doing, they introduce value-laden and highly differentiated solutions that are difficult to copy.

Doug, a lead innovation architect, shared his personal feelings of failure when he saw an exhausted and worried father carrying his heavily sedated son through the parking lot. His team of engineers had recently upgraded the imaging technology which now produced the most accurate images of its kind. He wanted to see the new MRI in operation and found, while the images were flawless, the experience of undergoing the imaging process was terrifying to a toddler. The attending nurse explained that 90 percent of children needed sedation. This was common.

While this may have been the normal experience in a clinical setting, the unnecessary pain and trauma were not acceptable to Doug. His empathy and personal values fueled an urge to create a different experience. That evening, he went back to the drawing board. Within days, new designs were drafted, and within weeks, new prototypes were ready. Within months, the redesigned MRI had proven to drastically reduce the need for pediatric sedation, setting a new clinical standard for the industry. The re-designed MRIs can now be found in pediatric health centers globally. To the competition, this single product decision may have seemed as if it had been years in the making, around fancy whiteboards and gourmet snacks, when in fact, it happened one evening in a parking lot.

Meticulous Planning and Frontloading of Targets

Top performers create the future by crafting plans three to five years at a time and by identifying the subsequent targets and capabilities to be achieved each year. They work to achieve the majority of their annual targets earlier in the year, accelerating performance in nine-month (versus 12-month) periods. This opens opportunity later in the year to make up for shortfalls, should they happen. They have time to observe and adapt to changes (learn), maintain a healthy and sustainable pace, and celebrate accomplishments.

Shane, a chief learning officer for a leading medical device company, has a keen ability to prioritize and collapse actions, so only the most impactful tasks are done. He knows the capability (skill) and capacity (time) of his team and their customers, and can accurately predict time to the minute it may take to complete a task. He invests time with his team to increase synergy and try new techniques. This allows him and his team to develop product and service delivery roadmaps with clearly defined priorities and actionable plans that deliver predictable, timely, and quality solutions. Having a clear vision of success, and well-defined goals and milestones to get there, allows them to be self-managing, autonomous, and empowered to make decisions.

Since the team values time as a resource, each hour is spent in meaningful tasks that advance the objective. Bottle necks are removed to drive flowing and focused execution. They avoid distractions and unplanned, irrelevant, or "pet" projects with hidden agendas. Each meeting has a purpose, agenda, and outcome. Time is spent doing value-added work, versus talking about what needs to be done. They understand the time and effort required to accomplish each task well and without cutting corners. Any deviation from their standards of safety, quality, delivery, or value is treated as a risk.

Top performers also understand the common pitfalls a customer may experience and set preventative measures to error proof the process. While planning, they study where issues might occur and develop alternate plans or back-up solutions. Their relentless focus on priorities enables them to scale up to meet even higher demand and double their profits year after year.

Transforming the World, One Leader at a Time

Jeff had been pulled out of retirement twice. At the time I met him, he was the chief learning officer and campus dean of an internationally renowned corporate university. He was hiring a program manager to launch a new series of workshops for emerging executives who would deepen their interpersonal acuity, develop inclusive and innovative leadership strategies, and practice more productive habits of mind.

On my interview day with him, I could tell he was very well-loved on campus. He knew the names of everyone in the C-suite and on the cleaning crew as well. He treated all with equal regard. He knew what was happening in their lives and what mattered to them. He advocated for contractors and employees alike. His head and his heart held an immense capacity to engage with and improve the experience of everyone around him, to hold space for, and to bring fresh, clear perspective on their dreams. He never missed an opportunity to be fully present. He was gentle in giving insight and generous in sharing his expertise. He saw pure potential in people and mentored them until they overcame limitations and blind spots. He had a unique way of helping others to stand fully in their role and of helping them broaden their vision. Everyone he coached would go on to achieve more than they could imagine. It was easy to see why he was chosen to launch new learning centers in Brazil, China, India, and the Middle East. He supported women's professional development programs within their communities, advancing the progress of women in business in Shanghai and Abu Dhabi.

When I was offered the chance to work on Jeff's team, it was an honor and a life-changing event. I was excited to bring new experiences into the curriculum, and I spent a lot of time advertising the program, the research, the techniques, and the benefits behind it. I treated the program as a business product, driving for enrollments, interviewing faculty, testing content, doing all the things an efficient program manager would do.

One day, over coffee, Jeff said to me, "Don't work so hard to push the ocean, take time to reflect on the waves you are creating." It was a gentle reminder that while we want all our leaders to execute flawlessly, it is important that they do not lose themselves along the way. We are greater than the goals we accomplish. Our power lies in our way of being, in who and how we are to others. Centered in our values and authentically expressing our talents, we influence and inspire others to reignite their own potential, and to be the best expression of their ideals and values.

I could tell story after story of the extraordinary men and women I've been fortunate to meet—top performers who have inspired greatness in others since what they do is undeniably rewarding. They seem to effortlessly achieve whatever they set out to accomplish, through detailed levels of planning, clear intention, and the laser-like focus it takes to make it all happen. They practice flexible and resilient habits of mind, and deeper levels of self-awareness and presence. They are clear about their mission and immerse fully within their environment. In turn, they are able to tune down distractions and engage others in a unique and inspiring atmosphere, creating meaningful and loyal relationships, where others will follow in their footsteps long after they have left.

For true top performers, life isn't about winning for selfish reasons. It is about creating a collective winning mindset that can be both profitable in business and gratifying as a way of life.

About the Author

Natalia S. Seybold is an executive transformation coach who has spent decades researching and developing techniques that have enabled top performing leaders to take their vision to the next level, develop winning business strategies, and deliver breakthrough results. She helps executive teams to achieve an indomitable market brand, sustainable financial outcomes, and enduring customer loyalty. Her clients are well known and sought after in their respective fields as highly skilled innovators who set new industry standards by re-imagining what is possible and making it real.

Natalia has bachelor's degrees in psychology and completed her MBA and doctorate in business at the University of Sarasota, Florida (Argosy University). She attained certification as master trainer and peak performance coach. She has written and facilitated over 50 workshops and executive development programs, which have been featured at internationally renowned corporate universities. Her programs have been awarded Best in Industry by Aon Hewitt and General Electric Company.

Email: hello@nataliaseybold.com
Website: www.nataliaseybold.com
Twitter: @natalia_seybold.com
LinkedIn: https://www.linkedin.com/in/nseybold/
Facebook: www.facebook.com/nataliaseybold

CHAPTER THIRTY

CHALLENGING LIMITS WITH A POSSIBILITIES MINDSET

By Vallerie Skelly
Founder, Skelly Performance Coaching Inc.
Cambridge, United Kingdom / Vancouver, Canada

When nothing is sure, everything is possible.
—Margaret Drabble

We go about our days invested in our individual plights, with the full intention of being effective in our interaction with others. This means showing up as our best self in order to make the biggest impact. We need our teams organized and working well to be constantly innovating, moving the business in ever-changing, competitive markets.

With so much daily pressure, we naturally take mental shortcuts to get through the clutter. What we may not realize is the mental shortcuts we take can be laden in unconscious expectations of others and ourselves. These expectations are littered in personal beliefs that can be rigid and defiant to change. This can hold us (and our peers) back from realizing our true potential, challenging limits, and achieving overall wellbeing.

The more we value things outside our control, the less control we have.
—Epictetus

Living for My Expectations

Without realizing it, expectations may be undermining your professional journey in life, dampening your progress and, thus, your personal fulfillment. We all have expectations that things should go a specific way. For example, I should get that promotion in a few months because I have been working on this project day in and day out. Or, I hit my sales target six months in a row, so I fully expect to get that big raise. Or, I've been spending months with Bill getting him up and running on this project, so he will surely back me up when I present my ideas at the next meeting.

Expectations themselves are not unusually threatening to us. But they become threatening when we become so dependent on their completion that we become disillusioned, disappointed, defeated, and even reactive when events don't go our way. When we feel disappointed by an outcome, it is likely that the expectation did not match up with our beliefs surrounding the situation. We then feel disappointment, and we carry that with us for days, months, or even years, depending on the depth of the felt experience.

Because expectations are wrapped in the future, they narrow our line of vision, stamp out our creativity, and close the door to innovative choices. When we mentally exist in future-thinking, we miss out on living in the present moment. By living in the future, we create stress and anxiety in our lives as the grip of expectations holds us hostage to an uncertain future that may not occur. While we are in its grip, our present behavior and thinking becomes rigid, causing us to react and behave more unfavorably rather than questioning for clarity and meaning.

In most cases, we are not aware that our expectations for the future have created a tightly boxed reality only known to us. This, unexamined and, therefore, unconscious reality, minimizes our effectiveness not only for ourselves but for the people around us. Because this reality is set in the future, we become stuck in drying cement. Others may try and persuade us to move, but living in the future has taken away our freedom of mobility, insight, and perspective.

Going one step further, expectations, when left unchecked, can inhibit our life's course, shaping the direction we take or don't take in our career and life. Years later, we may look back at decisions made and wonder why we didn't notice other opportunities.

When the Past Becomes Your Future

Expectations are tightly rolled up personal beliefs (something believed to be true, but with little proof) about how future situations and events will be experienced.

Are we a product of our past? A very natural part of being human is unintentionally and unconsciously carrying our past experiences with us. The accumulation and integration of our past experiences has created a habit of expectations. These habits have solidified their value in our daily lives, becoming a part of our belief system.

As an example of this, my father always believed that a clean and organized office was a sign of a person who took their work seriously. Now when I see others with a messy work environment, I get instantly frustrated as I expect that person will have terrible output. I have, in fact, created a rigid expectation through my belief about the meaning of a messy desk. Totally unintentionally, I even treat that individual differently than someone with a tidy desk.

Sometimes we expect too much from others because we
would be willing to do that much for them.
—Unknown

Our well-purposed and lived habits of expectations have gotten us to where we are today in our careers and personal lives. We have come to rely on our expectations, even creating rules and schemas about how the world should operate. We believe that every action will receive a certain reaction. For example, if I'm pleasant and cooperative, the next person should be the same. When I work hard, the next person will follow suit. Whereas it appears this behavior makes life easier to manage, it is, in many cases, leading us down the path of disappointment and frustration, with stress and anxiety looming close behind.

Expectations of Others

The rule of expectation is when we make decisions based upon what we think others expect from us. Basically, we form and carry out behaviors and actions based on what we believe others want to see in us and our performance.

When an employee is given the opportunity to speak at a general meeting, they may feel stress and anxiety leading up to the day. When they bring awareness to the feeling, they will realize the stress is driven by an expectation that they had better nail the presentation or their peers will think less of them and executives will criticize them and discount their value to the organization.

When we are consistently bombarded with these stresses of others perceived expectations, we can eventually shut down, decide to play it safe, or not participate at all. You see this exact scenario play itself out in sports, when an athlete has a goal kick or a hockey player has a breakaway, and they fumble the ball or puck, and miss the net all together. We use terms like "I was in my head" or "I choked."

Perceived expectations can have detrimental effects on our performance when our focus is removed from the well-practiced physical part of our sport, to thinking about not disappointing others. During a goal kick or an ice hockey breakaway, chances of scoring are greatly increased if the player stays in the moment rather than allowing emotions of celebration or defeat creep in regarding thinking about the outcome of the pending shot. In terms of a winning mindset, winning, in this moment, is taking the best shot possible (the action), not seeing the ball or puck hit the net (the result).

The Language of Expectations

You can hear the presence of expectations in the words we, and others, use in our daily lives. These words can be verbal but also notably occur in the form of self-talk. Phrases like "I need to," "I have to," and "I expect to" are very fixed and unyielding. This kind of desperate language gives the appearance of a person who is lacking confidence and control. Language like this is part of a one-dimensional mentality removing any opportunity of rephrasing or altering course. When we become aware that we or someone else is using this language, it is beneficial to ask questions that will create insights and awareness of this pernicious mindset.

- With "I need to …" ask: *Why do you need to do this? What would happen if you don't do it?*
- With "I have to …" ask: *What would happen if you didn't have to? What would happen if you didn't?*
- With "I expect to …" ask: *What will happen if that doesn't occur? How would you feel if you didn't expect this?*

Here are a couple further examples of self-limiting statements full of negativity that will have you questioning your competence and steamrolling your confidence.

- "I should be so much further along in my career."
- "I should have much more to show for the age I am at."

By questioning the terms you use, you create an awareness of your beliefs. This awareness brings with it clarity of thought, and it starts moving you towards other more positive forms of language. This process cracks open the door, so you can begin identifying different options and breaking the habits and rigid schemas of how the world should perform.

A Mindset of Expectations Limits Both Me and You

As discussed earlier, we create expectations based around our beliefs, then project them forward in the form of a highly anticipated outcome. This type of behavior limits our chances of observing all other possibilities and causes us to abandon creativity, human potential, and helpful collaborative relationships.

When you exist in a state of expectations, it robs others and you from living in the greatness of the present moment. Expectations consistently drive and then park the mind in the future, causing you to miss much of what is happening directly in front of you. Important leadership skills like active-listening become difficult to perform when you are not able to situate yourself in the present moment, missing and even dismissing others' expressed thoughts and ideas.

If we are not listening, we are projecting our rigid expectations onto others, limiting individual and group thinking in the organization. Similarly, when we expect others to behave in a certain light because of past dealings, we are painting a permanent picture of them, writing them off and any perspectives that could prove helpful. When this happens, we create an environment of incompetency, with mundane, sterile interactions.

Our expectations can create significant personal anxiety when the outcomes do not match up with our internally created schemas or beliefs. We run the risk of becoming detached and disillusioned. In a sense, we become blindfolded, living in a discontented one-pony show where frustration and unhappiness are the new normal.

These high expectations will almost never transpose into a greater level of wellbeing and happiness. They will also not help us to achieve or reach a higher level of performance.

A Possibilities Mindset—Expect Nothing. Be Curious About Everything

The Stoics were very enthusiastic about expectations, stating that because they are a part of our consciousness, we are able to control them.

The good news is, we do not have to continue down the dead-end road of living with expectations. When we acknowledge the inner tug-of-war between a mindset of expectations or possibilities, we begin to open the mind to a new reality, one where limits are pushed and questioned with adventure and curiosity.

By making a conscious decision to move towards focusing on what is in and what is not in our control, we start the process of relaxing our grip on the future and our need to set expectations.

We begin to understand that our actions, in business and in life, will create a reaction, and this is when we must detach ourselves from wanting control of the outcomes. By acting with our best intentions while remaining in constant contact with our values and those of the organization, we are advancing towards growth.

When you make a conscious decision to work hard to move a project forward, don't think about the expectation of a raise; think about how you are living within your values. Allow your personal win to be a job well-executed, not the result of a raise or accolades from others. When this happens, you are opening up the world to possibilities of furthering your career and wellbeing in a harmonious way. If, in the end, you don't receive a raise, then you will open up to other possibilities like making a conscious decision to ask for one.

A Possibilities Mindset

When I see possibility, I'm more likely to achieve it.

Roger Bannister was a British middle-distance runner and neurologist who went on to do the impossible when he broke the four-minute mile back on May 6, 1954. Before Bannister, it was thought impossible for a human to run a four-minute mile. Once Bannister broke the four-minute barrier, multiple others completed the same feat right after Bannister. What changed? What was once believed to be impossible, was now a new reality. A shift occurred as a possibilities-mindset of "what could be" emerged. Now coined the Bannister effect, this feat shone a light on the psychological barriers we carry within ourselves in the form of expectations. When we free our mind from the constraints of limits and the beliefs that support them, we enter the exciting world of possibilities.

A possibilities-mindset is firmly grounded in the present moment, where real opportunities exist and are discovered. Existing in the present opens your senses to a world of creativity and exploration, a place where there are no limits. In saying this, a possible mindset is a sort of awakening, bringing awareness to your thinking and, thus, leading you to question your beliefs.

We are not always in a place where we appreciate what we have when we are constantly expecting more. We see this when we compare ourselves to others regarding where we are stationed in life. Doing this, we end up missing out on the richness of our present environment. With a possibilities-mindset, we are less reactive and more curious; we enter a room with enthusiasm, wanting to understand and realize others' valuable perspectives.

The real fun starts when we think in terms of what "could be" as opposed to what "is." By thinking in these terms, we give ourselves and others around us permission to be creative and think outside the usual boundaries. Plus, we begin to listen with real intent to understand. A possibilities-mindset can still be future-driven by creating goals, the difference being we understand that this is what we "want" to happen. The goal we are setting is open-ended and modified as new information comes into play. This is an important part of the possibilities mindset as there are a lot of variables that can affect a goal.

Embracing Possibilities

First things first, let's perform a check-up from the neck up.

A quick and effective exercise that triggers the process of recognizing your thoughts is by simply wearing an elastic band or bracelet. When you feel an emotion, give the bracelet a little snap. This is your reminder to stop, *arret*, *detener* what you're doing and become aware of what is happening in the moment. Bring your awareness to the emotion that triggered this event. What were you thinking when this happened? Is the thought full of expectations about the future and the outcome of an event? If so, ask "Why do I need the event to turn out this way?" There will be an abundance of information that you will discover about your beliefs.

For example: I feel an emotion, and I snap the band, bringing my awareness to the present moment. I was thinking about my presentation next week and that if my audience doesn't find my information impactful, they will think I'm a failure, and they will discount my abilities.

With my pause, I now change to a possibilities mindset by remembering that I cannot control what people will think about my presentation. Therefore, I will remain in the present and stay within the realm of what is in my control. Meaning I will prepare well and do my best, then let the chips fall where they may. End of story.

Moving the possibilities mindset to focus on the benefits that align with your values and purpose is very important. In my presentation example, I might change my thoughts to: "This preparation and presentation will increase my knowledge, I will become a more experienced presenter, and this will further my business exposure."

By becoming mindful of our expectations, we can consciously decide to change our course towards a healthier, more effective way of thinking and behaving. A possibilities mindset is mixed with active-listening, curiosity, and divergent thinking. When our interactions exist in the present with a mindset of inclusivity and limitless possibilities, we start to bring it to the world rather than expecting the world to bring it to us.

About the Author

Vallerie D. Skelly is a high-performance and executive coach with Skelly Performance Coaching Inc. Val specializes in coaching business professionals and athletes to help them overcome their self-imposed limits, to achieve total confidence, purpose, personal authenticity, and presence. She has spent 20 years in management within the automotive industry where she learned a skillset necessary in creating a winning team and organization. Val followed up her management experience attending Cambridge University in the United Kingdom, studying coaching and cognitive psychology.

Val was a player and lead organizer of the world's longest ice hockey game, where 40 women went on to set a world record while raising awareness and donations for Cystic Fibrosis Canada. The game was played night and day ending after 234 hours and 65 minutes (10 days). An inspiring movie called *Lace Bite* about this feat is available on Amazon.

Email: vskelly@skellyperformancecoaching.com
Website: https://www.skellyperformancecoaching.com
linkedin.com/in/vallerieskelly
facebook.com/Skellyperformancecoaching
@Skellyperformancecoaching (Instagram)
@Skellyperformancecoaching (YouTube)

CHAPTER THIRTY-ONE

THE WINNING MINDSET IS A DISCOVERY MINDSET

By Jennifer Stirrup
Founder of Data Relish, AI, Business Intelligence
London, England, United Kingdom

"APPLY WITHIN"

You once told me
You wanted to find
Yourself in the world—
And I told you to
First apply within,
To discover the world
within you.

You once told me
You wanted to save
The world from all its wars—
And I told you to
First save yourself
From the world,
And all the wars

You put yourself
Through.

—Suzy Kassem

You might hear the phrase "growth mindset" quite often. Since Carol Dweck's 2007 book, *Mindset: The New Psychology of Success*, the idea of growth mindset has been used in different contexts from nursery schools to major corporations. Business leaders such as Satya Nadella, for example, talk about a growth mindset all the time.

The concept of growth mindset can be interpreted in a variety of ways. It can be described as individuals who believe their talents can be developed through hard work, good strategies, and input from others. It is often contrasted with the "fixed mindset," which is the belief that thoughts are innate and unchanging. As a consequence, the individual with a fixed mindset believes they have a ceiling on their thinking and cannot develop it further. In this situation, the individual has a negative thought-pattern. This person gives up on challenges easily and does not accept feedback. It's easy to see why it is preferable to say one holds a growth mindset rather than a fixed mindset since it is appealing to define oneself as having more positive characteristics than the negative characteristics associated with the fixed mindset.

Let's face it, who honestly wants to describe themselves as having a fixed mindset? The problem is that most people with a fixed mindset don't know it.

Growth Mindset "Lite"

The concept of the growth mindset is, at heart, very forgiving. When someone makes a mistake, that person moves on from the mistake (while adapting because of their growth mindset), and everyone forgets about it. Sounds great, right?

However, that's the *easy* part about a growth mindset, and it misses out the bigger meaning. You could call it "growth mindset lite." The more complete interpretation of the growth mindset has been missed somewhere. So what's wrong with the growth mindset? The reality is, people do not always learn from mistakes, even with a growth mindset. The growth mindset is a "get out of jail" card. It's the easy way to get out of bad behaviour, and repeating the behaviour. Also, if the person is focused on appearances, it pushes the onus on everyone else to forgive. Mistakes are repeated, and individuals chalk it up to just another lesson from a growth mindset person. Again, it becomes a talisman to fend off blame. In other words, they do not truly learn from their mistake, and they misuse the magic phrase "growth mindset" as an excuse to repeat the same mistake. Since people's memories are short, the misuse of the growth mindset as an excuse does not get picked up.

While being used as an excuse for mistakes, the whole point of having a growth mindset is missed—to have a growth mindset, you actually have to grow. Intentionally or not, people do not always learn from the growth mindset. Worse, it can even become a habitual excuse preventing growth rather than promoting it. Using the growth mindset as an excuse, people do not move forward to applying what they have learned. Instead, they get stuck in a growth mindset phase where they are using growth as an excuse, but they do not actually grow. How can we resolve the situation?

Growth is painful, and it happens when we are out of our comfort zone. Growth involves change. People do not like change, and they do not like to be changed. Change is a powerful mechanism. Change is the impulse that generates innovation for the leader and the organisation. Change also involves fear, defensiveness, and uncertainty, which is similar to the fixed mindset behaviour that people strive to avoid. Together, this creates a situation that does not promote healthy change, and encourages a response that discourages growth. Under these circumstances, how can we direct ourselves back towards a true growth mindset, which can also be called a winning mindset?

Moving Forward: The Discovery Mindset

How do you move forward to a winning mindset?

As leaders, we need to develop a "discovery mindset" before we can have a growth mindset. The objective of the discovery mindset is to be very clear on our goals by confirming our current status. Once we have a clear grounding, it is easier to find a path forward to our unique leadership style for ourselves and for the organisation we lead.

I learned that courage was not the absence of fear, but the triumph over it. The brave man [person] is not he [she, they] who does not feel afraid, but he [she, they] who conquers that fear.
—Nelson Mandela

Fear will always play a part in your life, but here is the secret: you get to decide how much fear will stop you. Take courage in slight improvements along the way, and have faith that you get what you work for and what you work at. Here's some advice to get started.

Give Yourself a Professional Review

Work to know yourself first and be honest about identifying what you are good at. To do this activity, it may be uncomfortable to admit to yourself that you are good, or not good at, at something. Journaling is a great way to see patterns in your behaviour over time. Our lives move so fast it can be difficult to see repeat patterns in our behaviour, making it more difficult to recognize them. Write it down. Over time, you can review your repeated behaviour patterns to yourself.

You Don't Get What You Want; You Get What You Work For

What are you working toward? Are you working on the right things? If you spend time logging your activities, you can see better, over time, what you are spending time on. Then, review your activities and work out what you could delegate or pass to someone else, so you can spend your time most wisely. With the data, you can hear the customer voice if you listen to it. By analysing your time carefully, you can work out what people, including clients, ask from you, and you can work to make sure that you can deliver what they expect. As part of the discovery mindset, you need to have a baseline to start from, so you can track your progress.

Discovery also means finding mistakes as well as achievements. You can't grow when you don't admit mistakes to yourself or other people. Don't just chalk up mistakes as being part of a growth mindset. Analyze and actively learn from them, sometimes by looking at your mistakes with other people. This might be a hard thing to do, but the mark of a leader is not to take the easy path.

Work to Identify How Others Perceive You

*O, wad some Power the giftie gie us. To see oursels as others see
us! It wad frae monie a blunder free us, An' foolish notion.*

This translates as:

*I wish for the power to give us this gift: Being able to
see ourselves the way other people see us.*
—Robert Burns

Journaling can help you to discover how others perceive you by helping
you to see repeated patterns in how people respond to you. If, for example,
one of your frustrations is that people (or your team) do not always do what
you request in the manner that you ask, then perhaps the outcome is that you
need to get better at setting direction and expectations. The discovery mindset
can help you to understand if your frustrations are generated as a result of a
reaction to you or your communication.

Work Out Which Skills Will Complement
You or Your Organisation

The organisation, or the individual, can develop a discovery mindset to identify better what other people need from them. For sales leaders, for example,
this will mean understanding your MVC—your most valuable customer.

Work out what skills you lack, and be very directed about what you need
to learn. CEOs don't write code during work, for example, since it's not a good
use of their time; they get someone to do it for them. Leaders add a distinctive
value, and your learning needs to be directed towards increasing that value.

Work Out What You Should Delegate and Let It Go

Saying no to something is a yes to something else. As a leader, you will find
it more fulfilling to have an impact that is unique and truly you. Don't waste
your valuable skills by side-stepping into an activity that isn't truly you. Part of
the discovery mindset is working out what you need to let go of. Delegation is
one of the toughest skills to learn, and it's particularly hard to let go of "work
but fun" activities. Let's be honest with ourselves; we all have guilty secret tasks

which are fun but do not contribute to providing maximum value from the time spent to produce maximum value.

As a leader, you can also apply this learning to organisations. If the organisation is focusing on activities that do not directly support the company vision, then they risk not fulfilling customer expectations.

How the Discovery Mindset Relates to the Winning Mindset

The discovery mindset is a journey of continuous detection to help growth. Reflection and meditation are daily practices, and they have real applications to our leadership, our life, and our organisations.

It's also important to watch out for fear, since it can be a brake that stops you, or your teams, from embracing change. Fear is a part of our life, and we can work to recognize it. Fear can be disguised as practicalities, and it is something that we can recognize in ourselves and in other people. Part of the growth mindset is the recognition that individuals can change and develop over time, and that will also involve patience and understanding.

Through this lens, there is a paradox in the winning mindset. We acknowledge that, in some areas, we are not winning. However, as we acknowledge this issue, we can plan to grow and move forward.

Collaboration, rather than competition, is the route to success in leadership. We can bring out the best in other people, by striving to bring out the best in ourselves. The discovery mindset asks us to acknowledge our relationship with ourselves, and also with other people, to recognize our interdependence in generating success. We can support others and be generous to ourselves too by working with others as best we can. This can involve getting real feedback, which is a gift.

The paradox about power is true power comes from giving it away to other people, not keeping it for ourselves. This is how we grow our influence, and we can do better for others by working on our discovery mindset, by discovering how to empower others. It is something that, as individuals and as leaders, we can work on for the rest of our lives. We want the things that are truly worth wanting.

Try again. Fail again. Fail better.
—Samuel Beckett

We fear failing, but the approach of living with a discovery mindset allows us to recognise failure and to grow and learn from our failures and weaknesses. We develop empathy and judge less, and understand more. It will be uncomfortable at times, but we are always moving forward. The discovery mindset is a process of continually testing and questioning ourselves, so that we continue to grow, and we make winning a normal part of our lives.

About the Author

Jennifer Stirrup is the founder and CEO of Data Relish, a UK-based artificial intelligence and business intelligence leadership boutique consultancy delivering data strategy and business-focused solutions. Jen is a recognized leading authority in AI and business intelligence leadership, a Fortune 100 global speaker, and has been named as one of the Top 50 Global Data Visionaries, one of the Top Data Scientists to follow on Twitter and one of the most influential Top 50 Women in Technology worldwide.

Jen has clients in 24 countries on five continents, and she holds postgraduate degrees in AI and cognitive science. Jen has authored books in data and artificial intelligence, has been featured on CBS Interactive and the BBC as well as other well-known podcasts, such as Digital Disrupted, Run As Radio, and her own Make Your Data Work webinar series.

Jen has also given keynotes for colleges, universities, as well as donating her expertise to charities and non-profits as a non-executive director. Jen's keynotes are about AI leadership, diversity and inclusion in technology, digital transformation, and business intelligence. All of Jen's keynotes are based on her two decades-plus years of global experience, dedication, and hard work.

email: hello@data-relish.com
website: data-relish.com

CHAPTER THIRTY-TWO

INVEST IN YOUR HEALTH: BET ON YOURSELF

By Serra Tumay, MS, RD
Sports Performance Dietitian
Delray Beach, Florida

Do the best you can until you know better. Then
when you know better, do better.
—Maya Angelou

During graduate school, my classroom education was coupled with hands-on experiences, involving fieldwork projects and nutrition workshops or presentations. With this, I had the honor of working with numerous schools and youth programs throughout New York City, delivering nutrition education classes to help students build a healthy foundation. The first lesson for each youth program (with participants' ages ranging from five to nine) was always the same regardless of demographic, location, or age group. I would bring four different fruits and vegetables to have the students examine and taste. We would then discuss their reactions and chat about the benefits of eating these foods. This little activity would help me gauge the students' prior experiences, if any, with these specific fruits and vegetables or similar foods. To my surprise, their reactions were very positive, with the majority having not tried the foods before, but willing and open to new tastes. However, out of the more than eight schools and nearly 300 students, one encounter stands out far above the others.

I had prepped for this session as I did for all the other sessions. To this particular school in the Bronx, I brought tomatoes, carrots, yellow peppers, and blueberries—aiming to showcase foods of different colors. Like always, I set up a station with samples of each for every student in the class. From the moment the lesson began, there was one student who made his aversion for these foods very outwardly apparent by yelling and crying. A negatively vocal student like this can easily offset the entire activity if their thoughts start to gain traction with their peers. To ensure this did not happen, I approached the student to understand his dismay. I was truly shocked when this fourth grader could not name any of the foods correctly, and instead kept calling them each "salad," including the blueberries. He kept repeating that he doesn't like salad, despite claiming that he had never tried these foods previously. By the end of the lesson, after seeing the excitement of his peers, he ended up not only trying a piece of each, but also asking for more carrots and blueberries.

While I was shaken by this encounter at the time, the more I started to run the scenario in my mind, the less baffled I became. On average, nutrition is not seen as a priority, especially at a young age. Ironically, that is the time at which it is most important. The nutrients children receive as they are growing will impact how well the brain and body develops. Not only that, but kids start to formulate life-long habits based on their experiences and surroundings. This student may have only seen fresh fruits and vegetables in salads prior to my lesson, leading him to the assumption that they are all referred to as salad. More research is constantly coming out about the implications of nutrition and food on our physical, mental, or social well-being throughout our whole lifecycle. To develop a winning mindset, we need the best physical and mental advantages as possible, and nutrition is one of the best ways to attain this advantage.

The same issues that were apparent in that fourth-grade classroom translate into the workforce. Due to our goal-driven society, health too often takes a backseat. We focus most of our time and energy aiming to fulfill performance markers that we hope will help us excel towards career goals. Constantly on-the-go, we strive to stay motivated and productive. However, peak productivity is influenced by our priorities—it is dependent on our choices in relation to our drive to succeed. In other words, even with the highest of ambitions, some of the choices we make may hinder our progress or stand in the way of greatness.

I unfortunately see this too often in my work as a sports dietitian. For every human, regardless of profession, our body serves as the vehicle guiding us through life. Just like any car needs fuel to drive properly, our body needs the right fuel in the right amount to perform at the highest level. While we can simply trade in or buy a new car in the event of any mishap, we are only given one body and, thus, must prioritize treating it well. If we are both the engine and driver of our own life, it becomes critical to invest in ourselves in order to bet on ourselves.

Return on investment (ROI) is a financial metric calculated by comparing the benefit of an investment to the cost of that investment. Although it is often used in the business sector, it has become the basis of all my initial conversations with clients. As a sports dietitian, it is my job to understand an athlete's needs and goals and then to structure an individualized nutrition plan, helping the athlete nourish, perform, and recover at an elite level.

The field of dietetics is quickly growing and evolving as more people see value in investing in their health. While the upfront costs may seem steep (nutrition services, gym membership, high quality foods, meal delivery, etc.), the benefits of the investment make it well worth it. An overall healthier lifestyle helps our body function properly, which results in feeling and thinking better, ultimately allowing us to perform more efficiently. This can lead to more work, raises, and promotions. Additionally, being healthy now will help prevent chronic diseases later in life, resulting in healthcare dollars saved in the long run. However, the ROI here is not strictly financial. In fact, the resulting mental health benefit is an invaluable asset. Feeling better physically can, in turn, increase our confidence, mood, and work ethic—all of which are critical factors to a winning mindset.

Having made a career out of this, I can confidently tell you there is no secret diet or cheat code to a healthy lifestyle. There is no shortage of nutrition information circulating the web, and this becomes overwhelming when deciding what to eat or what to avoid. For the most part, people already know what to eat to live healthy—more fruits, vegetables, whole grains, lean proteins, and less highly processed foods. Therefore, a lack of knowledge is not the problem. Rather, the issue lies in the barriers or distractions preventing us from adhering to a daily routine. Therefore, my role as a dietitian focuses on behavior change to help individuals prioritize nutrition and invest in their health. This is very different from simply telling someone what to eat. My strategy of aiding clients in behavior change has shown to result in long-term sustainable health habits and positive outcomes.

Stages of Behavior Change

In nutrition counseling, we use the transtheoretical model to assess an individual's readiness for change. This helps us determine how willing a person is to change a select behavior, which, in this case, is dietary habits. It is understandably difficult to initiate a behavior change, especially if you are unaware of the need for change or if you have been carrying out the same habits for many years. It can feel like a daunting and isolating step to take. Too often, people wait to intervene until there is a notable or serious problem at hand, i.e., an injury or chronic health conditions. Part of investing in yourself and your health is to be proactive rather than reactive.

Regardless of whether this is a personal journey or if it will serve as advice for someone you know, an important first step is to understand the starting point and associated feelings you have around your diet and health. Using this tool will help determine which initial steps to take towards a healthier lifestyle and more productive mindset.

The following include the five stages of change of the transtheoretical model:

1. *Precontemplation*
   The individual does not intend to make any behavior change in the short term. They may be unaware that their behavior is problematic or feel overburdened at the thought of change.

2. *Contemplation*
   At this stage, the individual may still feel hesitant to commit to change, but they are highly interested and aware. They intend on starting the new behavior within the next few months.

3. *Preparation*
   The individual is committed and has taken initial steps towards the behavior change, yet still lacks some skills or support needed to build sustainable habits.

4. *Action*
   The individual has very recently changed their behavior and is enthusiastic about adhering to the changes over the long term.

5. *Maintenance*

At this point, the individual has successfully maintained the new behavior for at least six months and intends to continue moving forward.

Sustaining Long-Term Behavior Change

According to behavioral theories like the transtheoretical model, behaviors are learned traits based on a person's internal and external environments. Internal environments refer to both physical and mental states, like height, weight, age, and genetic predispositions. The external environment focuses on a person's surroundings and how they adapt to them. It is influenced by factors like culture, socioeconomic status, schedule, stress levels, location, food access, education, employment, etc. Together the internal and external environments not only make up our behaviors, but also shape our mindset. Therefore, any intervention that impacts behaviors will also result in a shift in mentality. When adjusting dietary habits, both internal and external environments must be targeted to create a new sustainable routine. To make this work, two main things need to be addressed—how much you eat and what you eat. "How much you eat" should be closely related to the internal environment while "what you eat" is influenced mostly by external factors.

The amount of food a person needs is dependent on their age, height, body composition, physical activity status, lab work, nutrient deficiencies, and health conditions amongst other considerations. How much you really need may greatly vary from the amount you currently eat or think you need. This is the case for the majority of athletes I work with; they are under-fueling, especially the collegiate and professional athletes. There is a certain analogy I like to use when counseling to help them understand their true needs. Imagine if I give you a house, as well as $2,500 each month for its rent and utilities. You love the house and become accustomed to all its amenities and conveniences. Then, one month I tell you that I can only give you $1,800 each month from here on out. You will have to make some decisions for what to sacrifice. You have to pay rent to avoid eviction, so maybe you choose to get rid of cable and internet, or you decide to use less heat or air conditioning. This change will inevitably impact how you enjoy the house. You may be fine for the first month or two, but over time these compromises will become more detrimental.

This analogy parallels your body and the amount of food you need. Based on your internal environment as discussed above, you have individual caloric, macronutrient, and micronutrient needs to ensure that each body system works to its highest potential. Hitting all these markers with a balanced diet will help fuel daily tasks and help you feel your best. However, if you fall short of these needs, the body starts to compromise on some fronts. The modifications may be unnoticeable initially, but with time the health implications can become chronic and severe.

A team of professional health care providers, led by a registered dietitian, will be able to run the appropriate tests and work together to build a customized dietary routine based on your individual needs and goals. With this guidance and continued support, behavior change becomes seamless. But as previously discussed, the behavior relies not only on the amount you eat, but also what you eat. The goal with this is to choose foods providing nourishment, not just sustenance. Sustenance provides a means of getting by. Merely giving food to your body may feel satisfactory. It will provide the calories necessary to carry out basic tasks. However, optimizing your full potential relies on true nourishment, which provides the calories as well as essential nutrients.

To work effectively, each body system, ranging from digestion to cognition, requires specific nutrients, including carbohydrates, fats, protein, minerals, and vitamins. By choosing a variety of high-quality nutrient-dense foods, you are able to capitalize on opportunities to feed these systems with exactly what they need to work efficiently, immediately and in the long term. When each individual system thrives, the body thrives, and the mind thrives. By choosing to focus on adding the best fuel to your body through healthy, nutritious foods, you open your world to more possibilities, which increases your ability to live the successful, high-performance life available to you.

The Main Takeaways

1. We all know the human body is capable of extraordinary undertakings. There have been countless individuals throughout history that have pushed the limits of the mind and body. The mind is powerful, but for longevity and sustainable results, you need to invest in your health and take care of your body.

2. Health looks different for each individual; thus, your plan must be personalized. Nutrition is not difficult; it's a matter of behavior change and consistency. It is important to first recognize your readiness for

change in order to take the appropriate first steps towards a healthier lifestyle.

3. Working with a registered dietitian will help you recognize your body's true needs and will help you create an individualized routine to conquer your goals.

4. What you eat is highly influenced by external factors like location, culture, food access, etc. Amongst the options you have, it is important to choose nourishment over just sustenance. A well-balanced nutrient-dense diet will ensure that you are providing your body with the various nutrients it needs to work most efficiently.

5. Your mindset is shaped by your experiences as well as how you react to your surroundings. A resilient mindset coupled with a healthy body and lifestyle will lead to the most optimal results.

About the Author

Serra Tumay, MS, RD is the founder of Tohum Nutrition LLC, a nutrition counseling and consulting company that helps individuals and small businesses excel through food, nutrition, and wellness strategies.

Serra received a BA in sociology from New York University in 2013. She later went on to obtain a master of science degree in nutrition and exercise physiology from Teachers College Columbia University in New York City, where she also completed her dietetic internship, consisting of numerous rotations, including New York Presbyterian Hospital, FLIK Hospitality Group, and the New York Giants football team.

Before devoting her work fulltime to Tohum Nutrition, Serra worked as the performance nutrition intern for the NFL's Cleveland Browns and the Olympic sports performance dietitian at UCLA Athletics.

As a previous collegiate and professional women's soccer player, Serra is able to use her athletic background to relate with the individuals she works with. This, coupled with her education and prior experiences, allows her to use the latest nutrition research to individualize care for clients.

Email: serra@tohumnutrition.com
Website: tohumnutrition.com
Instagram: @tohumnutrition

CHAPTER THIRTY-THREE

ABUNKOKHELI

By Corina Zanner-Entwistle
Founder, Executive Minds Solutions
England, United Kingdom

The most difficult matter is not so much to change the world as yourself.
—Nelson Mandela

"Abunkokheli" means leadership the African way in
Xhosa, one of the tribal languages of South Africa.

As we sit in the stillness of a waterhole early in the morning, it's completely quiet except for the occasional chirping of a cricket or the sound of a lion in the distance. The tranquility is interrupted by the breaking of twigs as a large group of elephants approach at speed to the water—led by the confident striding matriarch. The elephant's heads bob up and down, and their trunks swing as they stomp, almost running, towards the water.

Amongst the other animals around the water, it is very clear which are in charge and in control. They all respect the elephants and make way for them. There are no signs of aggression. The only sounds are the chirping of the crickets and the splashing of the water as the animals drink and frolic.

One huge elephant wanders right up to our car—hovering high above us—reaching out with her trunk to investigate. We can almost hear our heartbeat as we sit in complete silence—not moving, hardly breathing—just observing, with the knowledge that these animals have the power to trample us in an instant. So, we sit quietly observing until she decides it's time to move on.

Some of the younger elephants begin to squabble, showing their strength and power. Ears flapping, they face each other head on, their trunks lifted into the air showing off their long tusks as they swing their heads in a sign of aggression. The dust rises from the ground and the trumpet sound slices through the silence. The other animals move off to the side to avoid being trampled. The matriarch approaches with calm assertiveness and the younger ones disperse.

My mind wanders off, thinking about leadership and the behaviour of humans. It occurs to me that the most respected leaders emerge not because they are the strongest or most aggressive, but because of the respect earned from others. They demonstrate leadership through their wisdom, strength, and extraordinary skills in problem-solving, emotional intelligence, decisiveness, patience, confidence, and compassion. Much of this comes down to "mindset"—the conscious awareness of our thoughts and actions that differentiate us from these prehistoric animals.

Mental Health

Next to the technical abilities and leadership skills, a leader needs to do their job well; I would argue there is one fundamental, basic attribute at the core of all good leadership from which all else can then easily flow—this is good mental health.

For entrepreneurs and C-suite executives, life often revolves around work, and when a problem arises, it can feel all-encompassing. With the success or failure of the organisation on their shoulders, many directors find it hard to prioritise their own wellbeing. There is still a huge stigma around mental health, but let me be clear ...

Mental health does not equal mental illness.

Leadership starts with being mentally, physically, and emotionally healthy. Chronically stressed and overworked leaders can quickly go into a downward spiral that leads to poor performance, poor leadership, and poor relationships. Poor mental health often leads to issues such as anxiety and depression—from this place, you never make your best decisions or achieve optimal results. By changing the way leaders think, feel, and behave from the top, they begin to change the way they lead, the way their teams engage, the results they get, and the relationships they have with the people around them. Leadership is not just about what happens at work—it's an interlinked "system" that flows in ebbs and waves through our social systems. Good mental health is a combination of physical, mental, and emotional wellbeing, and includes the way we use our brain's resources in order to perform at our best.

Be Positive

Being positive means even when times are difficult and challenging—and there will be those times; nobody goes through life without challenges—you are able to bounce back. There are times when it is normal to feel sad, overwhelmed, or stressed. For example, if somebody close to you has unexpectedly died, it would not be normal to feel happy. If you have an important meeting coming up or a presentation to deliver to senior shareholders, it's normal to feel a bit anxious. It's when these feelings become overwhelming to the extent that they begin to interfere with your daily life that they become a problem.

CEOs and other senior executives go to great lengths to maintain a facade of unflappable confidence, concealing any insecurities or anxiety. But this cycle creates dangerous problems both for CEOs, themselves, and the organisation. You simply cannot afford to ignore doubts and anxieties that put your organisation's success at risk—not to mention your own happiness.

Being positive comes down to knowing and accepting that difficulties and challenges "shall pass," and you will get through it, despite sadness, pain, stress, trauma, anger, or whatever else is going on. After all—you have survived and gotten through 100 percent of every challenge in your life up to now—so you will get through this too, even though it might be difficult, challenging, or stressful. Knowing that these feelings are a normal part of life and have an important function, and knowing that you have the resources to cope puts you in a much stronger position to do so when times get tough, and *that* is all about mindset.

Practising a positive mindset and focusing on good mental health during the "good times" puts you in a much stronger position during the "bad times." When we talk about mental health and mindset, we really are talking about creating habits and routines that help us through stressful and challenging times or situations and that help us improve and go to the next level during other times. Doing this is keeping a winning mindset, whether in good times or bad times. It does not mean we will not experience sadness, worry, stress, or trauma. These are all part of being human, but with a positive mindset, we are able to manage.

The world is not going to become any less complex or uncertain in the coming years, and to be able to adapt and prosper, CEOs must start by addressing their own resilience and wellbeing. If we are not mentally well, we will not make our best decisions or perform at our best. Just like we cannot run if we have a broken leg.

Rewire Your Brain

Recent advances in neuroscience show that neural networks grow new connections, strengthen existing ones, and build insulation that speeds transmission of impulses—but it takes practise! It does not happen by just changing a thought once and then expecting everything to change. You literally have to "train your brain," so it rewires itself and builds new connections.

For example, you are driving to work, a route you know by heart, and one day the road is closed, and you are redirected another way. The first day will be tricky for you to go the new route. You really need to focus on where you are going; the second day will be a bit more familiar, the third day even more so. By the end of the week, you probably know the route quite well. If you continue to use that route, you will get to know it just as well as, if not better than, the old route. To use the same idea with a walking path, the less the old route is used, the more overgrown it becomes until it is not even usable anymore, and the new route becomes the norm. The same thing happens with the brain. We have to set goals and actively rewire the brain until new habits, routines, thoughts, feelings, and behaviours become the norm. In short, we increase our neural growth by the actions we take and the number of times we repeat them. Your brain is like a muscle that needs to be exercised regularly.

Abolish Your Negative Self-Talk

If you are like most people, you have spent years programming your mind with negative self-talk and messages, listening to that negative programming, and now believing it. Once we take control of our thoughts, we can reverse this cycle. We tend to think that we first feel bad, and then the negative thoughts come. While this may well be the case, very often it is actually the other way around, which is hugely encouraging as it means that we are not helplessly left to deal with negative thoughts. I would, therefore, strongly encourage you to create a success statement. Keep repeating this to yourself over and over again until it becomes a habit, and when the negative thoughts creep into your mind, you immediately change it to your success statement. The aim of your success statement is to change your energy from going into a negative downward cycle, to something more positive that will keep you going—even if you don't 100 percent believe it. You are beginning to rewire your brain and change the habit of negative self-talk. It's not about denying reality and difficult situations, but rather about creating new thought patterns and reprogramming your mind.

Recharge Your Batteries

Every high-performance athlete takes time to recover after a competitive event. However, in the business world, people are expected to perform 24/7. It is a natural expectation to work late, be available after hours and on weekends, and to continue doing so even after the latest deadline or goal has been achieved. We live in a society that seems to believe that if you want to be successful, you have to work long and hard. And we wonder why people burn out!

Planning periods of recovery on a daily basis is essential for your mental and physical wellbeing—and wellbeing is essential for performance and success. Make sure you end your day at a certain time, and that during each day, you have a few minutes to do something you enjoy, no matter how small—even that five-minute cup of coffee out on the patio, a ten-minute walk or conversation with a friend—whatever it is, be creative and have a plan. Make sure to incorporate time to recharge daily, weekly, monthly, and quarterly. A few minutes to an hour a day (an hour in the gym, for example), weekends off, a day or two off after a big work event, a holiday or two during the year. These things may sound trivial but are actually essential for our mental health. Take the time to enjoy and reap the rewards of your hard work. These are the things that create a winning mindset and ultimately a winning business because when the leader models these practices, they filter down into the organisation and become part of the culture. This means the employees also have better mental health and work/life balance and, in turn, perform better.

My mind returns to the elephants in front of me, and I notice how they all stop simultaneously with what they are doing—some of them raise their trunks to smell the air. They listen, smell, and look around, using their senses to the fullest at these moments to become aware of one another, their surroundings, and the activities and direction of the herd.

It seems they are reminding us of the importance of taking time to stop, step back, and reconsider or reflect. For us, that means reconsidering and reflecting if the activities that keep us busy all day are the right ones and whether they contribute to our reaching our business and personal goals.

By taking a few moments each day to just *stop*, breathe, step back, and train your brain to think and behave differently, you can begin to create new habits and routines, and rewire your brain for success. I'm going to share with you my favourite technique called the Stop Technique. My mentor and trainer Dr. Leila Edwards taught me this, and it can be used to help you take action on a daily basis and start creating those new neural pathways. Enjoy!

The Stop Technique

The Stop Technique is incredibly simple, but also incredibly powerful. I teach it to all my private clients, and they all tell me how useful they find it. However, I must stress that it only works with repetition and practise. Neuroplasticity is about practise, practise, and more practise, so it then becomes your default mode under stress.

For the first week or two, make sure you do it as often as you can throughout the day, and then perhaps cut it down to three times per day. Set yourself reminders. Once you have mastered the technique, you can do it anywhere—at the computer or dinner table. Research has also shown that people who use this type of relaxation live healthier and longer. The Stop Technique activates the relaxation response, which is the opposite of the stress response, which we activate all the time through our thoughts, lifestyle, actions, and behaviours. The goal really is to get your body into a natural state as often as possible to function and perform at its optimum, which it doesn't do under stress, unless trained. After all, stress is really a survival mechanism, it does not need to be active all the time. We need to train our mind and body to relax. So, here is the technique:

- Say to yourself in your mind the word "STOP" and close your eyes.
- Take a deep breath in, and as you breathe out, think of relaxing your face, jaw, neck, shoulders, arms, and hands, imagining a wave of relaxation spreading over those areas.
- Take another deep breath in, and as you breathe out, focus on relaxing down the front and back sides of your body, down to your legs, through your feet, relaxing and releasing any tension or tightness down into the ground through to your toes.
- Imagine another wave of relaxation spreading through your body and at the same time pushing down any tightness and tension. Pushing down any negative thoughts, feelings, fears, irritations, or anything that might bother you—all the way down to the bottom of your feet.
- Take two small, quiet, easy breaths.
- Imagine there is a big vacuum cleaner or a big magnet at the bottom of your feet sucking up all those negative thoughts, feelings, worries, or tensions.
- Now allow that vacuum cleaner or magnet to disappear into oblivion— allow it all to go, disappear, allowing all those worries, stresses, strains, negative thoughts, and negative feelings to disappear into oblivion.
- Now picture a lovely scene you have visited before or want to visit, or picture the face of a loved one, maybe something that makes you smile or laugh.
- Now open your eyes and come back into the room feeling calm, refreshed, and ready to face the rest of the day, bringing back all those good feelings with you to the here and now.

You can become endlessly creative in the way you use the Stop Technique. You can use it in conjunction with your positive affirmation, or success statement that you set up earlier, or you can add to it a beautiful visualisation of your favourite place where you feel completely calm and at ease, a place where nobody wants anything, nobody expects anything, where you can just be completely calm and at ease, and spend a few minutes here. This could be a real or imagined place. You could visualise yourself feeling more confident in a particular situation or see yourself the way you want to be when you are at your best—you can do a combination of all of these, or you could cut it right down to a one- or two-minute exercise when you sit down at your computer before beginning to work or even during a stressful moment in a meeting. This is my quickest and easiest go-to technique when times are tough. Use it as often as you want or need, and notice how much better you feel after that first breath.

Back to Basics

A winning mindset is about remembering to go back and practise the basics that make us strong, that build resilience and the determination to drive forward no matter what. Being a good leader and having a winning mindset takes time, patience, and repetition. It is the ability to create calmness during a crisis as a result of raised awareness, moments of peacefulness, calmness, and great determination. It's about choosing to have a winning mindset.

Time to Move On

The matriarch elephant begins to walk away, signalling to the others it's time to move on. Those that are submerged enjoying the coolness of the water lift themselves up and out. These giants once again hover high above us and toss their heads towards us with one last glance as they stomp off into the distance. The matriarch and her assistants make sure no one is left behind, and everyone is safe. Within minutes the scene is clear and silence once again surrounds us with only the crickets and birds occasionally breaking the silence as if it had never happened.

About the Author

Corina Zanner-Entwistle, founder of Executive Mind Solutions, is an anxiety management and performance coach and trainer. Corina is known for her cutting-edge approach and powerful mindset strategies that help her clients achieve results—fast. Executive Mind Solutions provides exclusive consultancy and training to promote leadership and health and wellbeing for professionals and corporations.

Together with her master's degree in adult education and training, Corina has an impressive list of qualifications, including psychotherapy, hypnotherapy, family therapy, counselling, and NLP coaching. She combines her extensive training and experience with the latest psychology to provide individual clients and organisations with powerful tools to improve performance and productivity, enjoy better leadership and higher team engagement, as well as increased health and happiness, or achieve therapeutic goals.

Having lived and worked in various countries in Europe, Africa, and the Middle East, Corina is comfortable with national and international groups alike.

Email: info@execmindsolutions.com
Website: www.execmindsolutions.com
LinkedIn: https://www.linkedin.com/in/corina-ze-leadershipexpert/

CHAPTER THIRTY-FOUR
WINNING MINDSET

By Erik Seversen
Author, Speaker, Coach
Los Angeles, California

When your desires are strong enough, you will appear
to possess superhuman powers to achieve.
—Napoleon Hill

I've got some news for you. There really is nothing complicated about having a mindset that allows you to perform better and do things others think is impossible. Having a winning mindset is so simple, the message can be taught in a children's book.

Have you ever read *The Little Engine That Could?* If you haven't, I suggest you do. The most popular version was published in 1920 by Watty Piper, but written versions of the story appear much earlier. Basically, the story goes— there is a trainload of toys for boys and girls that needs to get over a mountain. The story's conflict is when the engine pulling the train breaks down. The toy dolls and clowns and engine (all of whom can speak) are stuck. After asking other large powerful train engines that pass, the train full of toys is refused help over and over until a little blue train engine who has never been over the mountain before comes along. When asked to pull the train of toys over the mountain, the little engine responds, "I think I can."

Through the entire struggle up the mountain, the little engine keeps repeating, "I think I can. I think I can. I think I can …" And the little blue engine succeeds in the seemingly impossible task. It was just the choice to believe that allowed the little blue engine to help get the train full of toys over the mountain. The simple message is that we can accomplish what we think we can.

Now let's leave children's stories behind for a moment and turn to arguably the most influential personal development book in existence—Napoleon Hill's *Think and Grow Rich*. This book was first published in 1937. It has been translated into hundreds of languages and remains a top-selling book over 80 years after it was first published. This book is the culmination of Andrew Carnegie's exhortation to Hill to create a philosophy of success and gaining wealth. Based on massive amounts of anecdotal evidence, the book has generated more millionaires than any other course on building wealth in existence. One of the main premises of the book is: if you can think of something as a possibility, you can achieve whatever it is.

> *Whatever the mind can conceive and believe, it can achieve.*
> —Napoleon Hill, *Think and Grow Rich*

It must be noted that Napoleon Hill didn't believe we just think things, and they magically manifest into our lives. He did believe, however, that we think things into reality, and through keeping a mindset of desire, determination, and drive, we can achieve anything we want since we are in control of our own lives and our own futures.

> *You are the master of your destiny. You can influence, direct and control your own environment. You can make your life whatever you want it to be.*
> —Napoleon Hill, *Think and Grow Rich*

Notice, Napoleon Hill doesn't say, you can make your life whatever you want it to be *as long as it is reasonable*. No, Hill clearly states that anything we can conceive and believe, we can achieve. Let me rephrase this because it is so simple, many people miss it—anything you can conceive and believe, you can achieve.

What is it that you would like to achieve? Take a moment right now, and ask yourself the question: what do I want to achieve? Is it winning a gold medal in the Olympics? Is it creating a new company? Is it making $100,000 per year? Making $1,000,000 per year? Why not? This isn't out of anyone's reach.

Napoleon Hill was one of the first to suggest the idea that we attract what we project. There are numerous books about themes such as willing things to happen and the law of attraction, and all of them begin in one place—the mind.

All of our successes start in the mind, and it is with a winning mindset that we can overcome the challenges that will occur as we conceive of goals that others might find unreasonable. I've spoken enough about theory, let me provide an example from my own life where I believed in an unlikely outcome, and I made it a reality.

I was a very poor student growing up. I even flunked the second grade. I wasn't lazy, but math, English, and science didn't come easily to me. Although I had wonderful parents, they were not involved in my school success, so I moved along grade after grade as an average C- student. Then, in the eleventh grade, something clicked, and I decided I wanted to become a college professor. (This was my first mental shift.) I said to myself, "College professors don't get Cs." With only a bit of extra work, I began getting straight As.

In my school, because I had an older brother and sister who'd already had it, I knew I'd have a 30-minute session with the school counselor to go over my options for college, etc. I was so excited for my session. I was engaged, enthusiastic, and I'd been getting straight As for a year. I also remember my older brother and sister coming home with arms full of brochures from colleges from around the country.

When Mrs. Elbert, the counselor, walked in, she sat across from me, looked at my transcript for a few moments, and asked, "Erik, what do you want to do with your life?"

I responded, "I want to go to UCLA."

"You will never get into a school like that" was her response. That was it. She pushed herself away from the table, stood up, and walked out of the room. I had no idea what to expect next. I sat there fighting back tears, wondering if she was going to come back to finish the meeting. She didn't return. After about 30 minutes, I composed myself and went back to class. But my mental transformation had already begun, and as an eternal optimist, I applied to UCLA.

UCLA rejected my application.

At this point, I could have caved in and "realized" that Mrs. Elbert was right, but I didn't. I went to a community college and continued to get As. I also realized that I'd have to do something different to get into UCLA. My next mental shift was that I envisioned the type of students who were accepted to UCLA, and I realized that getting As was not enough. I had to do something extraordinary. In my mind, I believed I could get into UCLA, and I wondered what I could do to set myself apart from the thousands of other straight-A students.

It was about that same time that I read the book *Things Fall Apart* by Chinua Achebe. I was a bit confused because the book didn't highlight African culture in the same way that my history and geography classes had done, so I had my plan. I'd go to Africa to see it for myself. By doing this, I'd not only satisfy a childhood dream of seeing lions, elephants, and giraffes, but I'd do something that would set me apart as I traveled to Africa to witness African culture for myself.

Growing up in Parkland, a suburb of Tacoma, Washington, in an average middle-class family, there were no resources to draw from to make this goal a reality, so I spent eight months doing two things: mowing lawns to make enough money for the trip and convincing my parents that me going to Africa alone was a good idea. In the end, after eight months, I couldn't afford the expensive plane tickets to Africa, so I purchased a ticket to London and hitchhiked my way down to Spain, took a boat across Gibraltar, and made it to Africa. I didn't stop at my arrival point in Morocco though. I walked and hitchhiked all the way down, through the Sahara Desert, to West and Central Africa passing through Achebe's native country of Nigeria.

To make a long story short, after Africa, I returned to Green River Community College, finished my associate's degree, applied to UCLA, and this time my application was accepted. I spent the next years living the vision I had seen for myself and graduated from UCLA with highest honors.

What is the point in sharing this experience with you? To start, notice that the first thing that happened was that I made a mental shift. I envisioned myself as a UCLA student, and I believed it was possible. This allowed me to continue working toward this goal, even when things didn't immediately materialize for me. The second thing that happened was I logically created a path I thought would lead me to being accepted to UCLA, and the third thing is I desired to go to UCLA so much, I dedicated myself to the long hours of study, the long hours of work, and the careful execution of my plan. With a winning mindset as my foundation, I pushed my brain and my body to the limit, spending every waking moment working toward my goal until the vision that I'd conceived in my mind became a reality.

My experience is not unique. I've seen people accomplish extraordinary things over and over again. The commonality that each of these individuals possess is a winning mindset, a belief that they can accomplish something, and the diligence to put in the work to make it happen.

Today, as I write this, my goals have changed. After years of teaching at the university level and years in working in business, my main goals are helping others through writing books, public speaking, and my education company. Each day, I wake up eager to get started, and each day I thank God for the progress I make as I reach short-term goals while working toward long-term goals. I'm not exhausted by these efforts because my actions are in alignment with my values, which I think is important. I step forward each day driven by a purpose greater than myself, which provides both internal and external rewards that fuel my desire to keep working, to keep growing my business, to keep helping others, to keep attaining goals that others find impossible. Whether it be my work goals, like making enough money to provide financial security for my family, or my adventure goals, like climbing extremely high mountains, I begin with my winning mindset and all of my actions after that seem to flow easily.

I pray that you now make the choice to live with a winning mindset at the forefront of everything you do. Whatever you can conceive and believe, you can achieve.

About the Author

Erik Seversen is on a mission to inspire people. He holds a master's degree in anthropology and is a certified practitioner of neuro-linguistic programming. Erik draws from his years of teaching at the university level and years of real-life experience to motivate people to take action, creating extreme success in business and in life.

Erik is an author of seven books, keynote speaker, adventurer, entrepreneur, and educator who has traveled to 86 countries and all 50 states in the USA. His travels and intersections with people have been a deep study of love, struggle, and ways of thinking that Erik relies on to tackle challenges in school, business, and life. His most current ambitions are sharing the lessons he's learned with others and climbing mountains. Erik lives in Los Angeles with his wife and two teenage boys.

Email: Erik@ErikSeversen.com
Website: www.ErikSeversen.com

DID YOU ENJOY THIS BOOK?

If you enjoyed reading this book, you can help by suggesting it to someone else you think might like it, and **please leave a positive review** wherever you purchased it. This does a lot in helping others find the book. We thank you in advance for taking a few moments to do this.

THANK YOU

If you enjoyed reading this book, you might also like the books in The Mind, Body, and Spirit series:

Book 1:
The Successful Mind: Tools to Living a Purposeful,
Productive, and Happy Life

Book 2:
The Successful Body: Using Fitness, Nutrition,
and Mindset to Live Better

Book 3:
The Successful Spirit: Top Performers Share
Secrets to a Winning Mindset

Manufactured by Amazon.ca
Bolton, ON